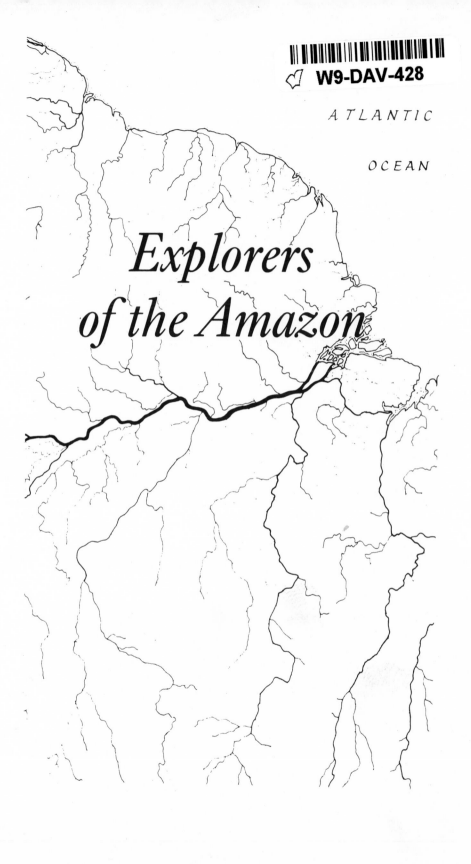

ATLANTIC

OCEAN

Explorers
of the Amazon

Explorers
of the Amazon

Anthony Smith

The University of Chicago Press
Chicago and London

The University of Chicago Press, Chicago 60637
The University of Chicago Press, Ltd., London

Copyright © Anthony Smith, 1990

All rights reserved. Originally published 1990
University of Chicago Press Edition 1994
Printed in the United States of America
01 00 99 98 97 96 95 94   6 5 4 3 2 1

ISBN 0-226-76337-4 (pbk.)

Library of Congress Cataloging-in-Publication Data

Smith, Anthony, 1926–
    Explorers of the Amazon / Anthony Smith. — University of Chicago Press ed.
        p.   cm.
    Originally published: London, England ; New York, N.Y. : Viking, 1990.
    Includes index.
    1. Amazon River Valley—Discovery and exploration.   2. Explorers—
Amazon River Valley—History.   I. Title.
F2546.S68   1993
981'.1—dc20   93-28121
                                                                        CIP

Contents

PACIFIC

OCEAN

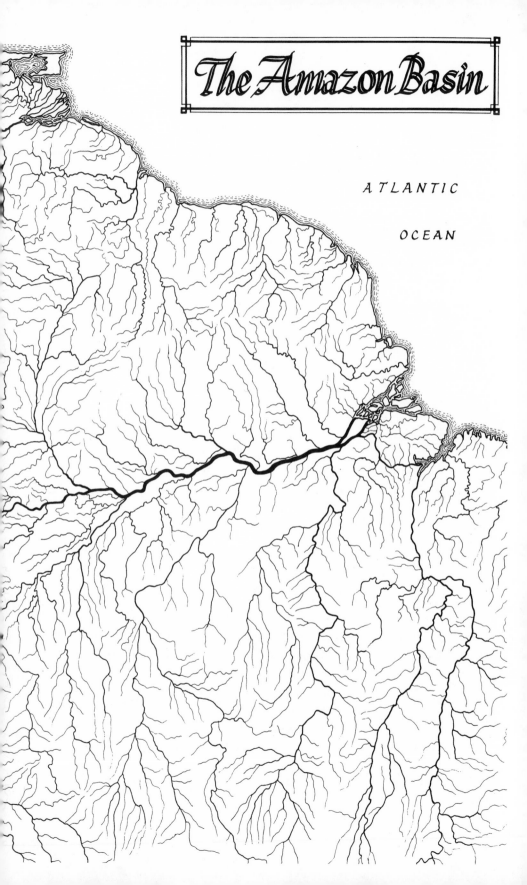

The Amazon Basin

ATLANTIC

OCEAN

Central and South America
Principal locations mentioned in the book

ATLANTIC OCEAN
(Northern Sea)

Havana
Bahamas
Mexico City
Acapulco
Leeward Is.
Lake Maracaibo
Isla de Margarita
Barbados
Cartagena
Caracas
Trinidad
Ciudad Bolívar
(Angostura)
Paramaribo
Cayenne
Buenaventura
Bogotá
Quito
Guayaquil
Cuenca
Manaus
Belém / Pará
(Fort Presépio)
São Luis
Iquitos
Recife
(Pernambuco)
Callao
Lima
Cuzco (Nuevo Toledo)
Lake Titicaca
PACIFIC OCEAN
(Southern Sea)
Potosí
Rio de Janeiro
Santos
(São Vicente)
Bay of Guanabara
Tucumán
Buenos Aires
N
1000 miles
1000
2000 km
Straits of Magellan
Cape Horn

Introduction

The Amazon is the superlative river, being greatest in so much. It drains more than half of South America. Even some of its 1,100 tributaries, such as the half-dozen that are 1,000 miles long, and the Madeira of over 3,000 miles, dwarf the rivers of other continents. No bridge crosses the Amazon for 3,900 miles, and ocean-going vessels can journey upstream for much of its length. Its basin contains ten times as many fish species as all the European rivers combined, and about 20 per cent of the world's river water. For all that, the Amazon is not well known. Even most Brazilians have never seen any part of it – neither the main channel nor any of its branches.

The individual stories of the Amazon's exploration inevitably reflect these vast dimensions. Would Francisco de Orellana have contemplated his voyage downstream, the first of its kind, had he known it would take him and his party nine desperate months? Does the tremendous separation of Monsieur and Madame Godin des Odonais, over two decades, make any sense save in the context of the world's greatest river? And how odd it was that, unwillingly but with fearful courage, Madame Godin became the first woman to travel down it. Of course its natural history attracted the globe-encircling naturalists of the nineteenth century, with the English doing more collecting along this river than most other nationalities put together. Eventually, as a different form of prize, they took its rubber seeds and killed off the corrupt, frenetic, genocidal rubber industry which had Manaus as its torrid capital.

For many portions of the world, their exploration by Europeans was a brief affair. The mystery of the Nile was speedily unravelled after brave individuals had ventured west from Zanzibar to encounter Lake Victoria. The first shipload of immigrants reached Australia in 1788, and within eighty years most of the major traverses had been achieved. Men first saw Antarctica in 1820 and had reached its pole within a century. However, the Amazon, always different, is still suitable for exploration some 450 years after a Spaniard sailed its length from west to east. No one went up it for another hundred years. No scientist came down it for a further hundred. No major collecting was initiated until the last century, and only in this century is it being realized quite how much has still to be learned about the Amazon basin.

Although most Amazonian forays, like those examined in this book, took place a long time ago, it is still possible to see the river as the early adventurers saw it. This is quite unlike standing on Manhattan and trying to visualize it from Peter Stuyvesant's viewpoint, or imagining Sydney Harbour when the first ships sailed in. On the Amazon there are sandbanks, floating logs, toucans pushing their bills through the air, the sound of parrots and macaws, much as these things have always been. The trees still line the river-banks, the Rio Negro is as black, and the caymans still stare as unblinkingly as when those first hungry boatloads of Spaniards could think of little else but food. As for the Putumayo, and the terrible things done there even within this century, where else in the world could a piece of land several times the size of England become the virtual property of one man? That river still looks much as it did before he took it, and then after justice had been enforced upon it.

The stories in this book are all particularly significant and encompass the centuries between 1540 and 1913. They blend into one another, even across such a span of time. The Spanish involvement with the river could not last. Too much was happening elsewhere. This vacuum was inevitably filled by the Portuguese. Neither Iberian country then had much time for science, and following the War of the Spanish Succession, so drummed into history lessons, France was quick to take advantage. Prussia trod in the French footsteps, with Germany in the ascendant when France was too embroiled in revolution. Humboldt inspired a generation of naturalists, not least the English, who almost took the Amazon for themselves. Once they had taken cinchona, it was inevitable that rubber should be next on the list.

Introduction

And it was no less certain that, when foreign rubber competition began to bite, Manaus would take wrongful steps to maintain its over-blown status in the world's economy. From Orellana and Aguirre to Teixeira, from La Condamine and Godin to Humboldt, and from Spruce and Wickham to Arana, Hardenburg and Casement, there is a thread binding each to each. There is also, flowing firmly past them all, the Amazon, the extraordinary river system linked with some of the most remarkable stories of exploration and endeavour, of courage and also disrepute, that the world has ever known.

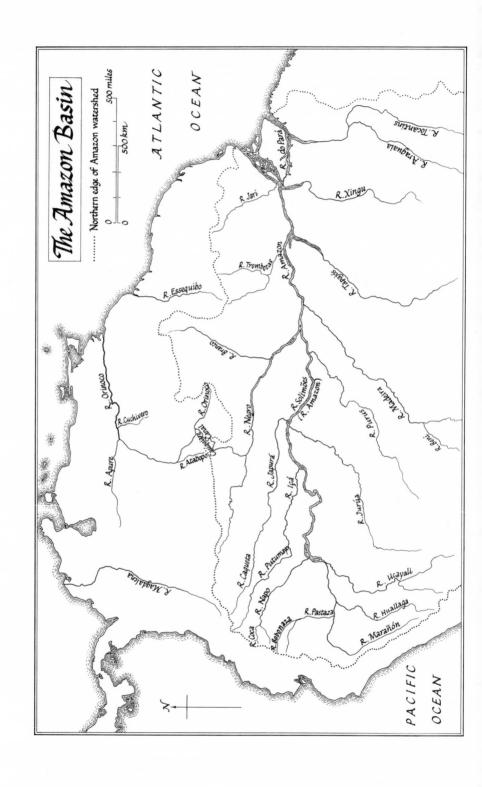

I

Pedro Cabral
STUMBLING UPON BRAZIL

In the year 1500, on 9 March, a fleet of thirteen ships sailed from Portugal. By 22 March they had reached the Cape Verde Islands, but they did not stop as provisions on board were still plentiful. Exactly one month later, on 22 April, floating grass was sighted and then, at the hour of Vespers, land. This was the official discovery of Brazil. The fleet's commander, Pedro Álvares Cabral, is therefore a hero of that country, and the first piece of land he saw – Mount Pascal – is similarly renowned. With his square-rigged ships, on that Easter Wednesday, he steered cautiously for the mountain and then anchored for the night some eighteen miles offshore. On the following day, after edging nearer the coast, his fleet eventually re-anchored in the mouth of a small river. A party went ashore in a single boat, and Nicolau Coelho became the first man from that fleet to walk upon the land that would become Brazil. He reported back to his commander that the people he encountered were amiable, naked and curious, never having seen such foreigners before.

That night was a difficult one. A wind sprang up, the ships dragged their anchors and Cabral decided to seek a better haven. An inlet sheltered from the wind was found some forty miles to the north. On 26 April, Low Sunday, Cabral went ashore, together with a large number of priests and friars from among his complement of 1,200 men. He had no stone (*padrão*) to mark the place, as was customary on voyages of discovery, but made the carpenter construct a wooden cross to serve as a token of possession. This was erected on 1 May after a Mass had been celebrated. He then named the land, not knowing if it was a huge island or a continent. *Terra da Vera Cruz* was his choice: Land of the True Cross.

On the following day, one vessel having been despatched to Portugal with this news, the remaining ships raised their anchors and set sail for the empty Atlantic once again. Watching them go, apart from the inhabitants, were two convicts, who were said to have been weeping. These men had suddenly been granted a measure of freedom probably unparalleled in mankind's history, being the only two people of their kind in a brand new world. In exchange for their liberation they were instructed to learn about the locality, the people and the language. Then, and who knew when, they and their information would be collected. If a tear was shed on that second day of May, 1500, it would seem entirely understandable.

Much less comprehensible, to anyone encountering this story for the first time, are many of the ancillary facts. Cabral was not on a voyage of discovery and yet hit South America amidships, as it were. He was *en route* to Calicut, on the Malabar coast of southern India. One of his thirteen ships had already been lost, and it could be construed that the overall commander was also lost when India-bound in that western South Atlantic. He did not even encounter Brazil where it juts most prominently towards Africa, but almost 600 miles south of that point and more than 5° further west. On his journey towards the east and India he was then about 30° west of his starting point on Lisbon's Tagus river.

Who was Cabral anyway, one is entitled to ask, as the nobleman springs from obscurity to command this considerable fleet? On board, in a humbler role, was Bartholomew Dias, famous discoverer of the southern end of Africa, the final cape, the 'cape of all the torments', as he called it in 1487. Poor Dias had not only lost authority but was lost altogether, aged 50, in a storm after Cabral's fleet had sailed south-eastwards from Brazil. Finally it is easy to wonder at Cabral's dismissive treatment of this major discovery – he stayed less than two weeks – and his rigid adherence to the Calicut destination. Could not half his fleet have sailed eastwards while the other half set about discovering what it had discovered, whether island or continent, ripe with riches or merely peopled with friendly, naked but worthless inhabitants? Modern Brazilians are enthusiastic about the finder of their land, and do not worry that he apparently cared so little about this encounter, and certainly dedicated so little time to it. Even in those heady days of long-distance navigation and discovery such meetings were hardly commonplace.

There are explanations, of a sort, for all these points, but it is important to remember at the outset both the rivalry and the togetherness of Spain and Portugal, the two major exploratory nations of the age. This Iberian unity led to the Treaty of Tordesillas, which effectively carved up the New World as if Iberians were the only contenders. It also led to each side respecting the other's allotted claim. Of necessity there was vagueness in the Treaty because it carved up a cake of unknown extent, but each side attempted to appreciate the Treaty's certain sentiments rather than its imprecision, the spirit and not the letter of this papal law.

The royal families of Spain and Portugal did their best to bind rather than separate their two nations, but their attempts are difficult to follow. In the year 1490 there occurred an important marriage between Spain and Portugal. (Being two years before Columbus's voyage to the New World, it was as if in anticipation of difficulties that might arise from an expedition led by an Italian, that had achieved support from Spain, having failed with Portugal.) The king of Portugal, João II, arranged for his heir presumptive, Afonso, to marry the eldest child of the Spanish royal family, the Infanta Isabel. Unfortunately, and initiating the confusion, Afonso died soon afterwards and João himself died in 1495. Next on the Portuguese throne was Manuel I and he, to put things right, married the same Doña Isabel, widow of Afonso. This marriage became even more important within a few days when her only brother died. Isabel was suddenly heir presumptive to the thrones of both Castile and Aragon. The many deaths were inconvenient but did permit repeated demonstration of this nuptial style of foreign policy. And never before had a foreign policy been quite so critical as during this major period of world discovery when – to list only the most crucial happenings – an end was found to Africa, a way was discovered to India, and great quantities of America were added to the map.

It might seem from all the various unions, and the determination to have more of them, that Castile, Aragon and Portugal were united peas in the same Iberian pod. The Treaty of Tordesillas, apportioning territories to the two nations, might therefore appear unnecessary. Portugal and Spain were as one, ruled during the period of discovery by the same king, and so the New World belonged to both of them. It did, in effect; but there was still rivalry, and the Treaty was designed to prevent squabbling by these two united but distinct nations.

The Treaty makes intriguing reading from our current standpoint. It is remarkably perspicacious about the New World and its extent, only two years after Christopher Columbus had first voyaged west. After all, he had encountered no more than an island or two and even believed he had arrived in some eastern part of Asia. If the new lands were Asia they were hardly unclaimed territories, ready to be carved up by visiting sailors on behalf of their European kings. Marco Polo had made this point abundantly clear two centuries earlier by detailing not just the colossal Mongol empire but also some of its powerful neighbours. Eastern Asia was never an empty land waiting for colonization, and yet the Treaty was written as if a New World had been found, as if Columbus's Asian assertions were unfounded. No one knew at the time how much land existed out there, or how much would exist on either side of any demarcation in the Treaty. Nevertheless the Treaty did carve up the New World as if it were new. It is as if its authors had been waiting for some voyage to give an excuse for drafting a piece of legislation that had merely been biding its time. It could not jump the gun, the one fired in 1492, but it was off the mark thereafter with extraordinary aplomb.

The Treaty was signed at Tordesillas, 100 miles north-west of Madrid, in June 1494. It apportioned to Spain all land west of a line 370 leagues from the Cape Verdes, and all nearer land to Portugal. Knowledge of the New World was then sketchy to say the least. Columbus was still on his second voyage. No land had yet been discovered within 370 leagues of the Cape Verde Islands, and the Treaty's seeming foreknowledge is therefore remarkable. However, once signed, its vision was neither queried nor explained. Cabral's voyage occurred six years later, but he was not looking for Portugal's entitlement. Instead he was assuming more and more water ahead of him when the look-out spotted Mount Pascal and Brazil was officially 'discovered'. *Descobrir* was the verb used, and there exists academic argument that it did not convey the same sense as the modern 'discover'. Rather than 'find by chance', it meant to 'uncover' or 'reveal' something or some place whose existence was already suspected or even known. Cabral's lack of astonishment at his 'discovery' of Brazil is more understandable with this meaning; so too his speedy departure for Calicut. Like all good academic arguments this one will probably never be resolved, and no one will ever know whether Cabral had expected such a sighting.

The despatch of one vessel to report upon the finding is interesting, but not helpful in the matter of Cabral's expectation or otherwise. It is referred to as a supply ship, and may well have been sufficiently emptied by then, the fleet with its 1,200 men being fifty-four days out from Portugal. There is no log of Cabral's voyage, and therefore a miserable lack of basic information, but at least letters have survived that were sent with the supply ship. One reveals an amazingly democratic attitude on the part of Cabral, who asked 'all of us whether it seemed well to send news of the finding of this land'. This letter was written by Pedro Vaz de Caminha and addressed to the king of Portugal, Manuel I, who was involved that year with his second marriage into the Spanish royal house. Whether or not the king approved of such democracy, he would have read that 'among the many speeches which were made regarding the matter, it was said by all or by the greater number, that it would be very well to do so' – namely to send him a letter about the discovery. In this casual manner, and following debate, the king of Portugal was graciously informed of the existence of Terra da Vera Cruz, a piece of land that subsequently became Brazil and which today occupies ninety-six times the area of its parent country.

The king also learned that, as a result of further democratic voting, the letter would not be accompanied by a couple of samples of the local population. There was precedent for sending natives back, notably from journeys to Africa; but Cabral and company thought it unhelpful, 'since it was the general custom that those taken away by force to another place' did not necessarily tell the truth. They tended to affirm that 'everything about which they were asked' did indeed exist in their land. To admit to gold, spices, precious stones and wondrous beasts raised the captives' chances of survival more than denying all these things. Cabral's assembly, standing by the wooden cross it had erected, thought that leaving two convicts was better than taking two initially incomprehensible and ultimately unreliable indigenes back to Lisbon.

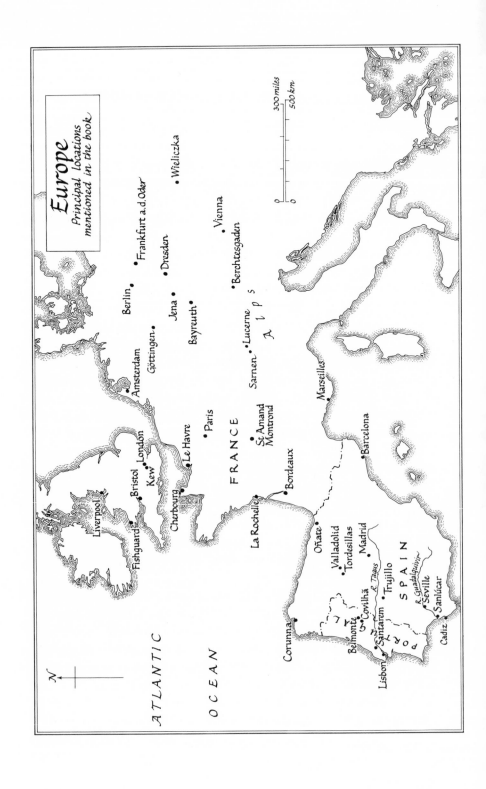

Europe
Principal locations
mentioned in the book

Pedro Cabral

The convicts would assuredly learn about the foreign land and could, in theory, impart their gathered information later on when, if possible, they were retrieved.

Unfortunately no more was heard of the two men. It is not even known if they saw the end of 2 May 1500, when Cabral sailed away, and it was subsequently learned that the people resident at Cabral's landfall, a tribe of Tupinambá Indians, did eat people. The letter to King Manuel makes no such mention, referring only to more attractive attributes such as decorative feathers, musical instruments, rafts and houses. Later travellers, less fleeting in their visits, observed tattooing, smoking and cannibalism. The convicts, therefore, had had every right to weep – and the eighteen other convicts on board, transported for just this kind of purpose, must have sighed with relief that they were not chosen as the first settlers of this new land.

Cabral's seeming unconcern for the continent he had encountered *is* surprising; but his voyage did come at the end of a heady decade of exploration, in fact the headiest there had ever been. On the African side Bartholomew Dias had discovered an end to the continent, or at least every indication that a route existed round it to the east. He had turned back at the Great Fish River, halfway between today's Port Elizabeth and East London. Although this river's mouth is on the same latitude as Cape Town, it lies 500 miles to the east; hence the promise of a coastline proceeding further north thereafter. Vasco da Gama then took advantage of the Dias findings and commanded the first fleet to sail from Europe for Asia. His voyage was not a complete success, in that many of the crew died and his goods for barter were not appreciated, but these mistakes were rectified as far as possible before Cabral was despatched two years later to the same destination.

Over in the west the decade's explorations had been even more dramatic. Christopher Columbus's voyage of 1492 had encountered the Bahamas, Cuba and Hispaniola (Española). His second and bigger expedition, which set sail less than seven months after his return from the first, demonstrated considerable haste and enthusiasm for the new lands. He revisited Hispaniola, off-loaded colonists, and then discovered the eastern part of that island, along with Puerto Rico (to Hispaniola's east) and Jamaica (to its west). On his third voyage, two years before Cabral's, Columbus travelled further south, discovering

Trinidad and setting foot upon the mainland of South America. That event took place on 5 August 1498, and therefore predates the earliest encounter with any piece of the North American mainland.

Although Columbus initially asserted that his expeditions had discovered some eastern part of Asia, this may have been partly to encourage his sponsors. To find a land whose virtues were already known must have seemed more attractive than to stumble upon one that was completely unknown. At the end of voyage number three, when sponsors were more assured, he pronounced that he had definitely met up with *otro mondo*, another world. By sailing through the Serpent's Mouth, a narrow channel between south-western Trinidad and the northern shore of modern Venezuela, Columbus entered the Gulf of Paria. It was within this bay, shielded from the Atlantic, that a boat went ashore to make the all-important landing upon the brand-new continent. (Columbus, having argued that Cuba was mainland, now asserted equally wrongly that Paria – the Indian word for this area – was an island; but it was certainly *otro mondo*.)

In 1499, one year before Cabral set sail, there occurred a greater flurry of exploratory activity than in any other year of that astonishing decade. Per Alonso Niño left Spain, along with instructions not to sail within fifty leagues of Columbus's landfalls. Niño instantly disobeyed, making straight for Paria, where he cut brazil-wood, traded skilfully for pearls and gold, and generally explored northern South America. (The enthusiasm for brazil-wood seems odd, when pearls and gold were available, but a fuller explanation will follow concerning both this wood and its all-important name.) Alonso de Ojeda, a former shipmate of Columbus, sailed a few days before Niño in the company of a map-maker, Juan de la Cosa, and Amerigo Vespucci, merchant of Florence (the Medici family's representative in Seville making sensible and vigorous use of his posting). On reaching South America Ojeda voyaged west with two ships while Vespucci turned south-east with the other two. This second foray is reckoned to have reached about 6°30′ south and therefore did not quite achieve the easternmost portion of Brazil or the site of modern Recife. The voyagers did reach the Amazon and the Pará, venturing up both of them in smaller boats to make better progress.

When Vespucci's main ships reached the strong northerly current sweeping up the coast of Brazil he was confused for the (to us) bizarre reason that Marco Polo had made no mention of any such current. As Polo's return journey from the capital of the Great Khan and down the China coast had begun almost exactly on the other side of the globe, namely one continent and one ocean distant, it is strange that anything tallied. Even the Pole Star had disappeared for Vespucci, a phenomenon not noted by the Venetian, and one wonders when Vespucci (or indeed anyone else) realized these American voyages had absolutely nothing to do with India, Cathay, or the Orient in general. Did understanding come as a thunderclap, or did the notion grow insidiously? Even Columbus fails to provide the answer, as his *otro mondo* was not necessarily a *novo mondo*; but there must have come a time when, to all observers, the distances and the facts did not add up.

The confused Vespucci turned upon his heels from 6°S to meet with Ojeda. These early explorers seem to have had less trouble in encountering each other than, say, modern city-dwellers who have arranged some detailed rendezvous. (Vespucci was to bump into Cabral's ships, for instance, over a year later when the former was heading for the New World once again, and the latter were returning from Calicut.) Vespucci found Ojeda off Hispaniola and learned of the rivers Essequibo and Orinoco, of friendly and hostile natives, of various gulfs and inlets such as Lake Maracaibo, and in general about Venezuela, so named by Ojeda because some dwellings stood in water, a 'little Venice' in their way. Slaves and pearls had been collected. The trip therefore made a profit, even though a number of the slaves died *en route* to Spain.

Within a mere seven years, therefore, of Columbus's earliest voyage, and only six after his return, the New World was suddenly crowded. One explorer beseeching the Spanish throne for funds had become many would-be travellers to the New World, and the Crown had been forced to issue licences to prospective voyagers. Columbus not only discovered new lands but apparently instilled in every man-jack of his crew a determination to return, to beg some vessel (or place in some vessel) and find more of what was plainly waiting out there to be discovered. Whether for fortune, fame, simple adventure, or to experience a different kind of life, there was a sudden and considerable enthusiasm for heading west.

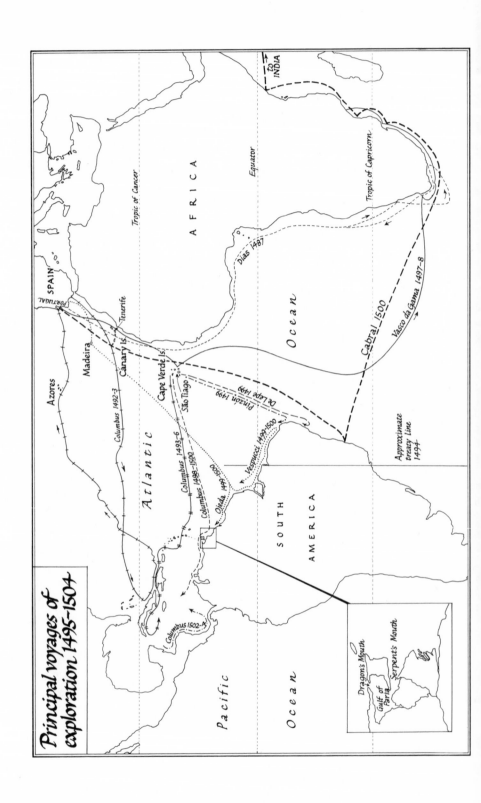

Principal voyages of exploration 1495–1504

Pedro Cabral

Apart from the Ojeda–Vespucci and Niño expeditions of 1499 there were those of Vicente Yáñez Pinzón and Diego de Lepe. Pinzón, who had been the *Niña*'s commander on Columbus's first voyage, sailed in 1499 to meet the South American coastline at about 8°S, more or less the latitude of modern Recife, and therefore further south than anyone else had been. He then voyaged north-west with the current before travelling past the Amazon, the Gulf of Paria and many of the same natives as had already been encountered. Then it was back home via Hispaniola along a route that had suddenly become commonplace. Lepe, who left Spain in December of that year, and who went even further south than Pinzón, landed and took possession of the new area by carving his name on a tree, an ordinary enough deed rendered extraordinary by the tree, which was of such size that sixteen men with arms outstretched were needed to encircle it. He too met natives as he sailed northwards, but they were learning fast in that exploratory end of the fifteenth century. They had already been visited by Pinzón and therefore met Lepe with arrows. He replied with superior firepower and took some of them as slaves before returning to Spain. The slave trade, therefore, first went from west to east, but was otherwise little different from the east–west trade that was to come. In both directions a high proportion died *en route* and the survivors never returned.

These four expeditions of 1499 – Ojeda, Niño, Pinzón, Lepe – all explored the continent of South America, and three of them certainly sailed along much of the coastline of modern Brazil. Cabral sailed the following year, and it is therefore strange that he, for Brazilians in general (and certainly according to all their school-books), is the acknowledged and undisputed discoverer of their country. He would not have known of Pinzón's or Lepe's voyages, since neither had yet returned, but he could have known about the findings of Ojeda and Niño, had he been interested. Their trips both ended months before he set sail. Perhaps he thought their discoveries interesting but irrelevant to a man heading for the Orient. The others – Columbus and his successors – were entirely wrong in imagining they had stumbled upon a westward route to the Orient, but at least they had been bent upon discovery. Cabral merely wished to get to Calicut; yet he, and not those who had already sailed by the Amazon, receives the credit for discovering Brazil.

The major factor in this pre-eminence is that his landfall was not a mere extension of previous landfalls. The four South American voyages of 1499 were all further probings following on from previous discoveries, notably those of Columbus in 1498. Cabral hit land in quite a different area, where none had been presumed. In 1500 only the northern part of South America had been investigated, and no knowledge existed of extra land further south. Hence Cabral's surprise, and hence his fame and glory. Or perhaps this rests solely upon his closer approach to Rio de Janeiro, more the heart and soul of Brazil to most Brazilians than the mighty Amazon. Cabral touched land only 6° of latitude north of that favoured spot. The bay of Guanabara, in which lies Rio, was to be discovered just two years after Cabral's journey, and this swiftly became a centre for colonization. Brazilian happenings, either on the Amazon or further to the north, have always seemed distant and even unimportant to the Rio citizen. Of those earliest voyagers only Cabral came near Rio, and the names of Lepe, Pinzón, Niño and Vespucci are hardly known. They might as well have discovered Cathay for all their local fame. Or maybe they were simply of the wrong nationality. Cabral was Portuguese. A Portuguese country, as Brazil became, had to be discovered by a Portuguese, however many Spaniards had been there earlier.

But why is he not ridiculed rather than honoured for encountering that land? He was, most assuredly, on his way to India when he chanced on South America. This event was undoubtedly caused by Vasco da Gama, his predecessor to India. He gave Cabral sailing instructions based both on experience and on an excellent assessment of wind and current in the South Atlantic. His recommendations on how and where to sail can hardly be bettered today. The routes currently favoured by both the US Hydrographic Office and the British Admiralty would have Da Gama nodding in agreement. This Portuguese navigator had learned a thing or two – and arguably everything of consequence – during his long voyage south in 1497 to take advantage of Bartholomew Dias's discovery that Africa had an end to it. He had set off to reach India by this all-sea route, excited that at long last the spices of the Orient would be acquired from, more or less, their source.

When he left the Cape Verde Islands in that summer of 1497 Vasco da Gama initially sailed south-east. This seems reasonable, not only because the shortest distance between two points is straight but because there was no longer any need to follow precedent. All earlier Portuguese captains had tended to follow Africa's outline but Da Gama could steer directly for Dias's cape. Unfortunately the shorter distance did not prove to be quicker: he experienced doldrums, tornadoes, one lost yard, and a current that remorselessly opposed him. The passage took ninety-three days before he sailed into St Helena Bay, some eighty miles north of Cape Town. He therefore had ample time to think of an alternative route and to come up with different sailing instructions for his successor.

These indicated that Cabral should sail from Portugal for São Tiago, the central and largest of the three southernmost Cape Verde Islands. If he still had four months' supply of water on board he should continue south without stopping. If any deviation became necessary, this should preferably be towards the south-west, so that the north-east trade winds would be behind his fleet. When these waned, however, and the fleet met the south-easterlies, he was to sail as close to them as possible. Finally, when his fleet reached the latitude of Cape Town (34°S), it was to head due east for that southernmost tip of Africa. These sailing instructions were undoubtedly instrumental in cutting down Cabral's sailing time. Vasco da Gama's ships had left the Cape Verdes in August 1497, returning to Portugal during the summer and autumn of 1499. Cabral passed by the same islands in March 1500, discovered southern Brazil, explored it (a little), headed south-east for Cape Town, travelled to Calicut, had considerable problems there and was still back in Portugal by July 1501, a matter of fifteen months rather than two years. Trading at Calicut involved Cabral in a minor war and the waste of valuable time, but he spent far fewer days actually at sea, thanks to the wisdom of his predecessor.

The encounter with Brazil therefore begins to make sense, even meeting it at 17°S, which is well to the west of its most easterly protuberance into the Atlantic. Cabral might have met it earlier had wind and current forced him further to the west, but he resisted their joint urging towards Brazil until the day of that all-important shout from the mast-head. Had he managed to claw his ships a few miles to the east and maintain a heading with slightly more south in it, he would have missed Brazil altogether and turned for Cape Town without an inkling that a tremendous continent had been lurking over his western horizon.

As Cabral explored a mere fifty miles of the South American coastline he could not know he had happened upon a continent; but the thought of him sailing extremely close to a land mass of over seven million square miles without (until that shout) being aware of its existence can strike us, with the world map at our fingertips, as extraordinary. However, two and a half centuries later James Cook probed deep into the South Atlantic and failed to find a trace of Antarctica's five million square miles.

Rather than being surprised that Cabral should encounter Brazil when on his way to India, we should now consider the meeting almost inevitable, bearing in mind Da Gama's instructions and the modest sailing abilities of fifteenth-century ships. For many degrees on either side of the equator the movement of air and water is to the west. The north-east trades blow down upon northern Brazil; the south-east trades blow straight at eastern Brazil. There is an inexorable urge to the west, whether for flotsam, primitive raft or the kind of vessel Cabral had under his command. No one knows precisely how close Cabral's ships could sail to the wind, but they were undoubtedly less efficient than many later sailing vessels that ran into trouble on this same lee shore. James Clark Ross, skilled in coaxing *Erebus* and *Terror* where he wished them to go, and on his way to 78°S, crossed the equator at 30°W. He thought this a mistake and recommended future sailors to cross no further west than 26 to 27°W on account of the strong current heading for Brazil.

That Cabral discovered a part of the South American continent by intent is an argument difficult to sustain. When off Pernambuco he was only a couple of hundred miles west of the route recommended for today's sailing ships. If he had been intent upon South America he was exceptionally casual about locating a piece of it. Once he had found it, the brevity of his stay can best be explained by his wish to trade with Calicut. He was scheduled to visit India rather than some other continent. On board his ships were gifts for princes, goods for exchange, scribes, supercargoes, seamen, soldiers, priests, and even the king's personal doctor. Admittedly gifts, soldiers and the like can also serve on a voyage of discovery, but the lack of a *padrão*, or stone pillar, is thought to be significant. Of what use is discovery if you cannot effectively mark the spot?

The Treaty of Tordesillas, already mentioned, deserves more attention. It is not odd that a new land should be officially shared between two friendly competitors, partly to prevent them turning unfriendly, but it is exceptional that the Tordesillas share-out was determined with such haste. It cannot be claimed that Columbus's initial discoveries – the Bahamas, Cuba, Hispaniola – effectively outlined the New World. As for their distance from Spain or Portugal, that was only imprecisely known. Latitude could be deduced with some accuracy, but not longitude, which had to wait for a reliable timepiece to be invented. And yet, despite such a quantity of lack, the Treaty carved up the not-yet-discovered new lands with unblinking exactness. The demarcation line of 370 leagues west of the Cape Verdes – east of the line for Portugal, west for Spain – was no hazy definition. The Treaty's signatories did not worry either that no land had been discovered east of the line or that no person could accurately position the line on the world's maps.

Nevertheless they did appreciate that the line, wherever it was, had to be agreed somehow by the two parties concerned. Spain and Portugal were each to provide ships, pilots, astrologers. These would sail initially to the Cape Verde Islands, starting point for the measurement. Then, and independently, they would sail west. If they were still at sea after 370 leagues, and both parties confirmed the distance, they would sail south until they met land. A stone pillar would then be set up to mark the spot. What is implicit in this proposal is the assumption not only that land did exist east of that meridian but that the meridian could be located by agreement of both parties. Samuel Eliot Morison, expert on early Portuguese voyages, has phrased this last point elegantly: 'Considering that no method of determining longitude by observation was yet known, that no two navigators agreed on the length of the degree, and that next to nothing was known about compass variation, the failure of this joint cruise to come off was a sad loss to the humors of history.'

Alas for humour, but it did not come off. Both Spain and Portugal realized in 1495 there was no sense in heading for land a precise distance from the Cape Verde Islands until it was known that land did exist in that area. 'Inasmuch as it would be unprofitable for the said

delles fob ac penas o b gnevoes uindos i renunciacoves no dito confeto decapitula
am i concordia emcima fepto conthuidos. Cpr certidam i corroboraco do quall
afinani esta nossa curta do nosso signal i amandamy feelar do noso selo do chumbo
pendente e fios defeda decores. Dada na billa defenuud a Cinq dias domes de setemb
Johanm triz afer. Anno do nacimento de nosso Snor Jhu x de myl uijlhiy anos

The seal and conclusion of the Tordesillas Treaty that carved up the Iberian world in 1494.

caravels and persons to proceed before knowing that there has been found an island or mainland in each one of the said parts of the said sea', the voyage should not take place. There was no purpose in dropping a *padrão* into the ocean, even if both parties could agree where to drop it. They therefore compromised. A demarcation commission would not set sail until somewhere suitable had been discovered, until 'there shall be known to have been found in which one of the said parts the said island or mainland to which they have to go'.

The postponement was entirely reasonable, but does underline the haste with which the Treaty had been assembled. The agreement was likely to be unfair, in that no one knew or could know how much land might be on either side of the line (that could not as yet be drawn), but no one could possibly know how unfair it might be. Columbus had discovered three large islands to the west of the line, but no one yet knew about anything anywhere else. Hence the argument which persists that Columbus was a bit of a charlatan, that in truth some knowledge did exist about the Americas, that sailors had already been substantially west of the Cape Verdes, that the famous explorers were simply confirming rumour, and that there was a belief, possibly handed down in folklore for generations, that land existed both east and west of the 370-league line.

There would have been little honour to be gained, and no new land to be cleanly won, if any captain had admitted to following rumour. It was preferable to forget existing legend, despite the plethora of stories about voyages long before Columbus. These accounts are short on detail, but so are those of many later, famous and generally accepted travels. There is no log-book (or *roteiro*) of Cabral's trip, for example. Lesser voyages are even shorter on material information, and there may have been deliberate suppression. Columbus is said to have interviewed five sailors shortly before his own first sailing. The men were the only survivors from a ship that had travelled far to the westward. Their whole journey had apparently been fraught with considerable difficulty, and the remainder of the crew had already perished from their exertions. After their interview with Columbus the remaining five also succumbed, despite having reached land, food, and everything else that should have speeded their recovery. The charlatan, by this account, was a murderer as well.

Explorers of the Amazon

Despite these intimations of prior knowledge, it should be noted that belief in large lumps of land has by no means always been based on solid evidence. The idea that South America existed – if there was such an idea before Cabral and co. turned it into fact – can be compared with the eighteenth-century notion of yet another continent lying in the southern hemisphere. The existence of Australia was then known, while Antarctica was still unknown, but the belief grew that a colossal and temperate southern land stretched right round the globe. It was thought to reach almost to South America and nearly up to southern Africa, and it certainly embraced Australia. Principal propagandist for this great new continent was Alexander Dalrymple, geographer, astronomer, Fellow of the Royal Society. He staked his enthusiasm and reputation upon it. Consequently, when in 1773 Cook sailed right through the regions where the continent should have been, Dalrymple was never able to forgive the great explorer for not finding what had not been there. That men of science could be quite so wrong in the relatively well-mapped eighteenth century makes it less surprising that south-western Europeans in the late fifteenth century could also believe in additional continents, whether or not supported by evidence. Pre-Columbian rumours of a new world on the western side of the Atlantic can therefore be considered probable rather than possible.

After Columbus returned from his first voyage in March 1493, having discovered evidence to replace some of the conjecture, he first spent time with the king of Portugal, Dom João. The king was not only interested but perturbed by the admiral's account. It appeared as if the explorer might have been investigating some portion of the king's Guinea dominion, a large territory under Portuguese influence. (It is difficult to appreciate how the world looked at the end of the fifteenth century when many captains believed the new discoveries in the west were part of either India or China. No wonder mere kings were confused and could worry that Hispaniola, off the coast of North America, might be some further region of Guinea and equatorial Africa.)

Dom João of Portugal listened to Columbus, worried about Guinea and thought of sending a fleet to examine what the admiral had discovered. Columbus then hurried off to Spain, to his sponsors. They too were worried and speedily acquired three papal bulls which definitely established the new discoveries as Spanish. This alarmed Dom João even more. He sent representatives to the Spanish court but they, as if to distract interest from the new western lands, spoke excitedly of greater riches to be gained from more southerly African exploration. Spain, concerned by Portugal's concern, then acquired a fourth bull from the Pope (a Spanish pope, as it happened). This was, in effect, a *carte blanche*. It permitted Spanish captains to claim not only new land belonging to India but any lands encountered when sailing towards the west or south, 'whether they be in western parts, or in the regions of the south and east and of India'. (It should not be forgotten that 'India' was an extremely vague term, almost all-embracing. Modern consequences of that casual attitude to the sub-continent's actual location are that all indigenes of both Americas are called Indians, the many islands and nations of the Caribbean form the West Indies, and much land to the east of India is, collectively, the East Indies.)

The fourth bull made certain that Spanish captains discovering land, whether to the west or south, or east of India, could claim it readily. Of course Portugal protested. It complained loudest about its African discoveries, the Guinea dominions, but it also wished for a slice of the new cake, whatever and wherever it was. The Pope, now pressed for another bull, this time by Portugal, was possibly irked by the quarrel. It was therefore reasonable that he should try to settle the issue once and for all. Spain and Portugal were the only two nations involved, so Spain and Portugal should share the inheritance. Instead of the imprecision – and unfairness – of the earlier bulls, urged upon him by Ferdinand and Isabella of Spain, there would be a clear division. Spain would have to yield – a little. Portugal would be allowed to consolidate her African holdings, and would gain perhaps a little, perhaps nothing, of the new lands. No one knows why the figure of 370 leagues from the Cape Verdes was selected for this compromise. It was presumably the result of bargaining – and certainly represented a gain for the king of Portugal.

Anyone trying to put this line on a modern map runs into immediate difficulty. The Portuguese league, unhelpfully different from all the other leagues (English, French and Spanish, for example), also changed with the centuries. Moreover, Portugal's *légua maritima* must not be confused with the *légua de sesmaria* (a land distance about twice as long) or the *légua de beiço*, charmingly defined as an 'indication of a vague distance'. In the fifteenth century a Portuguese sea league was one seventeenth and a half of a degree of sixty nautical miles. This became a sixteenth and two thirds of a degree in the next century, and then one eighteenth of a degree about a century and a half later. In those years it therefore varied from 3.42 nautical miles to 3.6 to 3.33. A modern Brazilian history book for schools proclaims with total certainty that the 370 Tordesillas leagues equalled 2,020 kilometres, namely 1,096 nautical miles (or 2.96 nautical miles to a league). So, not to prolong a paragraph already tortuous, it is as well to conclude that it does not really matter. No one could sail accurately to a point 370 leagues west of somewhere else, whatever kind of league they had in mind, whether early Portuguese, later Portuguese, Spanish, English, or even the *légua de beiço*, that most pleasing indicator of a vague distance.

A more intriguing point concerns the Cape Verde Islands themselves. They are 180 miles across, some 50 to 60 leagues. The Treaty of Tordesillas does not mention which Cape Verde island it had in mind. Plainly there was scope for bickering if no one knew the starting point of the agreed distance. Spain would want the line as far east as possible, Portugal as far west. As further difficulty there could have been disagreement between Spain and Portugal concerning the actual longitude of the Portuguese islands. If even the starting longitude is debatable, how much more so the concluding longitude?

A possible solution for some of the inherent difficulties in the Treaty's expectations comes to mind. Or rather it was brought to mind by a letter sent from an English merchant living in Spain to Henry VIII of England. This man wrote in 1527 that when 'the division of the worlde was agreed of betweene them, the king of Portingale had alreadye discovered certayne Ilandes that lye over against *Capo Verde* . . . So for that all should come in his terme and limites, hee tooke three hundred and seventie leagues beyonde *Capo Verde*'. The letter seems to suggest that Cape Verde is a place rather than a group of islands bearing that name. Within the Cape Verde group there is no one island acting as eponym for the archipelago as a whole. Instead it derives its name from the most westerly spur of the African continent, currently called Cap Vert (and near Dakar) but formerly Capo Verde. This landmark was well known to all fifteenth-century sailors on their way to Guinea, being the spot at which their compass heading moved fractionally to the east of south. It was a fixed point, making a more sensible datum than an undefined somewhere in a scattered group of islands of uncertain longitude. Nevertheless, and strangely, the islands are generally assumed as the starting point for those 370 leagues, even if no one ever set off from any one of them to measure the distance.

How much of the New World was therefore actually granted to Portugal and Spain by the Tordesillas agreement? By the most generous assessment (from Portugal's point of view), using a long league from the westernmost part of the Cape Verde Islands, the Tordesillas meridian runs approximately through the mouth of the Amazon and the state of São Paulo. Taking the least generous assessment (again from Portugal's viewpoint), with a short league from Capo Verde on the African mainland, the agreed meridian just slices through the most easterly portion of Brazil. By either measure Portugal did well in later years. The Portuguese element of South America, Brazil, is far larger than the Tordesillas treaty could ever have intended, being about half of the South American continent. Admittedly the areas that came under Spanish influence – the rest of South America, Central America, Mexico – are considerably larger, and were initially much richer, but it may have been the Pope's intent to give Spain the lion's share of whatever lay on the other side of the Atlantic. After all, Portugal was busy with Africa, and with India, and was not the first to discover the New World (having refused aid to Columbus). Spain did deserve – if the cake was to be sliced at all – the larger portion. Not only was the Treaty prescient, but it actually achieved more or less what was intended.

As a document, the Treaty is certainly all the more extraordinary and impressive for being signed in midsummer 1494. Its makers did apparently know there was land out there for Portugal and that this area was smaller than Spain's domain. Cabral's discovery was another piece of providence. He, a Portuguese, was able to claim land for his country in the zone allocated to Portugal by the Treaty. The encounter therefore seems almost pre-ordained. Both sides did their best in the years immediately following 1494 to respect the Treaty, to steer away from each other's allotted portions, to retreat if either side protested; but Cabral was not a part of that later manoeuvring. He bumped into Brazil, east of the Tordesillas demarcation, when on his way to India. Maybe the very aptness of this encounter has appealed to the Brazilians, so that for them Pedro Álvares Cabral is the one and only discoverer of their land.

As for the man himself, Cabral is poorly documented, being probably the least well known of all exploratory heroes of that time (and certainly since). For all their worship of Brazil's first official witness, most Brazilians have no idea where he came from, how old he was when he set sail, whether he sailed again, or when he died. They certainly do not beat a path to his grave (in Santarém, Portugal). Nor do they care about the rest of his voyage, with its loss of life and of ships. For them it is sufficient that he arrived, set foot ashore, sent word back of his discovery and claimed the land for Portugal. For those who want to know more, about the individual, or about the remainder of that all-important journey, there is some information. It does not tell the whole story – indeed there are great gaps – but at least a portion of our curiosity can be satisfied.

The personal unknowns are considerable. There is no contemporary portrait of the man. His birth year is vague. The facts about his life, both before and after his great voyage, are extremely slim. He had probably not been on any prior voyage. He certainly did not make another. No reason is given concerning his selection for the Orient. Neither is any reason given for his abrupt removal as commander of a second voyage, months after the appointment had been made and shortly before this second fleet was due to sail. He may have been tall, his father having been known as the giant of Beira, but there is no confirmation. After his first voyage he might have been indicted for its considerable losses, but he was not. On the other hand he was not greatly honoured on his return. He apparently wrote nothing about the journey, either at the time or on later reflection. He ought to be known as the man who set the seal upon the traditional spice trade, but his fame rests upon that brief, unintended, not wholly welcome, and not particularly illuminating encounter with Brazil.

Pedro Álvares Cabral was born at Belmonte, some ten miles north-east of Covilha and about as far away from the sea as you can get in Portugal. The date is thought to have been 1467. By the age of seventeen he had gone to serve João II, and he stayed on at court when Manuel ascended the throne. He was therefore well placed for interesting appointments. The obvious choice of leader for the fleet being assembled in 1499 was Vasco da Gama, slightly younger than Cabral and experienced both in sailing and in Calicut, having voyaged there two years earlier. Cabral could not have been appointed without Da Gama's blessing, and it is even suggested that Da Gama recommended him, believing that a more courtly man might fare better with Calicut's authorities. Da Gama had been wearied by the enforced bargaining and by the rigours of the extremely lengthy, scurvy-ridden voyage. Also in Cabral's favour were the 'presence of his person' (according to one contemporary), his two brothers in the king's council, his family's long record of loyalty to the crown, and presumably his ability at court, having served under two kings for over fifteen years. What he did not possess, apart from any nautical experience (which could be left to his captains), was acquaintance with wily, cautious, fearful and greedy foreign overlords, like the Zamorin of Calicut.

Cabral had no difficulty in recruiting the 1,200 men to sail with him. This sizeable band, about 0.1 per cent of Portugal's population, approved of Cabral's appointment, but they did receive a wage as extra inducement. (Not only did Da Gama's fewer sailors die in great numbers, but the survivors had to rely upon the king's subsequent generosity for any remuneration.) The size of Cabral's fleet, the number of men involved and the longed-for prospect of oriental trade led to a magnificent send-off from Lisbon. Allegedly 'all' witnessed the departure, and everyone was optimistic that spices, drugs and perhaps jewels would henceforth flow to Portugal by a route that, quite literally, circumnavigated the rich and unrelenting middle-eastern middlemen. It would be a long voyage but a short cut to wealth and prosperity. No wonder the Tagus echoed to the cheers of a nation. At one masterful, daring, cunning stroke the fleet would go round the merchants of Venice and Cairo, returning laden with everything the Orient had to offer, but much cheaper than before.

Cabral's impatience with Brazil therefore makes great sense. It had

An early rendering of Cabral's brief encounter with Brazil, when he landed, held mass, named the place, met friendly Indians, and then departed to the East.

come his way unexpectedly, and he behaved as befitted a chance discoverer who could not afford delay. He approached the land, found a secure anchorage, sent men ashore, held a mass, named the place, sent word of the finding back to Portugal, and then set sail once more, with no one but the convicts bemoaning his departure. The Orient was his goal, and not some unexpected piece of territory that might or might not be a continent and might or might not be of significance. The lure of India had lasted too long to be dashed aside by the palm-fringed shore of somewhere else. He ordered his helmsmen to turn towards the east, the discovery of Brazil having consumed just twelve days of his sixteen-month voyage.

The meeting with Brazil passed without incident, but the rest of the voyage was nothing like so straightforward. Ten days after leaving South America the crew sighted a comet and predicted difficult days ahead. These were not slow in coming. On 24 May a storm hit them, 'a head wind so strong and so sudden that we knew nothing of it until the sails were across the masts', according to an unknown chronicler of the voyage. Four ships were sunk almost at once, one of them captained by Bartholomew Dias, discoverer of the Cape towards which they were heading. The remaining seven could not set a sail for another twenty days and were dispersed. When the storm relented Cabral was accompanied only by two other vessels, with the remainder themselves split into a trio of ships and a singleton. These must have been terrible days for the young commander with only two other sails to see.

After rounding the Cape of Good Hope Cabral's diminutive fleet put in at Mozambique to make good the damage. Three more of his ships then joined them, meeting up in the providential manner that seemed to have been so simple to these early explorers. The fleet of six then sailed northwards up the coast of eastern Africa, reaching Kilwa on 26 July and Malindi on 2 August, the latter being most friendly towards the Portuguese. There was then the big hop across the Indian Ocean before Cabral could anchor off Calicut on 13 September, slightly over six months after leaving Lisbon. With half the ships and less than half the men that had started the voyage (there had been sickness *en route*), there was nevertheless considerable jubilation. Guns were fired. Flags were flown. Negotiations could begin.

These were such that Cabral might have wished for the relative simplicity of a storm at sea. Before any Portuguese could go ashore there had to be mutual hostages. Only then did Cabral land and talk with the Zamorin, Calicut's ruler. He speedily learned that India did not particularly welcome this Portuguese visitation. The spice trade was set in its ways, doing very nicely, and there seemed no immediate, or even long-term, advantage in selling directly to sea-borne western Europeans. There were many businessmen in the Persian Gulf, Aden, Cairo, Venice, who would be aggrieved at any loss of business and could take commercial reprisals. Anyhow Cabral set up a trading post on shore, as was the Portuguese custom along the coast of Africa. India's Arab merchants were particularly resentful of this encroach-ment and quickly made their point. They incited rebellion so that the post was suddenly attacked. Of the seventy men within it at the time, only twenty escaped to swim back to the ships. The losses included three Franciscan monks and Pedro Vaz de Caminha, author of the principal letter sent back to King Manuel reporting on the discovery of Vera Cruz.

Cabral waited on board awhile, hoping for some word – such as an apology – to come from the Zamorin. Nothing arrived, so revenge began. Ten Arab ships were seized, looted and burned. Without doubt it was Arabs who had instigated the uprising, but the Portuguese then attacked the city itself, bombarding it for a day. If Cabral had been given command for his skill as a committee man, as a diplomatic negotiator, he had forgotten all this in his lust for vengeance. The citizens of Calicut might have welcomed traders other than the Arabs, but the bombardment landing in their midst did not encourage such a response. They never forgot, or forgave, the attack.

The Portuguese, for their part, considered themselves perfectly entitled to effect such punishment. Not only had their men been killed, but they had the permission of the Pope to take over India's exports. Heathens had no right to stand in the way, and it was unpardonable that they should kill Christians. As the Zamorin must have connived in the Arab attack it was right that he, together with his city, should be taught a lesson. Cabral's skill as a diplomat was suddenly of the gunboat kind. Some of his predecessors had behaved similarly, and many of his successors were to do likewise as they too turned superior weaponry upon various forms of infidel.

Calicut a century after Cabral's visit, by which time it had become India's most celebrated emporium.

With only two of his ships laden, with Calicut reeling from the attack, and with further trading difficult for the time being, Cabral sailed for Cochin, about 120 miles to the south. In his orders he had been instructed to try this other port if Calicut proved unsatisfactory. News of Calicut's devastation had preceded Cabral's fleet, but Cochin's king welcomed it. The Zamorin was not everywhere popular along that Malabar coast, and Cabral was to benefit. The enemy of an enemy is a friend, and within two weeks all of the Portuguese fleet was fully laden. News that the Zamorin was heading south with eighty vessels at first prompted Cabral to seek battle, but discretion then prevailed. Leaving behind a number of sailors at Cochin, and taking hostages and an ambassador with him, he turned his ships west – for Africa and Portugal. The date was early January 1501.

There were further problems on the return journey. One ship impulsively sailed too near the east African coast, ran aground and had to be abandoned. Its crew were spread among the five remaining vessels. The fastest of these was permitted to go ahead to hasten the expedition's news to Portugal. It had to put in for food and repairs at the port of Beseguiche, near Cape Verde, and there encountered the remaining ship that had become separated from Cabral's fleet during the great storm off southern Africa on the outward voyage. This vessel, commanded by a brother of Bartholomew Dias, had visited Madagascar (the first from Europe to do so), called at Sofala (the most important east African trading port, which Cabral had not dared to enter) and then continued north to the Gulf of Aden before returning. As this reunion was occurring, with the traditional effortlessness of such encounters, three ships arrived under the command of Amerigo Vespucci. They were to explore and trade with Cabral's land of Vera Cruz, news of which had reached Portugal exactly a year beforehand.

Those earliest days of the sixteenth century were undoubtedly exciting, as ships returned with brand-new information, as fleets were despatched to follow up earlier findings, as these encountered the remains of earlier fleets returning with further news of an island such as Madagascar, of Arab trading posts, of a world that had suddenly been exposed to European eyes. The chat must have been tremendous. One wonders that anyone could bear to depart when there was so much more to tell, to hear, to think and ponder on.

Cabral's fleet, in its ones and twos, arrived back in Lisbon during June and July 1501, fifteen to sixteen months after its departure. There was both rejoicing and sadness at its return. The unhappiness was for the heavy loss of life, with the crews of four ships vanished utterly. There had also been casualties, as at Calicut, and great sickness during the lengthy voyages. The total is not recorded, but 75 per cent of the original complement are thought not to have returned. If there were 900 casualties this was a considerable loss, particularly for a country whose population at the time numbered little more than a million. The compensatory rejoicing was for the five ships that had returned fully laden, and also, in smaller measure, for the two back safely without cargo. A way to the east had been found. Trading in a direct fashion had been proved possible. The terrible Egyptian and Venetian monopoly had been broken. Portugal could now satisfy her own needs and become the great entrepôt for everything the Orient had to offer that could profitably be transported in ships.

The effects of this new sea route were to be felt in the eastern

Pedro Cabral

Mediterranean almost at once. During the final years of the fifteenth century, and immediately prior to Cabral's sailing, the Venetian galleys had been returning – mainly from Alexandria – with 1,500 tons of spices a year, principally pepper. In the four years from 1502 to 1505 their loads dropped to less than 500 tons annually. As the Portuguese wiped away their tears for the lost sailors they could happily anticipate such figures. Their little country had beaten the stranglehold. The mighty power of Venice, the trading authority of Cairo and Alexandria, the connivance of all the intervening businessmen, with goods changing ownership ten times between India and Italy, had all been humbled by one daring venture of commercial acumen. Lisbon and Portugal did weep, but cheered as well, loudly and at length.

There is no casualty list from the expedition but there is an account of the goods brought back (good news being more noteworthy than bad). Amerigo Vespucci, having encountered Cabral's ships at Beseguiche, and hearing of the cargo collected from Cochin, quickly dashed off a letter to his Medici patrons. He first details, not wholly accurately, the voyage itself, and then lists some of the goods returning with the fleet. These were, he writes, 'an infinite amount' of cinnamon, green and dry ginger, pepper, cloves, nutmeg, mace, musk, algabia (thought to be a source of perfume), *istorac* (an Indian medicine), benzoin, porcelain, cassia, mastic, incense, myrrh, sandalwood, aloewood, camphor, amber, *canne* (believed to be bamboo), *lac, mumia* (or extract of mummy, prized as a drug), *anib* (probably anil, or indigo), *tuzia* (probably *tutia*, or zinc oxide), opium, *aloe patico* (another kind of aloe), *folio indico* (indigo leaf) – and here Vespucci peters out, referring only to 'many other drugs which you know it would be a long thing to relate'.

Cabral's men must have been exultant when shopping for such items in India. Not only were they abundant, and displayed for all to see and buy, but the prices must have been a fraction of the cost of such commodities in Europe. Vespucci also wrote that 'of jewels I know only that I saw many diamonds and rubies and pearls, among which I saw a ruby of one piece, round, of the most beautiful colour, which weighed seven and one-half carats . . .' It must have been difficult for him to steer his vessels towards the unknown merits of the Brazilian shoreline, having been confronted with the known blessings acquired from Malabar.

When Cabral's ships had returned to Lisbon and emptied their holds of pepper, cinnamon, ginger and the rest, the rejoicing was prolonged; but what of the commander of the fleet? He received neither great rewards for the triumph nor castigation for his losses. He certainly was not acclaimed in the same way as Vasco da Gama, who on *his* return from India became Count of Vidigueira and was offered the captaincy of any future expedition to India. Yet although Cabral might have been criticized for returning with only five ships laden of the dozen that had sailed, he was more warmly than coolly received. As William Brooks Greenlee puts it (in the Hakluyt Society's biography), 'the losses and the inability of Cabral to attain his objectives were not his fault; they were his misfortune'.

Besides, it was a first try. Cabral had learned some of the difficulties and, particularly at Cochin, had paved the way for future trading. For eight months he worked upon the preparations for a further expedition, intending to be even more successful than on the first. Then, without historical explanation, the command was given to Vasco da Gama. There may have been intrigue behind this change of appointment – indeed, it is difficult to visualize the event without it. Perhaps Da Gama felt sufficiently recovered from the rigours of his own Indian voyage for a second attempt. Or maybe, as the discoverer of the spice route, Da Gama increasingly and jealously resented Cabral's exploitation of it. At all events Vasco da Gama did command the next venture, did succeed triumphantly, and effectively displaced Cabral as merchant adventurer number one.

Pedro Álvares Cabral, now aged thirty-five, left court after being replaced, never to return. A document shows that later on he was managing a small estate near Santarém, up the Tagus river. In about 1503 he married Doña Izabel de Castro, well connected and with some money of her own. They had six children: Antonio, who died in 1521 without issue; Fernão, who did marry and have children; Constança; Guiomar, who became a prioress; and Izabel and Leonor, who both became nuns. It is known that Cabral was alive in 1518 and was dead in 1520, but it is not known precisely when he died and whether he was aged fifty-two or fifty-three (assuming the birth year of 1467 to be correct).

They buried this first hero of Brazil in the Convento de Graça, now

Pedro Cabral

in the Asylo de São Antonio at Santarém. Later his wife and one of his children were laid to rest beside him in the same little chapel attached to the church. There is no major memorial, and access to his resting place is difficult. If any Brazilians do determinedly seek out the grave of their country's accepted discoverer they will eventually succeed. They will then read a tablet which makes no mention of his status in all Brazilian eyes:

Here lies Pedralvarez Cabral and Dona Izabel de Castro, his wife, to whom this chapel belongs and to all her descendants. After the death of her husband she was *camareira môr* of the Infanta Dona Maria, daughter of the King Dom João, our Lord, the third of that name.

The omission of Brazil's name from the tomb of Brazil's discoverer is intriguing, but perhaps its inclusion would have surprised Cabral even more. The leader of the first successful commercial expedition to the Orient, the first European to trade directly for spices and drugs, and the man who wholly upset the traditional system of eastern enterprise, would be astounded to learn that he is currently renowned for the twelve most unintended days of his sixteen-month voyage. Cabral's name will last for ever because it is taught to all Brazilians at school, a fact which would probably astonish no one more than the individual concerned – Pedro Álvares Cabral.

A contemporary memorial about Cabral's discovery is inscribed on a map published in 1502. It records the fact, but does not enthuse. It might even have been dictated by the commander himself.

The *vera cruz* so named, which pedralvares cabrall, *fidalgo* of the house of the King of Portugal found; and he discovered it going as chief captain of 14 ships which the said king sent to Calicut. And on the outward voyage he came upon this land, which land is believed to be mainland, in which there are many people, men and women, whom they describe as going nude as when they were born. They are more white than brown and have very long hair. This land was discovered in the era of 1500.

A possible mainland, equipped with naked, long-haired, whiteish people, is interesting, but a far cry from the Orient.

There remains one postscript to this tale – the naming of Brazil. Cabral was perfectly clear in his wishes; he called his discovery the *Terra da*

A posthumous portrait of Pedro Cabral, the man Brazilians have chosen to honour as the discoverer of their land.

Vera Cruz. The name was apt for various reasons. Firstly he and his men had been gazing for days upon the Southern Cross, the most interesting constellation of the Southern Hemisphere. Secondly

Pedro Cabral

Cabral displayed a banner of the Order of Christ, a red cross on a white background, on all the sails of his fleet, he being a knight of that order. And thirdly, with the new land encountered at Easter-time, the theme of the cross was entirely topical. One man even likened the fleet's (remaining) twelve ships to the twelve apostles.

Two letters sent back with the empty supply ship to Portugal's king named the find. In his letter Caminha referred to the *Ilha da Vera Cruz*, while Master John, author of the second, shortened this to *Vera Cruz*. Whether it was a land or an island, the correspondents were unanimous in their choice of name. It was *Vera Cruz*, and was therefore entitled to stay that way. The king then fudged the issue by informing the Pope that his new kingdom was the *Terra da Santa Cruz*, and it was henceforth given that name in all ecclesiastical writing. There was also a more popular or casual description, allegedly used by Cabral's crew on their way to Asia and even afterwards. Having been properly astonished by the macaws and parrots to be seen in the new land, they called it the *Terra de Papagaios*, or sometimes, as an abbreviation, Papaga. No trace, though, of any name like Brazil, not in those earliest days.

This name did already exist, after a fashion. Along with various other pieces of land imagined to exist in the Atlantic was one marked as Brazil. On a map published by Toscanelli in 1484 (eight years before Columbus's first voyage), the island of St Brandan, probably named after the sixth-century Irish monk, lies to the west of the Cape Verdes. Antilia is well to the west of the Canaries, and is said to have been an island of refuge from the Moslems, where seven bishops presided over seven cities. There are the Fortunate Islands, the Blessed Islands, and there is also Brazil. On that particular Italian map it is placed immediately to the west of Hibernia (Ireland), which itself is correctly detached from Britain. This island of Brazil not only appeared on maps but was referred to in texts, where it was said to have sands of gold-dust. As the world opened up, and reality replaced fantasy, Brazil was therefore a name looking for a piece of land, a name that appeared on maps alleged to have been drawn before Columbus ever set sail.

Coupled with this legend is the story of brazil-wood, which was already known from the Old World, its name being probably a corruption of the Arabic *bakkam*. The wood was prized for the deep-red dye it provided and came from a tree known to modern botanists as *Caesalpinia sappan*, one of the Leguminosae. When Cabral's men were shopping at Calicut, before the disastrous massacre, they noted that a *faracola* of brazil-wood cost 160 *favos*, about a third as much as opium and the same as camphor. (It may be wholly unhelpful to add that there were 20 *favos* to the *ducat*, and about 20 *faracolas* to the *baar*.) The Portuguese were informed that brazil-wood (*brazili*) came from Tanazaar, '500 leagues beyond Calicut'. Today this is Tenasserim, the coastal region of Burma lying to the south of Rangoon.

The 'brazil-wood' tree found by Columbus on his second voyage, and by subsequent travellers to Brazil (although not Cabral), is of the same genus as *C. sappan* but a different species: *Caesalpinia echinata*. Both have popular names, such as false sandalwood, East Indian sappan and Indian redwood, as well as brazil-wood. It was a little insulting to Cabral's *Vera Cruz* that in its earliest days the country was thought to be good for nothing but red dye. However, the trade in this wood did develop rapidly, with a notably large demand for it from Flanders. Gradually, and much to the disgust of church officials who persisted with the old religious name, the new Portuguese territory began to be referred to as Brazil. This then developed into Brasil, the current local spelling of the ancient word.

As for Cabral's choice, that still has a small foothold. Brazil's national flag is not among the most beautiful in the world, being a little cluttered, but it does include the stars of the Southern Cross. Cabral, like the ecclesiastics, might not approve of the change of name to Brasil, but he might still be gratified to note that all is not forgotten. In his fame as discoverer, and in the flag's undoubted cross, his memory still lives.

II

Francisco de Orellana
FIRST DOWN THE AMAZON

There are parallels between Cabral, effective discoverer of Brazil, and the first man from Europe to travel down the Amazon. (It is unlikely that any group of South American Indians ever paddled down the entire river, but the possibility should be left open.) Both Cabral and Orellana achieved fame almost by chance and unintentionally. Cabral did not expect to encounter Brazil; Orellana did not hope to travel down the world's mightiest river. Neither of them wrote an account of his travels. (Friars did the task for both of them, most flatteringly.) Neither leader was greatly praised by the home-based authorities for his South American efforts, nor did significant rewards come their way. Both men wished to command a further expedition, capitalizing upon experience and fame, but neither wish was satisfactorily gratified: Cabral was relieved of command shortly before the fleet set sail, while Orellana was given such inadequate backing that his Amazon return was foredoomed. Neither man's death was greatly mourned at the time, and the world in general does not know of either man as perhaps it should.

Francisco de Orellana was born in 1511 (when Cabral was aged forty-three and with eight more years ahead). Brazil's discoverer was Portuguese, but the conqueror of the Amazon was Spanish, from Trujillo in Estremadura. No one knows when he set sail for the New World or to which place he first travelled, but the year was probably 1527, when Francisco was a youth of sixteen. Although Peru, with its astonishing riches, had still to be invaded, there had been sufficient New World exploits (such as Hernán Cortés' conquest of Mexico) to create irresistible longings in every young Spaniard with the means and zest to head westward for fame, fortune, glory, excitement, and possibly some sort of governorship at the end of it all. More to the point in young Francisco's case was his relationship with the Pizarro family, many of whom were already in positions of consequence, notably in Panama.

Perhaps Orellana did first go to Panama to join his relatives. If so it is highly likely that he took part in expeditions to the north of that isthmus, the initial interest being in northern America rather than the south. Balboa had discovered the western ocean in 1513, but Cortés had subsequently diverted attention from it by attacking and subduing the Aztecs. Magellan then sailed through the straits that bear his name in 1520. He named the Pacific, and one of his ships eventually circumnavigated the world, but there was more than enough for other men to do in the Americas without following up his distant discoveries. However, he had demonstrated the tremendous extent of the southern continent. The Spaniards in Panama or Nicaragua (where Orellana is believed to have cut his teeth as a *conquistador*) would therefore have started probing southwards, particularly when rumours of Cuzco and the Incas filtered through to them. So they sailed further and further down the Pacific coastline, and in 1533 achieved their overwhelming conquest of the Incas. Francisco Pizarro's band of 150 men accomplished one of the most extraordinary feats of arms (and of treachery and cunning) in the history of the world by subduing Atahualpa's well-organized, powerful, rich and technically advanced Inca empire in six months. Accompanying the Spanish leader, notably during the attacks upon Lima, Trujillo and Cuzco, was Francisco de Orellana, then twenty-two years old. The young *hidalgo* won much honour for himself in these battles, and also lost an eye.

They do say that for mercenaries and the like, whose business is war, the arrival of peace is a terrible occurrence. For the *conquistadores*, whose war or wars had been so dramatic and so rewarding, the conquest of the largest Indian empires must have been devastating. What else could possibly compare, either in adventure or in recompense? For the one-eyed veteran, who had left Spain six years earlier and had seen more action than many a nobleman could hope for in a lifetime, the end of the war was not wholly welcome. He suddenly found himself no more than the builder and owner of a house in Puerto

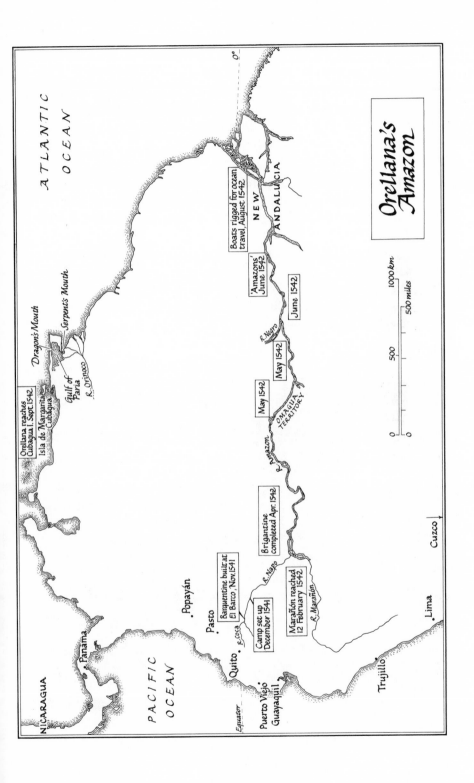

Orellana's Amazon

NICARAGUA

Panama

PACIFIC OCEAN

Popayán

Pasto

Quito

Equator

Puerto Viejo
Guayaquil

Trujillo

Lima

Cuzco

R. Coca

Camp set up
December 1541

R. Napo

Marañón reached
12 February 1542

R. Marañón

Barquentine built at
El Barco, Nov.1541

Brigantine
completed Apr.1542

R. Amazon

OMAGUA
TERRITORY

May 1542

R. Negro

May 1542

June 1542

'Amazons'
June 1542

Boats rigged for ocean
travel, August 1542

NEW

ANDALUCIA

0°

ATLANTIC OCEAN

Dragon's Mouth

Gulf of
Paria

R. Orinoco

Serpent's Mouth

Orellana reaches
Cubagua I. Sept.1542

Isla de Margarita
Cubagua

0   500   1000 km
0   500 miles

Viejo (on the coast of today's Ecuador). Years of relative retirement loomed ahead of him, years of inactivity and boredom.

Fortunately for such a man, there was to be further conflict, not just between Spaniard and Indian, but between Spaniard and Spaniard. When he was resting at his home there came news that Lima and Cuzco had been besieged by Indians. He immediately borrowed money, bought twelve horses, amassed eighty men and marched for Lima, which was under the command of Francisco Pizarro, blood relation and Inca conqueror. The two sieges were raised fairly speedily, although Orellana's part is unknown. He merely states, in a subsequent memorandum, that he 'left the said cities free from siege'. He next fought in the civil war between groups under Pizarro and Diego de Almagro, the former controlling the coastal regions and the latter the high sierra. These rival armies met at Las Salinas in April 1538, when

What could compare, in the eyes of the conquistadores, *with the spoils of conquest brought to them during the subjugation of the Inca empire?*

the Pizarros, under Francisco's brother Hernando, won the day convincingly. Magnanimity in victory was not a Pizarro characteristic, and Hernando had the sixty-three-year-old Almagro garrotted. The act caused ill-feeling and further side-taking among the Spanish, not only in the Americas but at home. There was such controversy that to have taken any part in the war was thought to have been dishonourable, or so says the explanation generally given for the fact that Orellana never mentioned the role he played. He had been in charge of 700 men, all sent by Francisco to assist Hernando, but Orellana expunged this particular action from any future memoranda. It was better to say nothing and remember nothing.

The war had been a warning for everyone, not least Francisco Pizarro, the governor of Peru. Idle *conquistadores* were not only bored but a likely source of further trouble. Therefore, as great tracts of land were in need of exploration, he despatched the heroes of the conquest to unknown areas of that part of South America. By this means they were kept busy, distanced from each other, rewarded in due course and given new realms to govern. Orellana was included in this skilful share-out. As he later wrote, he had to conquer, 'with the rank of Captain-General, the province of La Culata, in which I was to found a city . . .'. He conquered, and a piece of Spanish Peru became his property.

Later, when writing yet another memorandum for the king of Spain (and all others who might care to read it), he gave a not entirely humble account of the setting out and the conquering. First he had to find men at his own expense. Then, 'at the cost of many hardships', partly because the Indians were 'untameable and warlike', partly because of the 'rivers having great volume of water' and the 'region of marshes', he had fought his way into the allotted province. Its Indians had grown 'haughty', mainly through knowing a thing or two about those marshes. 'Two or three captains' had gone into that area, been routed and seen their men killed. Orellana, however, now aged twenty-nine, had managed to place 'the said province under the yoke' of Spain, and had then set about phase two, the founding of a city: 'I gave [it] the name of Santiago', in the founding of which 'I rendered great service to his Majesty', as it lay in 'a spot so fertile and so rich', and so 'conveniently placed' for the towns of Quito, Pasto and Popayán, that if it had not been founded there would have been 'great slaughterings of Spaniards and great destruction and losses'. In other words he had accomplished his instructions and, once more, was at a loose end.

At about this time, early in 1541, the unemployed Francisco de Orellana heard of an expedition being planned by Gonzalo Pizarro. It was just the sort of thing both men wanted. Gonzalo, a younger brother of the conqueror of the Incas, whom he had accompanied throughout the conquest, had recently been appointed governor of Quito and much of its surrounding area. He was therefore Orellana's immediate chief, as well as a relative and an old acquaintance from the same part of Spain. The planned expedition was of a kind (the only kind?) that would appeal to a *conquistador*. Its intent was to explore new territory where both riches and spices were alleged to exist. New conquest, new wealth and new trade – each was sufficient lure. The possibility of all three was overpowering.

The fact that new land for Spanish subjugation lay over to the east was the only certainty. The wealth and spices – allegedly gold and cinnamon – were less sure. There was rumour of both but the Spanish were insufficiently sceptical, even when information about such blessings had been tortured from captured Indians. The rumours told in particular of El Dorado, 'the Gilded One', a king who was periodically covered in gold dust, and then washed himself free of his coating in a sacred lake, where his ancestors had done the same for generations. To the Spaniards, the idea of a lake whose very sediment was gold must have been even more enchanting than the stories from Peru. There were also accounts, culled according to Gonzalo from 'prominent and very aged chiefs', of forests of cinnamon. The spicy bark of a tree could never be as exciting as gold, but any produce to undercut that from the Orient had considerable appeal, particularly back home.

Gonzalo Pizarro wrote glowingly to his sovereign about the region of El Dorado and La Canela, of gold and cinnamon:

I decided to go and conquer it and explore it, both in order to serve Your Majesty and in order to broaden and increase Your Majesty's realms and royal patrimony, and because I had been made to believe that from these provinces would be obtained great treasures whereby Your Majesty would be served and aided in meeting the great expenses with which Your Majesty is faced every day in his realms.

Such a promise from one who had seen Inca treasure laden for Spain

Francisco de Orellana

would assuredly have pleased its monarch, who was immersed, as always, in the unending problem of expense.

The Gonzalo Pizarro expedition was not interested in the Amazon, however much the two may now be linked. Its intent was wealth, glory, adventure and excitement, culminating in the administration of a tremendous piece of land. It was certainly no modest expedition. Gonzalo recruited over 200 Spaniards (the numbers cited vary from 'over 200', to 220, to 230, to 280) and collected almost as many horses. This added up to more men and horses than his brother had possessed when conquering Peru. At least the men came free of charge, save for the expense of paying some of their debts, but the horses cost a fortune. The party was also well armed, with arquebuses, crossbows and munitions. It was well supplied with pack animals, mainly llamas, and with food. There were 2,000 pigs, who would walk until they were eaten, and almost as many dogs, useful in hunting Indians. As for Indians, several would act as guides and over 4,000 others had been amassed to act in any capacity for which they might be needed. These last were shackled until the day, towards the end of February 1541, when the whole panoply set forth from Quito, a total – if beasts and men are added together – of over 10,000 marching, walking, riding, running, hobbling, limping forms of life.

Francisco de Orellana, who made all possible speed after he had heard of the enterprise, missed that impressive departure. After being invited to take part, he had not only to hurry to Guayaquil and resign his office, but to get money, buy horses, collect some men of his own, and hurry the couple of hundred miles from Guayaquil to Quito. In fact he left for Quito precisely when Gonzalo and the 10,000 assorted men and beasts were leaving it. By the time of Orellana's arrival the very last llama, dog, pig and Indian had vanished to the east. The remaining Quito citizens urged Orellana to forget the whole business. With such a small party he would not be able to resist the inevitable attacks, or so they said. He would succumb to every natural form of hardship and would certainly starve. It was doubtful, they added, whether even Gonzalo's great army would triumph – very doubtful.

The first problem was cold. A mere seven leagues from Quito (some twenty-five miles) both parties had to cross a snow-covered range, and a hundred of Gonzalo's Indians swiftly died. Then there was forest, through which a path had to be hacked. And then rivers, over which bridges had to be built. And finally came Zumaco, just thirty leagues (110 miles) from Quito, where a rest was not simply desirable but vital for the exhausted contingent. The difficulties, according to a chronicler of the time, were 'such that anyone but Gonzalles Pizarre would have abandon'd such an Enterprize as seem'd to be opposed by both Heaven and Earth'.

Pizarro then explored ahead with a smaller party. He soon found some cinnamon trees and demanded of the local Indians where these grew in greater abundance. Despite having them tortured he learned nothing more, but did succeed in antagonizing the local population. With the area up in arms, and the trees so thinly placed, he returned to Zumaco, forgot the cinnamon idea and turned to that of El Dorado. This second story grew with the telling. The king, it was said, wore nothing but gold dust, smeared on with an oil. He preferred this covering to any ornaments or apparel, even if these were also made with gold. And his washing was not on rare occasions, but every single night. It is understandable that cinnamon trees waned in their importance when the Spaniards were confronted by such a tale.

Orellana was united with the main body of the expedition at Zumaco. His contingent had been less encumbered with pigs, Indians and the like, but had only numbered twenty-three soldiers. Consequently it had been set upon repeatedly, as had been forecast. Also, as Pizarro had already travelled that same route, not only antagonizing the neighbourhood but, locust-like, stripping it of food, Orellana's worries concerned starvation as well as Indians. A reception party was despatched by Pizarro from Zumaco to meet up with the newcomers. Orellana was glad of their welcome but gladder still to fall upon their food. When he and Pizarro eventually stood face to face, Orellana was dubbed lieutenant-general, or second in command. The promotion may have been pre-arranged, or given as reward for such a courageous pursuit. At all events this high appointment made the subsequent happenings, with their alleged treason, yet more significant.

Despite the two groups' mutual happiness at their union, and the small boost this gave to the expedition's resources (in men, if nothing else), their pleasure in the enterprise was on the wane. The rain grew heavier every day. 'A few' Spaniards were dying, following those 'many'

Indians who had already perished. As a third reason for disquiet, the local people could not assure Pizarro of better conditions ahead, or a healthier climate, more suitable conditions for his horses, or valleys rather than mountain-tops, despite the burning alive of some of those questioned. Pizarro fared no better when reconnoitring again with a small force, and only managed to secure good news when returning to Zumaco along a different route. A local chief, Delicola by name and undoubtedly wiser or better prepared than some of his fellows, disregarded the truth. He told Pizarro of rich regions towards the east, of great settlements ruled by powerful overlords. As reward he was kept alive by the Spaniards. Ever ready to hear good news, and to believe it, they now forged ahead in the recommended direction, fought more Indians, threw a bridge across a river, and eventually found a few insignificant dwellings with extremely modest provisions. It is not mentioned what happened to Delicola, but Indian deaths were rarely recorded even in numbers, let alone by name. Delicola's death, for the crime of raising false hopes, can be assumed as assuredly as if he had told the truth in the first place.

A further reconnaissance was then despatched, with fifty men under the command of the 'camp-master'. They returned after two weeks, with news of a 'great river', of houses on its banks and of 'many Indians wearing clothes'. (The fact that this news was encouraging shows how far the original promise of gold and spices had receded. Survival was now paramount, the problem of food critical.) The entire party headed for this river, 'passing through great marshes and . . . many creeks'. Then, as further indication of a changed attitude, Pizarro attempted to befriend the 'quite civilized' clothed Indians. Barter trading proceeded until most of the Indians disappeared, possibly finding their share in the commerce inadequate. The Indians who stayed had no choice. Pizarro made certain that the chief and elders could not vanish. As these local people had never met anyone resembling the Spaniards, there must have been initial curiosity on their part, plus a willingness to learn about foreign ways. The Spaniards, on the other hand, had been meeting Indians of one sort or another for years, and were rarely slow in teaching them about their different attitudes. There was soon a considerable battle raging between the 'quite civilized' clothed Indians and the extremely hungry, invading Spaniards.

A new problem, not encountered in the mountainous areas further to the west, was the local Indian expertise with canoes. Rivers were now the highways, rather than old or fresh-cut paths. In one place some 150 canoes, all laden with warriors, flaunted this form of sea-power while the invaders struggled on the shore. Gonzalo took stock of an unpleasant situation and decided to build a boat. Various names, such as 'brigantine' and 'barquentine', are given for the type of vessel he ordered, the various translators of contemporary accounts having differing preferences. Such nautical names have acquired greater precision over the centuries, so that brigantines and barquentines are now defined as two-masted and three-masted vessels respectively. Plainly Gonzalo's men built nothing of the sort: masts would have been an encumbrance (trees, overgrowth) and also useless, since there was hardly any wind in those regions. What they actually constructed was a little boat, a *barqueta*. Its dimensions are not known, but it probably had cross-members and could be propelled by about twenty men while carrying a quantity of stores. With higher gunwales than the local dug-outs, it afforded more protection and undoubtedly tipped the balance of power towards the Spaniards.

The expedition's principal chronicler was Friar Gaspar de Carvajal. Originating from the same Spanish city as Gonzalo Pizarro and Francisco de Orellana, he was a trifle older, being about thirty-eight when the expedition began. He had left Spain in 1536, and had earned some fame by vigorously defending the right of asylum in his monastery when a prisoner escaped into it. (He needed that fortitude as he was to lose an eye in the forthcoming adventure.) As a recruit for Gonzalo's company he made an obvious choice. The custom of taking a friar on military exploration was already well entrenched. Such men represented the Church and acted as recording scribes, many of the leaders being either illiterate or too busy. There was also a suggestion of objectivity in having an allegedly impartial observer to glorify your exploits. In fact these friars generally so identified themselves with their various leaders that any hint of neutrality became buried beneath effulgent and high-toned praise. The chroniclers were also diplomatic, putting their leader's point of view on any controversial matter. This was certainly true over the issue of the boat, for Carvajal knew its building would be a matter of contention. He therefore set the story straight, right from the outset.

'Orellana was of the opinion that the boat should not be built,' wrote the friar. He added that the lieutenant-general favoured a retreat to the savannah country in the west, believing that roads should be found which would lead forward to the settlements, and that Gonzalo should change his mind. When this last point could not be effected, 'Captain Orellana . . . went throughout all the camp securing iron for nails and apportioning to each [soldier] the timbers that he was to bring, and, in this manner and with the labour of all, the said boat was built.' This official narrative therefore affirmed that Orellana had stood against river transport, had argued the point, and had then yielded to the wishes of his commander obediently and energetically. The fact that Orellana subsequently took the boat, apparently abandoning Pizarro, and did make total use of the river to achieve both fame and a place in history – well, Carvajal had done his best to offset the inevitable accusations of betrayal. According to the journal it had not been in Orellana's mind to travel anywhere by water, let alone down the world's greatest river. He was even against the building of the *barqueta*, and said so at the time.

The creation of the boat underlines the considerable change in the expedition's fortunes. There had been 10,000 assorted men and animals at the departure from Quito. Now, at a village appropriately dubbed El Barco, only seventy leagues (256 miles) from Quito, much of the expedition's optimism was being pinned on a single craft, 'water-tight and strong, although not very large'. The contingent would have needed an armada at the outset; now one small boat was all-important.

Very shortly afterwards the pigs were entirely consumed. Most of the Indians had already perished. (Being highland people they swiftly succumbed to fevers when no longer at altitude.) Quite a few Spaniards had died, killed by Indians, by disease. A greater number of their horses had also died. Whether the boat could transport twenty individuals, as most chroniclers suggest, or double or treble that number, its modest capacity proves how times had changed. Into it were loaded a number of the sick, a quantity of the equipment (such as axes and adzes) and some able-bodied men to assist in its propulsion. The rest of the party, namely all the Spanish still with horses, the surviving Indian load-carriers (male and female) and the remaining dogs (eaten when the pigs had been consumed), had to make their way as best they could, downstream along the banks.

Travel in a tropical forest is never easy. It is particularly difficult near the rivers, where swamps and ox-bows, tributaries and profuse vegetation all compete to antagonize those on foot. Moreover the rivers meander, and their followers must do likewise if not to lose their way. With the boat on the water, and the remaining men, women and animals proceeding as best they could by land, the expedition progressed a further fifty leagues or so. During this progress the Spaniards encountered no more inhabitants and hardly any food. It was ten months since they had proudly left Quito and they were now to reach a turning point, certainly in the history of the Amazon and more so in the lives of the two leaders, Orellana and Pizarro. These two men, so soon to separate, would never meet again. More to the point they could never have met again save with weapons in their hands.

Mutual hatred, with terrible accusations of deceit and perfidy, were to simmer thereafter down the centuries until José Toribio Medina took it upon himself to set the record straight. This late-nineteenth-century Chilean was determined to remove the stigma attached to Orellana. He had been particularly piqued by a major magazine article of 1892 entitled 'La traición de un tuerto' ('The Treachery of a One-eyed Man'), and his rebuttal was published in 1894. In the end, having produced the first scholarly account of the sixteenth-century journey, he vindicated both Orellana and Pizarro. Each man, in his opinion, had done what was both right and sensible at the time.

Of the two individuals it is easy to prefer Orellana. He was more intelligent and actually took trouble to learn the Indian language. The tongues changed, of course, as the journey progressed, but no member of the expedition could ever converse with the local people better than he could. He cannot have been the handsomest of men, as blinding damage to one eye rarely enhances beauty, but his efforts on the Amazon show a quality of leadership and engendered loyalty of the highest degree. His pathetic end is also endearing in its fashion. As for Gonzalo Pizarro, he was as much *conquistador* as his more famous elder brother. Intensely brave, a first-rate horseman, dashing in manner and appearance – he would have been a military leader without his astonishing family to bring him to the fore. Another Pizarro, writing thirty years later, called him *apretado y no largo*, close and not generous. He also 'knew little', which was probably just as well. To know more might have created excessive caution, not the first requirement of a conquering explorer. He was later to take over Peru by force, courageously but none too wisely, and was killed soon afterwards. Both he and Orellana were dead within eight years of their parting, one shortly after defeat on the battlefield, the other having failed to overcome a terrible environment. Death is not always so explicit in defining the kind of life it is bringing to an end.

The parting of their ways came when foodstuffs were at their lowest, along with the expedition's morale. The date was Christmas 1541. After almost a year of hardship the Spaniards had encountered no gold, no El Dorado, only a few unprofitable cinnamon trees, and no wealthy communities. The explorers could barely keep themselves alive, let alone obtain 'great treasures' whereby the king of Spain would be aided 'in meeting the great expenses' which faced him every day. As the crow flies, or as the condor makes the journey, they were just 200 miles away from Quito. There was no immediate prospect of improvement in their lot unless food could be found. Hence the decision that a small contingent should take the boat, hurry downstream, somehow find supplies and bring replenishment to the main party.

This decision was to be so crucial it is perhaps best to let both sides tell their stories. According to Pizarro:

There came to me Captain Francisco de Orellana, and he told me how [he had questioned] the guides that I had placed in his charge . . . in order that he might talk to them and from them get information regarding the country beyond, as he had nothing to do, for it was I who looked after matters pertaining to fighting; and he told me the guides said the uninhabited region was a vast one, and there was no food whatsoever to be had this side of the spot where another great river joined up with the one down which we were proceeding . . . Captain Orellana told me that . . . he was willing to take upon himself the task of going to search for food . . . and that, if I would give him the brigantine, . . . he would go in search of food and would bring it for the relief of the expeditionary force . . . and within ten or twelve days he would get back.

Explorers of the Amazon

Pizarro's lieutenant-general has to speak through Carvajal's journal:

Captain Orellana, seeing what was happening and perceiving the great privation from which all were suffering, and considering that he had lost all that he had had [at the start], thought it was not becoming to his honour to turn back after so great a loss . . . So he went to the Governor and told him how he was determined to leave behind him the little that he had with him and go on down the river and that, if luck favoured him to the extent that he should find an inhabited region and foodstuffs . . . he would let him know about it . . . and thereupon the said Governor told him to do whatever he thought best; and so the said Captain Orellana picked out fifty-seven men, with whom he embarked in the boat and in certain canoes which they had taken away from the Indians, and he began to proceed down-river with the idea of promptly turning back if food was found.

There does seem to have been agreement. It was Orellana's idea and Pizarro gave it his support. The fifty-seven, who are all named in the records (save for two Negroes in the party whose names are never given), took with them three arquebuses (guns that needed support) and 'four or five' crossbows. Most of the weapons, all of the horses, and the remaining men, about 140, stayed with Pizarro. He was later to assert that Orellana had taken 'all the arquebuses and crossbows and munitions and iron materials', but this does not seem to have been the case. It is the only point of disagreement in the two accounts; the rest is accord. Orellana had to sail downstream, find what food he could and report back as soon as possible. Many another expedition, conscious of the lumbering presence of the entire force, has despatched a smaller party to forage for supplies. It is a wise solution, or perhaps the only possible solution.

The leave-taking must have been quite a spectacle. Going down-stream, apart from the boat, were ten canoes of fifteen that had been purloined. Some of these were attached to the main vessel, while others were paddled independently. On board, apart from Orellana, were the Dominican friar, Gaspar de Carvajal, another friar named Gonzalo de Vero (of the Order of Mercy), several of the sick and a greater number of healthy soldiers to make up the complement of fifty-seven men. (Carvajal initially refers to sixty, but this does not appear to be correct. What is certain is the absence of Indians. It might have been wise to have taken some as guides, in that several had known of communities

Francisco de Orellana

A Spanish arquebusier of the sixteenth century, as drawn for George Millar's Orellana.

downstream, but perhaps space was at a premium and the river's current a guide in itself.) On land, watching this departure, stood an equally hungry but three times greater body of men. It was correct for Gonzalo Pizarro, the governor, to stay with the larger force, but it must have been galling for him, the powerful adventurer, to watch his lieutenant setting forth. If food was to be found, the men with Orellana would be first to assuage their appetites. Those left behind could only wait, and hope.

Carvajal does not write of that farewell. On the second day the boat struck a midstream tree trunk and had a plank stoved in. This was repaired and once again they pushed out into the middle of the river. The current was faster there, urging them more swiftly towards inhabited territory and the likelihood of food. The trouble with such travel, of course, is that the speedier the flow the harder the return. To paddle downstream at three knots with a two-knot current means an agreeable haste of five knots. To travel upstream with the same parameters will take five times as long, the paddling being almost negated by the current. If the flow is swifter the progress up-river will be non-existent. Carvajal does not specify the river's speed, save that it was 'fast', or the boat's, but does express disquiet. 'Although we did wish to go back up the river, that was not possible on account of the heavy current . . . To attempt to go by land was out of the question.' 'I am in blood stepp'd in so far that, should I wade no more, returning were as tedious as go o'er,' wrote Shakespeare a few decades later. It would seem, on that tributary of a tributary of the Amazon, on the Rio Coca leading to the Rio Napo of today, that returning would be rather more than tedious. It would be quite impossible.

After a week, and realizing the gathering problem of return, one canoe-load thought it heard the sound of drums. The date was 1 January 1542, suitable occasion for a change in circumstance. With some of the men 'eating hides, straps, and the soles of their shoes cooked with certain herbs', with others 'so weak they could not even stand', and with a few taking unfortunate pot-luck over various forest roots that poisoned them 'to the point of death', it is extremely understandable that wishful or hallucinatory thinking made some of them hear drums. Everyone immediately rowed faster, but the day ended with no more distant beats. The next day was even quieter.

However, late that night, and allegedly first heard by Orellana himself, the drumming grew more positive. It could no longer be attributed to the light-headedness of hunger. Guards were posted in case the Indians should attack. Orellana did not sleep. He must have been relieved at their impending change in fortune, either for good or ill. Anything was better than inexorable decline.

At first light, with arquebuses loaded and crossbows poised, the Spanish moved downstream. After two leagues they encountered four canoes of Indians. These turned tail, as well they might on meeting a flotilla of armoured, bearded strangers, the like of whom they had never seen. Soon drums were being pounded on every side, and there was no misreading them. Orellana urged his men to greater speed, intending to arrive at the first village before the general call-to-arms had been effected. The Spaniards, leaping ashore in a disciplined manner, quickly had the village to themselves. There was food in abundance, being cooked and in store, and also 'beverage'. Orellana made certain the inevitable counter-attack would not take them unawares. Then the men began to eat, their 'shields upon their shoulders, their swords beneath their arms'.

As the previous ten months had never been characterized by an excess of food, as horses, dogs and then boots and roots had been on the menu, the joy of discovering whatever that village had been preparing for itself must have been extreme. Even at this first encounter the leadership of Orellana was demonstrably different from that of Pizarro, now languishing 200 leagues upstream. No Indians were captured, garrotted, thrown to the dogs or imprisoned. Instead, when some shyly returned in canoes, Orellana attempted to speak with them. He 'gave them something from his supplies', 'took away their fear', 'cajoled them' and asked them 'to go get the overlord'. This they did, and he 'came right away, very much decked out'. After mutual embrace the chief was given clothes 'with which he was much pleased' – surprisingly, if he was well-attired – and offered whatever the Spaniards had spare when a year out from home. The captain, single-mindedly, asked for food in return. He was rewarded with 'an abundance, including meats, partridges, turkeys and fish of many sorts'. As exchanges go, it was a bargain for the Spanish; donating old belts and shoes for good food was greatly preferable to eating them.

The bonhomie continued, but Orellana remained vigilant, arranging 'watches both by day and by night'. On the second day at the village four more chiefs arrived to meet Orellana. He spoke to them 'at length' (and one wonders if Pizarro ever exchanged a single word with any Indian). Rather high-handedly, Orellana took possession of all their land in the name of the king of Spain. Perhaps they, for their part, did not understand everything said to them, for they continued bringing food in particular and aid in general. It was the first village that had treated the Spaniards in such fashion. It was also the first to be encountered under Orellana.

By now the point of no return had been reached. The fact of finding food and regaining lost strength ought, in theory, to have made more feasible the retracing of their steps. In practice it merely emphasized the impossibility of return, however full their bellies and their boats. The 700-mile journey back to Pizarro's camp was three times as far as Pizarro was from Quito. The fast current would either hinder or negate (probably the latter) the benefits of river travel, and Orellana now knew that the intervening land had no food. His contingent had been in favour of turning back before encountering that bountiful village. The very lack of anything to eat had made a return seem preferable; anything seemed better than going on and on. On meeting that village, on eating and drinking to their stomachs' content, a retreat seemed valueless. Not only would everyone probably die on the journey upstream, but, knowing of Pizarro's lack of food, they could not believe he was still waiting for them. Either he and his men were dead or they had travelled elsewhere.

For all the logic of the situation, Orellana, the second in command, knew how his failure to return would appear to Pizarro. He had been entrusted with the boat, with canoes and fifty-seven men. He had offered to find food and to send at least word back to his commander. No message of any kind had been sent to Pizarro, who must have seethed as the days passed, as no word came and his men grew weaker. For Pizarro only two possibilities existed. Either Orellana and his men had died or they had found food and disregarded their promises. By incurring Pizarro's wrath and running the risk of being branded a traitor, Orellana was not simply losing the favour of one man. He was forsaking all he had gained – his position in Peru, his wealth there

Francisco de Orellana

(largely in the form of Indians), his prestige, his everything. To fall foul of the Pizarro family, certainly in Peru at that time, was to lose all hope of gain and probably one's life.

Those quick to label Orellana treacherous – and for three and a half centuries that was one of the milder epithets – could have spent more time considering the option he had chosen (or had had imposed upon him). As options go the adjective soft does not immediately surface. He had absolutely no idea how long the downstream journey might last, how many tribes of Indians he would meet, how warlike they might be, or whether there would be great areas that were short of people and starved of food. Were there waterfalls, terrible rapids, wild and frightening beasts? Did the river lead pointlessly to some unknown inland sea? Had Orellana been able to open a modern atlas and observe that he was somewhere in today's eastern Peru, and had he measured well over 2,000 miles of river ahead of him, he might have been yet more alarmed. Even when he did debouch into the Atlantic there would still be the problem of that ocean, of journeying on to Spain, or to Panama, or anywhere else that seemed feasible.

The food village was called Aparia. It was there that Orellana, further to vindicate his position, recommended a return to Pizarro's camp. His men opposed this, stressing 'how much more danger of death there would be for us if we were to go with Your Worship back up the river'. However, as they too were unwilling to be branded traitors, either to Pizarro or to Orellana, their petition concluded that they would follow him wherever he chose to go. Orellana, they argued, ought not to put them in a position where they would be compelled to mutiny. Aparia and its thatched roofs must have seemed very far from Spain, but everyone knew that all decisions taken in that distant village would be thoroughly, critically and mercilessly examined when the group returned home. Even if the chances of that happening might have seemed slender at the time, it was correct to take precautions against subsequent recrimination. A judgement against them would make them wish they had perished in the depths of South America. Hence their attempt to make it plain that they were loyal, both to Pizarro and to Orellana. Proceeding down-river seemed to them not just the wisest course but the only course, however much it contradicted Pizarro's original instructions.

Finally, in an attempt to show democracy at work, Orellana resigned his appointment as lieutenant-general, the post given by Pizarro. His men, now reduced by starvation to forty-seven (excluding the two friars), then demanded his continuance as leader. All swore 'by God ... by the sign of the Cross, and by the four sacred Gospels' that Orellana should be leader. He too swore, and signed his name, everything being written down by the expedition's appointed 'scrivener', Francisco de Isasaga, for later scrutiny.

These ceremonies over, 'and in order not to lose time nor waste the food in vain', the survivors prepared for the journey ahead, all thoughts of return now truly vanquished. Certainly there was much to be accomplished, particularly when they decided to build a bigger boat. Water-travel had now changed from a temporary expedient to a means of existence. By boat they would journey to the Northern Ocean, as the Atlantic was then called. By boat they would sail from the river's mouth to wherever seemed most sensible. The modest barquentine constructed at El Barco should therefore be replaced by something more suitable for such a voyage. The small canoes, having been appropriated from Indians, were no better than all other local craft. They were never intended for lengthy journeys and would also be inadequate should the Spaniards be attacked further downstream by a fleet of such dug-outs. A better boat was the undoubted answer, for both travel and survival.

However, much easier said than done. No member of the proud force that had left Quito almost a year before could have expected the search for cinnamon and gold to be transformed into boat-building. There is no written mention of anyone carrying carpentry tools other than axes and adzes. (Indeed there is frequent mention that the Spaniards carried only shields and weapons.) A difficult requirement for the boat was nails, which meant the manufacture of charcoal, plus some bellows to assist in heating iron to its melting point. These ventilators were created from buskins, the calf-length or knee-length form of boot (and one assumes some men were bootless afterwards). Despite 'weakness' and the men being 'not expert in that line of work' there were 2,000 'very good' nails to show for their labour after twenty days.

Unfortunately, the rightful residents of Aparia were becoming increasingly conscious of the Spanish intrusion. It is frequently said

never dismisses a peril with a merry quip or understatement. Instead he takes pains to mention the pains, scarcely noticing the geography or the vastness of the river on which he is voyaging. He becomes more excited when, after two weeks on the greatest river in the world, 'four or five canoes' were seen, visibly laden with food. This proved to include partridges 'like those of our Spain, save that they are larger', and turtles 'as large as leather shields'. Orellana gave presents in return for the food, a gift from the area's overlord, confusingly named Aparia like the village left behind twenty-four days earlier.

The three and a half weeks had been fairly tranquil. Their most disturbing incident had been the temporary separation of two canoes carrying eleven men. These had gone too far ahead, had become lost among some islands and were not seen again for two disconcerting days. Orellana immediately ordered that no canoe should ever be more than a crossbow-shot distant from the barquentine. New rules, with tough penalties, were having to be instituted for a wholly new environment. High on the list were those that encouraged the friendliness of the Indians. Orellana always tried to speak to them, to assure them of his peaceful intent, to request a little food. Word must have progressed ahead, causing Aparia (sometimes called 'the Great') to anticipate their requirements by loading those four or five canoes. If food was what the foreigners wanted, so be it. Give them food and urge them on their way.

However, Orellana liked the idea of tarrying a while in Aparia's kingdom. Such immediately proffered hospitality should not be disregarded. These new Indians might in time also consider the Spanish presence to be irksome, but that possibility could wait. An immediate problem was the building of the second and larger boat. For that task he needed friendly Indians and a ready supply of food. It seemed as if such a village was near at hand. He therefore spoke with the canoe-men and asked to see their overlord. The Indians paddled home with the Spaniards following. At the village scores more Indians climbed into canoes 'in the attitude of warriors'. Orellana, ever a mixture of gentle diplomat and man of action, immediately ordered his rowers to proceed 'at full power'. As a conseqence the Indians 'seemed to get out of the way', as well they might before a bunch of armed and bearded strangers. The old *conquistador* method of attacking while the other side hesitated worked once more in the village of Aparia the Great.

Explorers of the Amazon

Orellana then moved from war, or the threat of it, back to diplomacy and conversation. Carvajal was rightly approving of his captain's fluency: his 'understanding of the language was, next to God, the deciding factor by virtue of which we did not perish'. Orellana told the Indians to have no fear, to approach more closely, and to let him speak with their overlord. This chief then leapt on land from a boat, asked permission from the Spaniards to sit down (while his followers stood) and immediately ordered more foodstuffs, such as turtles, manatees, fish, roasted partridges, cats and monkeys.

To the Spanish in general, after all their privations, this must have seemed heaven on earth. To Orellana it was too good an opportunity to miss for further gain. He spoke of Christianity, a single God, the error of worshipping stones and images, and how the Spaniards were children of the sun. The Indians allegedly marvelled greatly, manifesting great joy and believing the invaders to be saints or celestial beings. Orellana knew, as his fellow countrymen had already learned in Mexico, in Peru, in much of the West Indies, that to be revered (however temporarily) solved all manner of problems. The Indians promised food on every day. They vacated their village. They listened quietly while their land was officially possessed in the name of the king of Spain. And they watched as a tall cross was erected, at which they 'took delight'. In short, everything was set for the building of the boat, referred to now as a brigantine as distinct from the barquentine, their principal vessel since taking to the river at the end of the previous year.

Carvajal did not pay much attention in his journal to the union of the Napo with the Amazon, on which they would travel across most of the breadth of South America, but he cared considerably about the construction of the newer, bigger, better boat. One of the party, Diego Mexía, took charge. There is uncertainty whether he was a woodsman, a stone-cutter or even a carpenter, but he certainly knew how the boat tasks should be carried out. Some men were each to bring a frame and two futtocks (curved or middle timbers), others the keel, still others the stem pieces. More men had to cut the trees, make the planks and generally prepare the wood. Carvajal stresses the 'considerable physical toil' involved, the ever-present possibility of Indian treachery, and how the wood had to be fetched from afar 'because it was winter'. (This point is not explained.) When each man had finished his particular labour he was given another, the making of more charcoal, the creation of yet more nails. Not only did everyone wish to finish the task but the virulence of the mosquitoes was spur to their endeavour, and the vessel was launched thirty-five days after work had begun. It had been caulked with cotton and tarred with pitch, the Indians supplying the necessary materials 'because the Captain asked them for these things'. This point is also not explained. A healthy dug-out does not need such water-restrainers, but perhaps the local craft did crack from time to time. The Indians evidently did know what was needed for the brigantine, and where to find it.

The completed vessel was of nineteen *joas*, 'quite enough for navigating at sea'. One longs to know its dimensions but, alas, these *joas* do not clarify the matter. They are additions to the main timbers at their upper extremities where they constitute the sides of the ship. A *joa* is not a measurement. In Carvajal's un-nautical context he is probably referring to extensions on the nineteen ribs: a sizeable boat, therefore, but of unknown size. Opportunity was also taken to mend the smaller boat, which had begun to rot. As their stay at the bountiful, friendly and co-operative village happened to coincide with Lent, there were frequent services. Each man confessed his sins to one or other of the two friars (and one does immediately wonder what a *conquistador*, who may have quartered Indians, considered to be sinful).

More amazing, at least to those who had seen only black hair, brown skin and short stature among Indians, there walked into the village one day four men of quite a different hue. They were quite white, had very fine hair reaching to their waists and were taller by a span than the 'tallest Christian'. Whether this means a span taller than very tall Spaniards, or a span more than the most lofty among Orellana's men, it is still astonishingly tall. Even southern Europeans, not the tallest from the continent, tend to be taller than South American Indians; but for the tables to be turned by a span (generally assumed as the stretch of a hand – some nine inches) is extraordinary. Their whiteness, as against the traditional Indian duskiness, fans the flames of surmise for those happy to believe that groups from the Old World made colonizing contact with the New World long, long before Columbus stole all the renown.

The four fine-haired, white-skinned giants were well mannered, splendidly dressed, 'decked out in gold' and – never a point to be missed by the diarist friar – loaded with a great quantity of food. Orellana spoke with them, as always, and after much civility the four men departed, leaving behind a quantity of food but no information. As to their tribe, or its location, the Spanish learnt nothing. Nor, apparently, did they ask their village hosts for additional enlightenment. This was the first occasion ever recorded by Europeans of white people emerging from the Amazon forest. It was certainly not the last; the sightings and the stories have, yeti-like, steadfastly continued. Never is the evidence wholly convincing, but never will the stories go away. One does wonder particularly at Carvajal's account. There was ample excitement in his river tale for it not to need embellishment. So one can only suppose the men did truly appear, were whiter than most Indians, were richer (in their gold), were longer-haired and taller, and simply went away.

On 24 April Orellana and his men set off again downstream. They travelled with the new boat, the smaller barquentine and an unspecified number of the original ten canoes. Initially they met more friendly (and food-donating) Indians but, with the passing of Aparia's territory, the flotilla passed into an uninhabited region. Once again, ever ready to stress difficulty, Carvajal dwells on shortage, with 'more hardships' and 'more hunger' than before. For the first time he mentions fishing, but does so only to detail its poor success in these particular waters. Many an Indian, observing the forest as a giant market, rich with every need, must have been astonished by the Spanish difficulty in living off the land. However, it may be that this uninhabited region did indeed lack sufficient resources even for Indian livelihood.

The Amazon can be short on fish, particularly during the wetter seasons when so many of the river's inhabitants leave the mainstream and take to the flooded areas relatively rich in food, but any reader of Carvajal's account begins to suspect, sooner or later, that fish were a sort of penance, to be eaten perhaps on Fridays (as dictated by the Church) but not every day. The suspicion grows stronger when he writes of hoping to find – at such and such a place – 'some kind of food, or fish'. However, it was a fish, a considerable fish of five spans (or almost four feet), that not only gave him one of his better stories but, inadvertently, belied the lack of sustenance.

Francisco de Orellana

'Proceeding along, harassed by our usual suffering and great hunger . . .' the story begins, determined as ever to make the most of adversity. The same Mexía who had been so masterly over the boat-building shot at a bird with his crossbow. A vital portion of the bow, a catch to hold the string in place, then fell off to be immediately lost in the Amazon. Carvajal does not mention whether the part was replaceable, but the intimation is otherwise. Another Spaniard, by name Contreras and equally eager to supplement the food supply, happened to be fishing at the time. The fish he landed shortly afterwards, a considerable catch of 'five spans', was not only far larger than had been expected but had swallowed the hook. Dissection was necessary and, during this probing, the crossbow's catch was discovered within the animal. Carvajal was not only astonished, as well he might have been, but also relieved, 'because, next to God, it was the crossbows that saved our lives'. (Orellana's linguistic skills have already been described as, next to God, the saving of them all. While the expedition proceeded, many more things were, next to God, due to save the expedition.)

The Orellana party had not yet encountered any antagonistic Indians. Pizarro apparently encountered nothing but antagonism. It is easy to suspect that Orellana's different methods – more love, less war – were responsible for his better fortune. However, he next met a stretch of river under the command of Machiparo. This ruler was no Aparia, kindly sending food and offering assistance. Instead he despatched canoes full of fighting men. According to other Indians on the river Machiparo had 50,000 warriors under his command, all aged from thirty to seventy. Only a fraction of this number were sent against Orellana, but the warrior-laden canoes must have been a formidable sight, all gaily coloured with each individual carrying a man-sized shield of lizard skin and manatee hide. Orellana instantly switched from diplomat to man of war. He ordered the two boats to be bound together for a better defensive centre, commended himself and his men to God, and prepared for battle.

Unfortunately for the Spanish, this attack came when their gunpowder was damp. Arquebuses were therefore useless, leaving firepower in the hands of the 'four or five' crossbowmen, including the archer whose trigger catch had been so providentially returned. There is no mention of ordinary bows, whose swift rate of fire had proved advantageous time and again on European battlefields. The onus fell fair and square upon the crossbows. Although slow to use they proved effective in finding their mark. After each firing the Indians would retreat until, reinforced with further canoes and courage, they again attacked within range of the crossbow bolts. As Orellana was being besieged and harried from both land and water he decided to effect a landing. More of his men could then give an account of themselves.

His original idea had been to find food in Machiparo's kingdom, rest for a few days, and proceed down-river when suitably refreshed. Reality proved different. Only half of the Spaniards were able to land effectively, the others having to defend the beached boats. The land party, under the leadership of Alonso de Robles (recently appointed Orellana's lieutenant), attempted to clear the village and find food. The Indians initially retreated, but fought like men who, in Carvajal's phrase, were 'vexed to abandon their homes'. They were also, one assumes, vexed to abandon their food supplies, which proved to be considerable: meat, fish, biscuit and turtles in pens, enough to supply 'an expeditionary force of one thousand men for one year'. Cristóbal Maldonado and a dozen men, designated by Robles as food collectors, had to compete in their task with scores of Indians about the same business. When upwards of a thousand turtles had been amassed, Maldonado gave up food collection and attacked the 'two thousand' Indians who were his rivals. During this fighting two of the 'companions' were wounded and the Indians were routed. Food gathering could begin again, but once more the Indians attacked. This time six men were wounded, including Maldonado whose arm 'was pierced' and face 'hit with a stick'.

The main contingent under Orellana was also having trouble. Some Indians had made a detour until a 'squadron of 500' was suddenly standing in the village square. Orellana, caught without his armour on (and one wonders about opportunity, let alone reason, for removing it), rallied his men and succeeded in repelling the Indians. It is extraordinary how frequently a modest Spanish force, whether in Mexico, Central America, Peru or here upon the Amazon, managed to rout a much more numerous enemy. Superior firepower was sometimes the answer, but an aggressive skill must also have been crucial. Carvajal commends one man in particular, Blas de Medina, who fought with

The Spanish first fell upon their knees, as one chronicler phrased it, and then fell upon the Indians.

nothing more than a dagger and yet survived with no more than a 'thigh pierced through'. By this stage of the battle against Machiparo's men, eighteen of the Spanish had been wounded, one seriously.

Any idea of rest at this village was now abandoned. Maldonado, of the food-raiding party, reported that the Indians were massing in a nearby gully. The men already wounded constituted a third of the Spanish force. There was also the realization that much more of Machiparo's kingdom lay ahead. To win at this first village, but possibly to have more casualties, would surely mean losing at the next assault that came their way.

Orellana made his departure in style and with cunning. Initially the stolen food was loaded on to the boats. Then the wounded were carried on board wrapped in blankets, as if they too were sacks of corn. Orellana wanted to avoid a display of limping men in visible distress.

Then the remaining companions embarked 'in good order' before setting off, as always, downstream. The arquebus powder was now dry, and the guns and bows were, 'next to God', their salvation. Carvajal had little compassion for the Indians defending their homeland and their food. He does not mention the number of Indians killed. Instead he pronounces them evil or wicked and never credits them with courage in the face of a superior fighting machine. Certainly these Machiparo Indians gave the Spaniards a difficult time for the rest of that day and during the night. Moving steadily downstream was like passing a line of angry hives. Each set of inhabitants would rush for their canoes, fight as best they could, and then drop behind while others took their place. For the Spaniards there was no such respite. They fought continually until, at noon on the following day, Orellana took refuge on an uninhabited island in the middle of the river.

The men were resting and preparing food when even this haven became unsafe. Three times they were attacked, and three times the Indians were driven away. Further resting was now out of the question. While the Indians were preparing a further assault, both from the island's other end and by canoe, the weary, hungry, battle-sore travellers were forced once again to head downstream. Encouraging the enemy were some sorcerers, 'daubed with whitewash', blowing ash from their mouths. Having made one complete circle around the Spanish flotilla the whitened figures cried out to their warriors. Drums were beaten, trumpets and wooden bugles blown, and the Spanish once again were fighting for their lives. Worse was to come in the shape of a narrow, well-defended section of the river. Poised high among those on land was their obvious leader, standing arrogantly to witness the destruction of the invading force. At this crucial and frightening moment one arquebusier, Hernán Gutiérrez de Celis, took very careful aim. The proud Indian leader received the shot right in the middle of his chest. His men immediately 'became disheartened and 'gathered round to look at their overlord'. The Spanish took instant advantage of the respite, steering and paddling for the wider water. Eventually, after being harried for two further days and nights, they sailed beyond Machiparo's domain. One Spaniard was to die from his wounds, a modest price for having passed the most belligerent Indian community Orellana and his men had encountered since taking to the water five months earlier.

Out of the frying pan into the fire. The territory ruled by Machiparo lay next to that of the Omagua. At the very first village of this new kingdom 'many warriors' were lined up. It must have seemed to Orellana as if the Machiparo saga was to start again. He therefore resolved to attack this village without delay, capture it and earn some peace. His men were not so much short of food as short of time to eat it, their fighting being so remorseless. The Omagua village had been fortified 'on the model of a garrison', a fact which turned to the Spaniards' advantage once it had been captured. The place could more easily be defended, gaining them the relaxation for which they longed. An attack upon the moored boats soon after this rest had begun was so fiercely repulsed, 'some damage' being done to the Indians, that no more significant attacks were forthcoming. The Spaniards could rest, at last. They enjoyed their good lodgings, ate all they wanted, and thoroughly appreciated the change in circumstance.

Orellana and his companions had now achieved, by their reckoning, 340 leagues (1,250 miles) since leaving Aparia's village, but had little idea how much river still lay ahead of them. It is difficult for us to know precisely where they had reached at this stage, but it was certainly above modern Manaus and probably about 63°W, Quito being 78.30°W and the Napo's union with the Amazon 73°W. They had done well but may even have known, insofar as longitude could be determined in those days, that the Amazon's mouth was 900 miles due east of their position and many more via the river's convolutions. Whatever the actual distance, they surely knew the journey was far from over. Better, therefore, to get on with it. When rested and well fed, notably from some excellent biscuits found within the garrison, they returned to their boats and the river. The date was 16 May 1542.

Eighteen days later, on 3 June, they encountered the Rio Negro and gave it that name (the only name they coined to have survived into modern times). It was black as ink, said Carvajal, and flowed so abundantly and with such violence that it did not immediately mix with the Amazon, but formed a streak for over twenty leagues. (It is not quite that black and the visible distinction between Amazon and Negro does not continue quite that far, but the union *is* most impressive and Carvajal was entitled to stretch the point on encountering this stupendous natural wonder of the world.) The journey from the biscuit garrison to the Negro had been the mixture as before: hostile Indians, fierce engagements, the need to capture villages and steal food. The belligerence shifted to amicability when they had moved from the land of Omagua to that of Paguana, the latter being rich in silver, in fruits (pineapples, pears, plums, custard apples – all 'of very good quality') and even in llamas, far from their traditional Andes. One important advantage was the steadily increasing width of the Amazon. If there were unfriendly villages on one bank the travellers moved towards the other, staying out of range, out of contact or even out of sight.

The further this journey down-river progressed, the more its captain, Francisco de Orellana, becomes a shadowy figure. He never speaks directly through Carvajal's journal. He is omnipresent and yet mute. Like the chronicler he was interested in the acquisition of food, but he was also concerned with a hundred other matters – the remaining stock of gunpowder, the serviceability of their various weapons, the quantity of crossbow bolts (on which, next to God, they placed so much reliance). Orellana did eventually present a lengthy description of his voyage to the Council of the Indies, but this no longer exists among the archives. Certain individuals interviewed Orellana after his return and did write down his story, but these accounts are also indirect, being hearsay more than reported speech. One longs to know what Orellana thought of his men, of that decision to leave Pizarro stranded, of his chances when beset so repeatedly by warlike Indians. In particular one would like his version of the expedition's famous encounter with the Amazons. Did Carvajal write the truth? Were there indeed warrior women? And what did Orellana think of the controversy on this matter when he and his friar were later castigated as liars? Or was the whole story grossly and subsequently exaggerated, being no more than a minor incident that should not have named the largest river in the world? When Orellana reached the Negro, the Amazon encounter was shortly to occur. One suspects that Orellana did not care greatly whether those who attacked his boats were men, women, giants or dwarfs. His sole and steadfast intent was to extricate himself and his companions safely from the 'inland sea' and somehow lead them back to Spain.

Nevertheless, it was shortly before the expedition reached the confluence of the Madeira, the huge tributary arriving from the south-west (which Orellana named the Grande), that he and his men first heard of female warriors. At one particular village, where the Indians spoke rather than fought, these peaceable people explained how they had to pay tribute to certain ruling women. This entailed a regular supply of parrot feathers, not as adornment for the rulers but to decorate their places of worship. Right from the outset the Spanish referred to these people as 'Amazons', and of course one wonders why. There is a similar Indian word (in Tupi-Guarani) meaning tidal bore, used also for those living in the affected area. And there is the old Greek story of warrior women living in Scythia (now mostly in the Ukraine). To this legend is added the notion of their name deriving from *a-mazos*, or 'no breast'. Whether there ever were Scythian women who valiantly removed one mammary gland to improve their archery (which does seem unnecessary) will never be known. What is known is that Carvajal names these South American women 'Amazons' the moment he first writes of them. No one in his party, it seems, ever called them anything else.

Hearing of them did not immediately lead to meeting them. Several leagues and many more villages had first to be negotiated. For instance, there was the place where, following an ambuscade, the Indian overlord urged on his men 'with a very loud yell'. A crossbowman put paid to his yell, causing most of his men to flee and others to fight 'like wounded dogs'. This battle ended when the Spanish burned the Indians' homes. 'Praised be our Lord', for a lot of food was found. At another village the captain had to hang a few captive Indians, mainly to discourage others from attacking the travellers, who only wanted all their food.

The downstream Indians, receiving word of the Spanish much faster than any barquentine could travel, became more cunning. One village appeared deserted. Orellana 'understood' the 'base action' that had been planned and was safely out of range when 5,000 rose up, relieved perhaps at the lack of contact but disappointed by the failed subterfuge. A wide berth was also given to an area speckled with gibbets. Dead men's heads had been nailed to them. Then a girl 'of great intelligence' was captured. Using her wits to the full, she spoke of people living nearby who were exactly like the Spaniards. Carvajal promptly assumed these were survivors from an exploratory party that had left Seville under the command of Diego de Ordaz to sail up the Rio Marañón (the Amazon) from its mouth. In fact that expedition, which was shipwrecked in 1531, did not get so far. In any case, 'as we were not concerned with this matter', the Orellana party did not investigate. It sailed on, leaving yet another mystery, or just an intriguing story concocted by a clever Indian girl.

Finally, shortly after raiding a village which had a 'very good wine resembling beer ... [so that] our companions were not a little delighted', they came across the 'Amazons'. The Spaniards had been searching for a peaceful spot to celebrate and gladden the feast of 'Saint John the Baptist, herald of Christ', when they saw ahead of them many large and white-shining villages. Their inhabitants were waiting for the invaders, having been forewarned. Orellana attempted a peaceful solution, but was mocked by the Indians. They said (and maybe Orellana had captives on board to help with translation) that the Spanish were to be seized and taken to the 'Amazons'. 'Angered at their arrogance', and not immediately curious about the women, Orellana summoned his artillery. The crossbows and arquebuses inflicted their customarily effective brand of damage. The Spanish then beached their boats so that all the men could have a hand in the fighting. Each man had armour, as Carvajal had already revealed, but to what extent is not mentioned. Was it just helmet and breastplate, or more? It is tempting to imagine greater protection, because on this occasion the 'great horde' of Indians who were formed in a 'good squadron' fired arrows to 'rain' from the sky. These should have slaughtered the Spaniards. In fact only five men were injured, including the friar. An arrow 'went in as far as the hollow region' (wherever that is) and 'would have been the end' of him but for the 'thickness of [his] clothese'.

These Indians fought with tremendous courage. It must be explained, wrote Carvajal, why these men defended themselves in this manner. Knowing of the Spaniards' imminence in their area they had hurried to the women for help. At least a dozen women were seen to be lending assistance, not only fighting in front of the men but clubbing any individual who dared to turn his back upon the Spanish enemy. Their appearance, as described by Orellana's friar, is certainly impressive.

Francisco de Orellana

These women are very white and tall, and have hair very long and braided and wound about the head, and they are very robust and go about naked, [but] with their privy parts covered, with their bows and arrows in their hands, doing as much fighting as ten Indian men, and indeed there was one woman among these who shot an arrow a span deep into one of the brigantines, and others less deep, so that our brigantines looked like porcupines.

And that's that, save that 'our Lord was pleased to give strength to our companions, who killed seven or eight ... of the Amazons'. The controversy began after the account of Orellana's exploration had become common knowledge. No one suggested he had not seen women fighting, as such a sight had already been observed in some of the Windward Islands, and near Cartagena, for example. Few bothered to question Carvajal's possible magnification of their strength, but many agonized over their name. Was Orellana right to call them 'Amazons', a title already credited to a group of people who may, or may not, have lived to the north of the Black Sea and who may, or not, have cut off a breast to facilitate their shooting?

Orellana paid a high price for this usage of a name already known. When he emerged from the river Marañón, as it had been called by those who found it from the sea, many rewarded his success by designating *his* river the Orellana. The title lasted for a time, but slowly lost favour. It was increasingly replaced by the name we use today, however wrongfully. Orellana had been careless to dub those women 'Amazons', and it had been wrong of Carvajal to follow his captain's lead. Female warrior Scythians, whether or not they ever lived, are irrelevant to this river on the other side of the Atlantic. However, it is today, and presumably always will be, the river Amazon; and although some of it is also the Marañón, and some the Solimões, none of it is now the Orellana.

A couple of weeks after encountering the fighting, clubbing, strong-armed women, Orellana had opportunity to learn more about them. Not only were he and his men able to rest on land without being attacked, but a captured Indian was questioned. (Considering the lack of a common language it is amazing, not to say unbelievable, how much detailed information the Spanish acquired.) Apparently the fighting women were unmarried but did bear children. No man lived in their villages, and no male visitor or servant or warrior was permitted to stay within their precincts between sunset and sunrise. When men were required for mating an assault was made upon the territory of a neighbouring overlord. Males were captured, taken to the female villages and, when the women found themselves pregnant, their 'caprice having been suited', returned unharmed to their own country.

The women's leader, named Coñori, ate with utensils of gold and silver. Some other 'ruling mistresses' did likewise, whereas the remainder used wooden vessels. All their houses were built of stone 'with regular doors'. The villages were linked by roads, guards being stationed at intervals who forced everyone entering the villages to pay a toll. Within the tribal places of worship, all painted and decorated, were many gold and silver idols in the form of women. The ruling clique had blankets of llama wool as covering from the breasts down, and also crowns of gold. These dignitaries were transported by 'camels' and other animals as 'big as horses' with long hair, which 'we did not succeed in understanding'. (Among the camel family are four South American species: llama, guanaco – the tallest, alpaca – the strongest and shaggiest, and vicuña – with the finest and lightest wool. The Amazonian species was presumably one of these.) The captured and talkative Indian also revealed – somehow – that many an Indian travelled far to satisfy his curiosity about these women. Those who did so 'would go a boy and return an old man'. (The point is not clear. Did the journey entail that number of years, or did the women retain the men until their youthful ardour had expired?)

Unfortunately the Orellana experience was never duplicated, in that no other explorers ever met these strong, long-haired, well-endowed matriarchal rulers. To see a dozen such women, to shoot seven or eight of them, to rely on hearsay in general and one talkative Indian in particular – it all makes frustrating reading for those of us living four and a half centuries later. The women were heard about, were encountered, were shot at, were discussed later, were identified with Greek legend, and consequently had this alien name given both to them and to the river flowing past their territory. The rest is silence.

It must of course be remembered that Orellana was on no fact-finding anthropological tour. By this stage, with thoughts of gold and cinnamon long since abandoned, the expedition's solitary wish was to

Descriptions of the Amazon women were in short supply, a fact which liberated artists from restraint in portraying them.

reach home safely. Therefore food was gathered, stolen, and fought for when need be. The Indians were by-passed, cajoled or attacked as the situation demanded.

From the Machiparo kingdom onwards, when fighting for food became the commonplace, Orellana's men equipped themselves with shields. If arrows were to rain upon them the Spaniards needed every protection. Writing of an encounter at a village whose bowmen put up a particularly vigorous barrage, Carvajal exaggerates a touch, asserting that arrow density prevented the Spaniards from seeing each other. Perhaps he can be forgiven hyperbole, or visual misjudgement, for one such arrow struck him in the head. It went through 'to the other side, from which wound I have lost the eye, and [even now] I am not without suffering and not free from pain, although Our Lord, without my deserving it, has been kind enough to grant me life so that I may mend my ways and serve Him better than hitherto'. His was the only injury on that occasion, despite the arrows blurring each man's sighting of his neighbour, but thereafter he and Orellana were as one. They had each lost an eye, Orellana before the expedition, Carvajal during it, and they must have looked a formidable pair, the friar and his captain, the leader and his scribe, both seeing eye to eye.

Whether because of his painful wound, or from the monotony of repetition as village after village attacked the passing travellers, Carvajal's account of the voyage now becomes less detailed. Odd incidents are reported – a tribe with short hair and black-stained skin, another that ate human flesh, a clever shot with an arquebus that killed two Indians with one firing – but for the main part he gives thanks to God and wonders for what purpose he and his companions have been saved. He is outraged by the use of poisoned arrows. First Antonio de Caranza, native of Burgos, surrenders his soul to God. Next García de Soria, from Logroño, gives up 'his soul to the Lord' even though the fatal arrow 'did not penetrate half a finger'. Orellana ordered a protective fencing to be built around each boat. This certainly helped, as did the policy of sailing as far as possible from every village unless hunger dictated otherwise.

At about this time the Spaniards first detected the flowing of the tide and 'rejoiced not a little'. With most rivers, tidal flow does not extend far inland. However, on the Amazon the tides reach much further than the length of the entire river Thames. The early rejoicing was, therefore, a little premature, as the river travel was not yet over. At one 'evil' village the smaller boat had a plank stoved in during an engagement. The mishap necessitated more charcoal, more nail-making, eighteen days, and 'no little amount of endeavour'. Later on, reduced by then to eating small snails and red crabs the size of frogs, the companions spent fourteen more days making their vessels fitter for ocean travel. This 'continuous and regular penance' entailed the creation of cordage from vines and sails from blankets, plus a general attention to seaworthiness. The river travellers departed from that spot on 8 August 1542, almost nine months from the previous December when the very first boat had been launched.

'We had no pilot, nor compass, nor navigator's chart of any sort, and we did not even know in what direction or toward what point we ought to head.' The river journey had been one formidable accomplishment. Orellana had performed extremely well in keeping his band together, with the loss of only three men killed by Indians. To have reached 50°W and the Atlantic, having started from Quito, almost within sight of the Pacific, ought to have entitled them to rest from their triumph. Instead they had completed no more than one section of their journey. A portion of ocean was now ahead of them. 'We passed out of the mouth of [the] river from between two islands,' wrote Gaspar de Carvajal, '. . . on the 26th of the month of August, on Saint Louis' Day.' Quite a different assortment of perils lay in store.

Orellana had been captain for so long it is easy to forget he was only a lieutenant separated from the main party. Whether Gonzalo Pizarro had been abandoned maliciously (as was generally alleged) or through unavoidable force of circumstance (as Medina asserted so vigorously), the fact remains that he had been left to his own resources. It so happened that he staggered back into Quito during the very month of August when Orellana and his men were emerging from the river.

Pizarro made great play of his lieutenant's desertion. He told his story in a letter dated 3 September 1542, addressed to his 'Sacred Cesarean Catholic Majesty', the king of Spain. It is difficult to imagine Pizarro telling the entire truth, and some aspects of his tale are frankly unbelievable. He wrote that Orellana not only took all the craft (every stolen Indian canoe plus the barquentine), but *all* the armament of the expeditionary force. Carvajal, on the other hand, states that Orellana took only ten of the fifteen canoes, three arquebuses and four or five crossbows. On his river foray to find food he may well have taken every canoe, but it is less credible that the exploratory, food-seeking contingent should remove all the artillery, all the powder, all the iron, leaving the larger party with nothing of the kind.

As to events after the parting, Gonzalo Pizarro reports how he stole five more canoes. He then sent a small group with these canoes to search for food, but it returned after six days without even helpful information. Pizarro therefore undertook a search himself. Within a short time, and aided by half a dozen men, he had found food 'in abundance'. Nevertheless, even with all this nourishment, he did not think it right to pursue/follow Orellana because (and the same point is made repeatedly) the rebel had taken everything: 'I had no chance of being able to go on any further.'

Pizarro therefore started upon the return journey. This meant initially crossing the Napo, all the men in canoes and the horses as best they could. The crossing took eight days and lost them several horses. The number of men who set out on the return is not known precisely – there had been deaths ever since the departure one year earlier – but it was probably in excess of a hundred. Some eighty horses survived the river crossing, but not for long. Despite a discovery of food, which was largely a manioc (cassava) plantation, the horses were all consumed in the next few weeks. In his letter to the king, Pizarro does not particularize his hardships – he had no faithful friar to keep a log – but stresses repeated bridge-building, wading through marshes 'up to our waists and even higher', the death of 'a few Spaniards' from hunger, and the lack of armament except for swords and staves.

Eventually, after retracing the 270 leagues they had accomplished from Quito to the point of return, the survivors stumbled, limped, slouched into that city. The date was August 1542. It had been February 1541 when the 2,000 pigs, 4,000 Indians, over 200 Spaniards and almost as many horses had departed. The half-naked, emaciated men who returned numbered nearer eighty. It was a humiliating experience for Gonzalo, arrogant member of the Pizarro family. It would have been more so had he known that, in the very month of that Quito return, Orellana was setting forth upon the Atlantic Ocean. He knew no details, but was aware that his lieutenant had stolen a march on him. Orellana was to be the hero of what once had been Pizarro's enterprise.

On Saint Louis's Day, 26 August, Orellana might have been excused if he too had wished to be back in Quito. Drifting and paddling downstream was one thing. Sailing and paddling out at sea was quite another. The boats were turned northwards, as might be expected, and stayed near the shore, as might also be expected, although occasionally losing sight of it. The larger vessel had been named the *Victoria*, the smaller the *San Pedro*. Both were to lose sight even of each other three days after arriving in the Mar del Norte, the Northern Sea, the Atlantic. The separation happened at night on 'the very day of the Beheading of Saint John'. (Pizarro was then busy composing his complaining letter to his king, which was finished five days later.) Those on the *Victoria*, including Carvajal, assumed the others had 'got lost' (thereby abetting a long tradition of others getting lost but not

Francisco de Orellana

oneself). After nine solitary days 'our sins drove us into the Gulf of Paria'. Some sort of magnetism operated from this area. It had been much visited at the turn of the century (as described in the previous chapter) when the continent of South America was first being explored. Being driven in proved to be much easier for the exhausted Spaniards than coming out; but, eventually, after seven days continuously at the oars and eating only fruit, the *Victoria*'s men emerged triumphantly from the Mouth of the Dragon. It was then but a short haul / sail / drift to Cubagua, near the Isla de Margarita, lying 150 miles to the west of Trinidad.

Carvajal states in his journal how many great favours had been granted during the journey, but one of the greatest lay in store at Nueva Cadiz. Both boatloads of Amazon survivors were astonished and delighted to meet their fellows, each party having been given up for lost by the other. The *San Pedro* had arrived two days before the *Victoria*, having taken just seventeen days from the Amazon's mouth. 'So great was the joy which we felt . . . I shall not be able to express it.' It was a tumultuous ending to a quite extraordinary voyage, begun nineteen months earlier without anyone even suspecting the outcome, and begun with gold and spice in mind rather than thoughts of any river, let alone the largest in the world. To Orellana must be given great credit. Amidst innumerable perils the majority of his party had survived. The number Pizarro lost is not known, but was about ten times as great. And credit should also be given to Brother Gaspar de Carvajal for donating to posterity such a graphic account. He may have lost an eye but never his loyalty, his humility or sense of style. The journal's concluding words are wholly in keeping with the remainder:

What I have written and related is the truth throughout; and because profuseness engenders distaste, so I have related sketchily and summarily all that has happened to Captain Francisco de Orellana and to the *hidalgos* of his company and to us companions of his who went off with him [after separating] from the expeditionary corps of Gonzalo Pizarro, brother of Don Francisco Pizarro, the Marquis, and Governor of Peru. God be praised. Amen.

The personalities cannot be left there, whether snarling and recuperating in Quito or roistering on Cubagua. Their subsequent activities must be recounted, and how and when they met their deaths. There is not only Orellana himself, who could not let the Amazon alone, but his friar and his men, some of whose lives were documented thereafter. And there is also Gonzalo Pizarro, not a man to resist further adventure for long, but he did not have long to live after he and his fellow survivors had struggled in such disarray back to Quito.

Gonzalo did not just lick his wounds that August of 1542; he also heard the news. Top item was the death of his brother, Francisco, the conqueror, the Marquis of Peru. The civil war of 1538, in which Orellana had taken part and which had resulted in a Pizarro victory over Diego de Almagro, had been brutally concluded. Hernando Pizarro's garrotting of the vanquished rival had caused loathing, for him in particular and the Pizarros in general. Hernando had travelled to Spain in 1539 to arouse support, but was imprisoned after the king had heard from Almagro sympathizers (and was not released until 1561, aged sixty and broken in health). The Almagrists' longing for revenge then focused on Francisco. They united around Diego's son, born to a Panama Indian. Francisco was aware of the growing danger but took no precautions. On 26 June 1541 he was attacked in his palace by twenty Almagro supporters. He had time only to strap on his breastplate and kill one man before himself being killed. The young Diego de Almagro was then proclaimed ruler of Peru. On this day Gonzalo was still struggling eastwards and had not yet split with Orellana.

An emissary from Spain, sent by the king to settle Peruvian problems and counter the rebellion, quickly rallied royalist support and marched into the country, gathering strength as he progressed. It so happened that the emissary's forces conquered the rebel Almagrists one month after Gonzalo's return to Quito. Gonzalo just had time to throw in his lot with the king's representative, as he was naturally opposed to the Almagro men who had killed his brother.

Seeds of the next rebellion were sown the following month, in November 1542. New laws were enacted at Barcelona to prevent the maltreatment, and the keeping in servitude, of Indians. In future the indigenous people would have almost the same status as Spaniards – if the laws were obeyed. The Iberian conquerors and settlers of Peru were not the only colonials to resent long-distance government. Besides they liked slavery. It was a form of wealth (especially now that the Inca gold had been consumed). The Barcelona legislation was therefore an affront to their dignity, their way of life, their growing independence. Opposition rallied around Gonzalo, last of the four Pizarro brothers still in Peru. His supporters particularly disliked the king's new viceroy and even managed to banish him in September 1544. Dashing, impetuous, belligerent, rich and still young – rebellion was the life for Gonzalo, and far better than grubbing around for roots or eating noxious beasts in those sodden jungles 200 leagues from Quito. He entered Lima, the capital, firmly leader of the new rebel cause.

The deposed viceroy had no wish to stay deposed. He gathered an army, headed south from Panama, crossed Peru's northern border, collected more men as he marched, and finally encountered Gonzalo's army near Quito on 18 January 1546. The viceroy was killed, an act which further entrenched Gonzalo Pizarro as king of Peru. Letters sent back to Spain by him were now less complaining, more arrogant, but still faithful after their fashion: 'I have never in word or deed offended against your royal service . . .' Unilateral independence of a kind had been declared, and considerable attention was therefore paid in Peru to the possibility of a Peruvian dynasty. Gonzalo had never married but he did have children, notably Francisquito. This boy, whose mother was a Christian Indian, had been legitimized and was therefore heir apparent. (His mother was almost bound to have been an Indian. The *conquistadores* did not take women with them to the New World, and the first European woman to reach Quito arrived there in 1546.)

Unfortunately, as Gonzalo must have expected, Charles of Spain did not relax while news of an independent rival kept coming from Peru. He sent a further emissary who, like his predecessor, began by amassing a royalist army. Gonzalo's initial popularity had waned in the interim, and for good reason. His rule had been brief, but long enough for him to have executed 340 Spaniards. Nevertheless, he still had supporters and he won the first battle against the emissary's forces. At the next encounter, near Cuzco on 9 April 1548, he was much less fortunate. While forty-five of his men were being killed, most of the remainder switched sides. In this battle the Spanish king's representative lost only one man and captured Gonzalo. Judgement was swift. The dashing, handsome, impulsive *conquistador*, one of the band that had attacked and destroyed the Inca empire, was executed on the following day. The kind of courage needed to conquer Peru was, in the end, the death of him.

Like Pizarro, at the time of the expedition's departure from Quito Friar Gaspar de Carvajal was young, vigorous, courageous and well known, but there the similarities end. No one could ever have confused the Dominican monk with the hot-headed Pizarro. When Carvajal arrived at Cubagua, once he had rejoiced at seeing the other boat, he too caught up with the news from Peru. He heard of Francisco's death, and also that of Bishop Valverde, his good friend and prelate, who had been killed by Indians. These two deaths encouraged him to go back to Peru instead of returning to Spain, as might have seemed reasonable after such an expedition. He was, therefore, witness to many of the turbulent events leading to Gonzalo's death. It is not known if Carvajal met his former captain again or had occasion to put to him Orellana's side of the separation. In fact not much is known about his post-Amazon life, save that his position and influence gradually grew with his advancing years. In 1575 he was even writing to the Spanish king, stressing the unfortunate lot of the Indians (those new, unwelcome laws from Spain had been far too liberal to gain general acceptance) and urging that they should not be compelled to work in the mines. Nine years later, aged eighty, Gaspar de Carvajal closed his remaining eye for good, dying peacefully in the monastery of Lima.

For most of the fifty-six other members of the Amazon expedition, apart from the three known to have been killed and the eleven (it is generally thought) who died from hunger during the earliest days of Orellana's captaincy, nothing more is recorded about them. They became as silent as the two Negroes who, according to Medina, lent efficient service as oarsmen, but whose names do not appear in any document. Of those whose progress in life is better known, at least to the extent of one signature on a document, the majority returned to Peru. A few even fought against Gonzalo Pizarro in his battles against the emissaries; none fought for him. None became rich, three petitioned the king for some sort of pension when in their sixties, and one man declared himself 'very poor and plunged into debt', though he had once owned 700 Indians. Only two, apart from Orellana, are known to have returned to Europe, both apparently settling in Portugal. It is easy

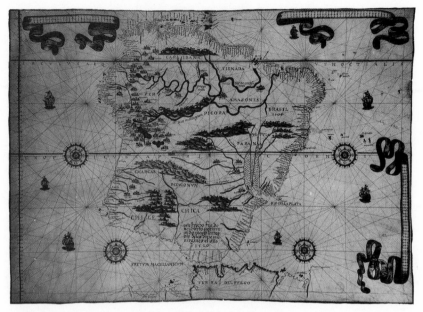

For a time after his exploratory voyage the Amazon was Orellana's river, or Rio de Oregliana, as in this Spanish map of 1587.

to suspect that, for all the companions, nothing so dramatic as sailing down the Amazon ever occurred again in any of their lives. They must have told their stories over and over, in Spanish America, in Spain, in Portugal, until – sometime during the 1580s – the last of the river explorers died. By then both their captains were long since gone.

It was at Cubagua, after collecting his thoughts, that Francisco de Orellana decided to return to Spain. He wished to petition the king and, with royal backing, to explore further the Amazon's vast domain. On his return it was unfortunate that his first port of call, after a difficult Atlantic crossing, was in Portugal. The king of Portugal eagerly offered hospitality, detained the explorer for a couple of weeks, and generally extracted useful information. A wealthy Portuguese official promised considerable assistance should Orellana embark upon a return journey. Apparently unaware of the political consequences of his voyage, or of the error in arriving first in Portugal, he eventually set off for Spain. The capital then was Valladolid, 100 miles north-west of Madrid, and he arrived there during May 1543.

Just down the road from Valladolid, fifteen miles to its south-west, is Tordesillas. Pope Alexander VI's Treaty, signed there half a century earlier, had certainly not been forgotten. Its allocation of territory had put the lower Amazon within Spain's slice of South America, and the Portuguese were most aware that Tordesillas had granted them an extremely modest slice of the New World cake. As the years progressed they began to hope that at least some of the Amazon might fall within their grasp. At the Spanish capital Orellana's wholly Spanish exploit along the Amazon was thought to be slightly embarrassing rather than a triumph worthy of every accolade. The king's secretary argued that the new discovery would turn out to be more prejudicial than advantageous, but there was also a muted wish to gain a further point over Portugal. Perhaps Orellana should be encouraged to go back after all?

Eventually, after nine months' gestation, a royal decree was issued to Orellana. It permitted him to explore and settle New Andalucia, the territory around the Amazon river. As contracts go it was as ungenerous as they come. Orellana was obliged to take 200 infantrymen, 100 horsemen and the material to construct two river-going ships. On his arrival at the Amazon he was to build two towns, one just inside the mouth. As for salary, or any degree of financial support, this was to be paid from the profits of conquering and settling New Andalucia. Orellana had, therefore, to supply the money to mount the expedition, provide the energy to make it work, possess the courage to see it through inevitable perils, and then successfully find some wealth within the new domain. The king, for his part, would receive eleven twelfths of the revenue from the adventure; Orellana and his men could keep the rest. The contract was, to make the point again, as ungenerous as could be.

Five days later, on 18 February 1544, Orellana formally submitted his acceptance. (It is almost possible to hear chuckles emanating from the royal palace.) Unfortunately, Orellana's misfortunes did not end there. He learned that an inspector-general, in truth a spy, had been appointed to monitor his expedition and even give orders. Orellana's request for guns from the king was bluntly refused. He was not permitted to force sailors to accompany him, even though the press-gang was in common use and had filled many a fleet with men. And he could not employ a Portuguese pilot, an important prerequisite as

Francisco de Orellana

Spanish sailors did not know that piece of coast. Perhaps a man who (apparently) never grew discouraged during the entire Amazon voyage, as Indian attack followed Indian attack, could be expected to triumph over even the most miserly royal patronage. Indeed, in May 1544, after acquiring two galleons (of 240 and 96 tons) and two smaller caravels, he announced his imminent departure.

Orellana not only possessed a blind eye, he had one mentally. No pioneering expedition can ever be fully prepared and Orellana was willing to overlook certain details. His impatience to set sail was partly a wish to leave behind all those carping at his unpreparedness. Without doubt there were dissenters. Not every palace official was in favour of the venture, and the king received frequent rumour that all was not as it should have been. A royal commission was therefore established to learn the truth. It discovered that Orellana still owed money for his ships, that his fare-paying passengers were growing concerned at the lack of provisions on board, that he had no sailors as yet, and that the merchant financiers of the enterprise were withdrawing their support.

His stepfather, Cosmo de Chaves, then stepped in. He raised 1,100 ducats, which were immediately needed, and set about collecting more. By October – six months after Orellana had announced his departure – the ships had been paid for and sailors had been recruited. More good news came in the well-founded rumour of a Portuguese fleet, also with four ships, about to sail for the Amazon with similar intent. The Spanish king was advised to provide more support for Orellana, thereby forestalling the Portuguese. Simultaneously he was still receiving less than satisfactory news about the Spanish fleet's readiness. One report concluded: 'I am unable to give [any further clearer account] at this point, because in truth I do not understand either Orellana or the affairs of this fleet, nor do I believe that he understands them himself.' In November Orellana compounded the general anxiety by marrying. The girl, Ana de Ayala, was very young and 'exceedingly poor'. There was concern at her total lack of dowry, and also that the bride would be sailing to the Amazon, along with a couple of sisters-in-law. A dowry would have been timely, particularly when the larger galleon had to be rejected owing to its condition. Then, with impeccable timing from Orellana's point of view, the captain of the Portuguese fleet arrived in Seville. Such blatant spying on behalf of a rival power, *the* rival power, encouraged Orellana's creditors to let him depart from Seville. His reduced fleet travelled fifty-five miles downstream to the river-mouth port of Sanlúcar.

When on the verge of departure, and despite the Portuguese spying, Orellana had to submit to a final inspection by the king's officials. They discovered a shortfall in men (the stipulated 300 soldiers were not all on board), in horses (with only twenty-four out of the 100), in guns, in provisions, and even in the eight friars he should have embarked. Orellana made excuses, said Sanlúcar was a good place for purchasing provisions, and reported that the friars were only waiting for his order. The bureaucrats were not impressed. Worse still, they discharged all those sailors who proved to be English, Portuguese, Flemings or Germans. An exception was made for the Sicilian master of the flagship; without his expertise it could not have sailed. As it was, the ships became woefully short of sailors, their complements – including cabin-boys – ranging from eleven to eighteen.

Orellana was bluntly informed (in secret) that he could not sail. If he did so he would be deprived of all those benefits the king had bestowed upon him, such as getting his own money back eventually. One month later the inspectors made another visit to satisfy themselves that Orellana's deficiencies were being made good. What they saw did not encourage them. Allegedly, Orellana was ashore in Sanlúcar. They looked for him there and learned he had gone to the ships. The king's officials once more examined the ships but, yet again, failed to discover Orellana. In their frustration they ordered all of Sanlúcar's pilots, on pain of punishment, not to take any of the Amazon fleet over the bar. Orellana's thoughts or words are completely unknown, but his actions are sufficient record. During the morning of 11 May 1545 he and his ships sailed two leagues outside the port. They waited at that distance until six in the evening. Then they hoisted sail and disappeared from view.

Fifteen months had passed since Orellana had received his decree from the king, and that had not been granted until nine months after he had asked for it. His patience – with merchants, officials, sponsors, inspectors – had been stretched to breaking point. To have to finance an expedition was bad enough, but to yield all hope of regaining that outlay showed his outraged desperation. By this act of defiance he was also forfeiting the possibility of any future royal favour and could consider himself *non grata* even in Spain itself. Circumstance had made him traitor, as with his departure from Gonzalo Pizarro. He had survived that misadventure, and perhaps events would vindicate him on this second escapade.

Orellana and his ships arrived off the coast of South America shortly before Christmas 1545, three years and four months after he and his boats had emerged from the Amazon. He was arguably in a worse state on his re-arrival than when leaving the river. Nothing had gone right for him. From Spain he had sailed first for the Canary Islands, hoping there to make good some of the deficiencies on board. In the end, due to all kinds of ill fortune, three months were wasted. He then sailed for the Cape Verde Islands, hoping for better luck; but, with further setbacks, he merely consumed two more months. During these delays he lost ninety-eight men from sickness, a further fifty from desertion (including three of the captains, who had plainly lost their nerve) and one entire ship. He cannibalized its equipment to improve the other three, a replacement having been found for the deficient galleon. Then, somewhere in mid-Atlantic, one ship vanished, carrying with it seventy-seven people, eleven horses and a boat to be used on the Amazon. Already, therefore, Orellana had lost – in one way or another – over four times as many men as he had brought safely down the Amazon.

He then proceeded up-river with the remaining vessels. In the first three months of 1546, as well as travelling a hundred leagues, his men built a second river-boat to replace the one lost at sea. Some of its material had been brought across the Atlantic; the rest – including some of the nails and planking – he ordered to be stripped from one of the ships. Then, as he had done repeatedly four years earlier, Orellana set off with some companions in the completed boat to search for food. A total of fifty-seven men had died from hunger during the first three boat-building months upon the Amazon, and more were to die during this exploratory foray. Unfortunately the boat party failed to find food, and its members therefore fell upon the dogs and horses brought across the Atlantic. All the details of this second Orellana expedition are vague, there being no official account. Nevertheless, the broad facts are clear enough. It started disastrously and continued that way.

Explorers of the Amazon

The expedition's ending was fairly swift. One day, when the river-boat and a ship were on the Amazon, the ship was driven ashore after its restraining hawser had broken. (Time and again the lack of initial cash leading to poor equipment is critical. The explorers were even using cannons in lieu of absent anchors.) The marooned men found refuge on an island one league distant from their wrecked ship and there encountered friendly Indians. Orellana and a smaller group then set off again in the river-boat, partly to find the Amazon's principal arm and partly, as ever, to locate food. Having failed on both counts, they eventually returned to the shipwreck camp but found it deserted. Its population of some thirty Spaniards had grown impatient. They had stripped the wreck of useful timber and built themselves a boat. This enabled them to search for their commander while he, in his slightly better boat, was looking for them. The Spanish endeavour, aimed at conquering and settling New Andalucia, had become two hungry, wretched boatloads of men paddling about not far upstream from the Amazon's muddy mouth and looking for each other.

The secondary boat of shipwrecked men soon gave up the search. They proceeded downstream and discovered more friendly Indians. Six of the twenty-eight on board elected to stay with them. Four others absconded a few miles further on, not liking the prospects that lay ahead. Indeed the boat did meet with great difficulty, notably in a mosquito-ridden mangrove swamp where, not for the first time, the crew believed their days had ended. Finally, much as Orellana had done four years earlier, they managed to claw up the coast before arriving at the island of Margarita. Just as the two Orellana boats, the *Victoria* and the *San Pedro*, had been reunited on the island of Cubagua in 1542, so did the shipwrecked survivors of 1546 discover twenty-five of their companions already arrived on Margarita, having travelled there on a ship of the original fleet. Among them was Doña Ana de Ayala. She had learned before leaving the Amazon that her husband had not succeeded in finding the main channel, that seventeen of his men had been killed by Indian arrows, and that Orellana had died, partly from illness but also from grief at the loss of so many men. The date of his death, aged 35, was sometime in November 1546.

It is so easy to find fault with failure. Orellana's expedition to New Andalucia had been foredoomed, mainly through the king's lack of support and partly because of Orellana's inability to provide the necessary funds. At every stage the venture could and should have been cancelled. The enforced economies – of men, provisions and quality of ships – proved catastrophic. A different kind of leader would have retreated when confronted by such a quantity of lack, but Francisco de Orellana was not that kind of individual. He had kept a body of men together when achieving one of the most daunting river journeys of all time, but he could not triumph over the merchants, the palace officials, the inspectors of Seville. They and his impetuosity combined to kill him at the mouth of the river which no longer bears his name.

Precisely forty-four people survived this ill-prepared expedition and a ship was later sent to Margarita to collect them. However, some preferred to settle in Central America, in Chile, in Peru. As for Doña Ana, she became the companion of a survivor, Juan de Peñalosa. Together they went to Panama, where they apparently lived for the remainder of their days. Her age was always a bit of a mystery. She claimed in a document twenty-seven years later that she was then thirty-five. That would have made her only eight when she married Orellana. Assuming she was then fourteen, 'very young' but not as young as eight, she would have been forty-two in 1572, when there is the last official mention of her. She may have lived much longer, perhaps until the seventeenth century, and may also have been the final survivor of either Orellana expedition on the Amazon, the one a triumph quite unparalleled and the other a disaster, sadder and much sorrier than most.

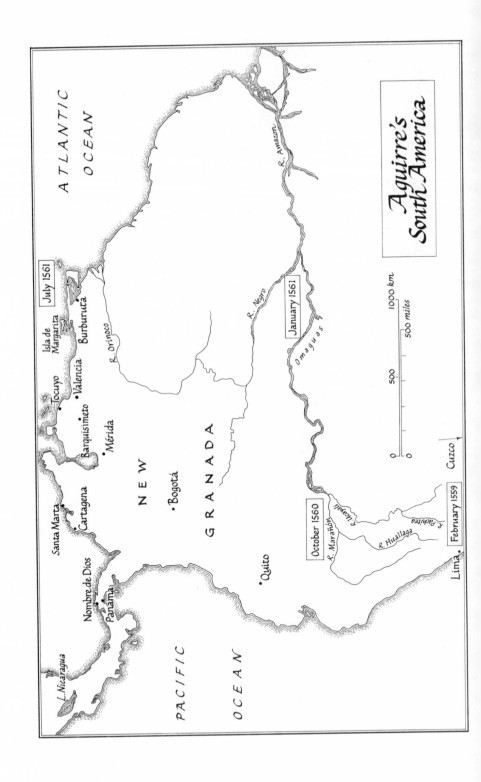

ATLANTIC
OCEAN

PACIFIC
OCEAN

R. Amazon

R. Negro

Omaguas

January 1561

R. Orinoco

Isla de
Margarita

Burburuta

Tocuyo

Valencia

Barquisimeto

Mérida

Bogotá

NEW

GRANADA

Santa Marta

Cartagena

Nombre de Dios

Panamá

L. Nicaragua

July 1561

Quito

October 1560

R. Marañón

R. Ucayali

R. Pachitea

R. Huallaga

Lima

February 1559

Cuzco

Aguirre's
South America

1000 km

500 miles

500

0

0

III

Lope de Aguirre
WHO KILLED EVEN HIS DREAM

Despite the brilliance of Orellana's first expedition there was little in this exploit to attract successors. Such mention as there had been of decked-out Indians, of ruling princes and astonishing women was more than offset by the constant battles, the ever-present hunger and a steady need for the helping hand of God. Orellana's second expedition, so steeped in death and failure, reinforced earlier conviction about the Amazon. The river basin was undoubtedly big and impressive but it held little prospect for immediate gain. It is therefore surprising that the next major foray down this mightiest of rivers occurred only thirteen years after Orellana's death; but its leaders were no ordinary men, and Aguirre was the most extraordinary of them all. Even in a period of butchery and conquest, of rebellion and perfidy, his exploits were in a class of their own. Other expeditions experienced loss of life, change of leadership and even murder. That of Pedro de Ursúa and Lope de Aguirre, which departed from Lima in February 1559, seemed to experience little else, particularly murder. In fact it becomes increasingly astonishing that anyone survived to tell its tale.

In the first full-scale English account of Ursúa and Aguirre, published in 1861, there is a lengthy introduction by Clements R. Markham. This man knew South America and acquired fame by stealing cinchona seeds to set up a quinine industry. He was to become president of the Royal Geographical Society and also the driving force behind Robert Scott's Antarctic adventures. Yet he manages to call the Ursúa–Aguirre venture 'romantic', using the word three times on his very first page. Its story, he writes, 'is fitter for the pages of King Arthur's romance than for the sober narrative of facts'. He adds that in this 'cruise of Aguirre all that is wildest, most romantic, most desperate, most appalling in the annals of Spanish enterprise seems to culminate in one wild orgie of madness and blood'. It certainly did culminate that way. It was undoubtedly desperate, appalling and wild. And perhaps the reader of this account will judge whether it was romantic in the slightest degree (or whether the word had a different meaning in 1861).

The story, romantic or not, had its origins in the region now occupied by Venezuela. The first major explorers of this area were German. Before long they had acquired a reputation for cruelty, mainly for their treatment of Indians who became sick or tired. The German expedient, simpler than opening all the fetters for a batch of men, was to sever the offending head from its body. The remainder of the enslaved party could then proceed unencumbered, with little time wasted. Not every knight was quite so callous, but all spent considerable energy in exploration, in capturing and utilizing Indians, in gathering such riches as could be found, and in promoting the idea of an El Dorado, a 'gilded one', a goal of unimaginable wealth.

In time the Germans' days were numbered, the last two knights having their heads sawn off by the soldier Carbajal, who had seized power in Venezuela. Carbajal himself was executed in 1546, but none of this killing contradicted the idea of extreme wealth somewhere in that general area. The rumour had certainly prompted Gonzalo Pizarro's expedition, and it continued to fascinate the young, the adventurous, the greedy or the power-hungry (a list that includes almost everyone). The more that men strove for wealth, and died, or were killed, or merely failed to find it, the more others were eager to follow. If there is smoke there must be fire. If there is killing, and tyranny, and enforced change of leadership, there must be reason; and what better reason than gold? Peru had disclosed one astonishing source. There must be another – somewhere.

The continuing unrest in Venezuela caused Spain's Council of the Indies to send emissaries, with the Council frequently being forced to send new ones when distressing rumours reached home concerning the conduct of some earlier representative. They despatched Luis Alonzo de Lugo in 1542 to administer New Granada (Bogotá and its environs), and three years later had to send Miguel Diáz de

Armendariz to check on Lugo. When Armendariz arrived at Cartagena, principal port of that coast, he realized there was sufficient work
for him solely in the coastal area. Therefore he asked his nephew,
Pedro de Ursúa, to organize Bogotá. Ursúa did so skilfully, having
been swift to find a pretext for arresting Lugo. By the time Armendariz
arrived, New Granada was being well administered.

Plainly the nephew Ursúa was not from the ordinary mould. All
kinds of adjectives were used about him that were not over-employed
concerning most administrators of the time. He was said to have been
generous, honourable, perfect, possessed of sweetness of temper, and
a universal favourite. A single one of these descriptions would have
marked him as exceptional. To merit them all, as he allegedly did, was
quite extraordinary. The only criticism ever made of him concerned his
youth. Someone so young should not be able to conduct affairs so well.

As one further source of astonishment, the young Ursúa survived
the recall of his uncle, Armendariz, in 1549. (Ursúa was then only
twenty-four, having been twenty when sent to settle Bogotá.)
Armendariz was initially reprimanded only for sensuality, an uncom-
mon form of accusation, but further charges were then laid against
him, notably by his successor, yet another emissary. On Armendariz's
return to Spain he was fined so heavily that they took the cloak from his
back to help make up the sum. His successor, a severe man by *all*
accounts, was subsequently executed for rebellion and cruelty. Meanwhile the good, young, amiable Ursúa managed to survive all the
confrontations, despite his close relationship with one of the principals.

In 1549 he was appointed to lead an expedition against the Musos
Indians. There was fierce fighting, but a kind of truce followed when he
was able to invite some Musos chiefs to a pageant. The sweet and
perfect Ursúa then killed them all. It was a 'felonious act unworthy of a
soldier of honour', according to one contemporary chronicler. Ursúa
founded a city at the spot, but unsurprisingly received no peace from
the Musos. They even succeeded in burning down his new city three
years after its founding, and the resident Spanish were forced to
withdraw. Despite Ursúa's provocative and 'felonious' act, he was then
appointed mayor of Santa Marta. This coastal town lay to the east of
Cartagena near mountainous country where the Tairona Indians still
ruled the land. (Their stone pathways, stone-based homes and stone

93

water-courses were first excavated by Colombian archaeologists in the late 1970s. This work proved the tribe to have been most skilled at living and growing crops in that steep forest land where heavy rain is a daily occurrence.)

In 1552 Ursúa set out to conquer the Tairona. Initially he did well, in that the Indians retreated. Later, with his lines of communication stretched, and suffering constant harassment from an enemy well acquainted with forest conditions, he became feverish. The sickness struck at a particularly difficult time, with the Indians defending a narrow, rocky pass which the Spaniards had to negotiate. Ursúa was armed when the enemy attacked, but only half dressed. Nevertheless, he and twelve other men were able to climb the rocks, withstand a hail of stones and eventually reach the commanding summit. From there, and after three hours of fighting, his party was able to scatter the Indians. The victors then retreated to Santa Marta, having won many battles but not the war. Others could defeat the Tairona; Ursúa had had enough of them. (Later they were defeated, mainly by smallpox and dogs. The disease debilitated the villages and the dogs sought the remaining warriors, much as hounds locate a hunter's prey.)

Pedro de Ursúa, still in his twenties, then decided that further action would be more rewarding in Peru. He therefore sailed away, arriving first in Panama. There, his renown having preceded him, he was intercepted. Panama's ruler, with the problem of runaway slaves on his hands, asked him to lead an expeditionary force against them. Ursúa agreed and found himself up against another wily enemy. The 200 Spaniards he led were all better armed than the opposing slaves under their leader, Bayano; but Bayano interspersed his steady retreat with sudden pin-prick attacks. This time Ursúa's enemies were not a powerful tribe defending their homeland. They were a bunch of desperate men without friends in any direction and, in time, were all killed, captured or returned to their owners. Within two years the Bayano war was over, a victory for the ruling Spanish and another feather in Ursúa's cap.

Once again he started for Peru, not knowing what kind of employment might lie ahead of him. And, once again, he was to find favour in the eyes of the country's ruler. Plainly he did have charm, generosity and the rest, never having trouble in securing support from those in charge. (Or maybe they swiftly found some task for this eager, likeable, aggressive individual who might turn some tables against them if under-occupied.) The viceroy of Peru gave Ursúa command of a major expedition that would search for El Dorado and the Omaguas. That golden legend, so promoted by the German knights, so dominant in everyone's thinking, would persist until someone discovered either its truth or its falsity. As for the Omaguas, the powerful people encountered by Orellana, they were thought to hold the key to great tracts of the upper Amazon, such as the secret of the 'gilded one'. Both the legend in general and this tribe in particular were thought to be eminently worthy of a determined investigation. Who better, therefore, to lead this venture than the man, now aged thirty-four, who was so personable and had been so victorious? And who better to have out of the way, rather than restlessly unemployed?

It is this expedition that provides the subject matter of this chapter. Just as Gonzalo Pizarro's venture ultimately became known, and with good cause, as Orellana's exploit, that of Pedro de Ursúa became attributed, and with equal reason, to Lope de Aguirre. Orellana took over when fate caused him to do so; Aguirre just took over. Without doubt Ursúa did possess many noble qualities, but his final expedition was to expose one fatal weakness: he seemed to know nothing about the qualities of others. In all of his exploits thus far he had not chosen his subordinates, he had simply been instructed to command them. They were greedy, aggressive, loyal, long-suffering, courageous and, in their understanding of the word, honourable, but by 1559 the major conflicts that had wracked Peru were ended. In their wake was left a different kind of individual, no less greedy, but less loyal and certainly less honourable. For his expedition from Peru the good and generous Ursúa had to command some of the very worst of them. The worst of all, by far, was Lope de Aguirre.

This man's *curriculum vitae*, had such a thing existed in those days, would have made frightening reading to any prospective employer.

Born 1509 (approx.). A Basque and known as 'the wolf'. Travelled from Spain to New World in 1534. Initially employed as tomb-robber. Protested to governor at uneven division of spoils. Was dismissed and posted to interior. Refused to go, mutinied, seized a ship, sailed to nearby colony and organized official protest concerning governor. Protest successful, governor dismissed, but protest earned no recompense. Sailed for Peru five years after its conquest, having been appointed *regidor* of Nuevo Toledo (Cuzco).

Worked there as breeder and breaker of horses. Served with Gonzalo Pizarro during Indian wars, suffered greatly (half the Spaniards dying), but again earned no reward. Sided with king's emissary in subsequent campaign against Pizarro, but was compelled to flee, eventually to Guatemala. Joined expedition hoping to find outlet from Lake Nicaragua to Pacific, but failed to find any such outlet. Seized city of Nombre de Dios in king's name, but defeated by rebellious governor of Panama. Fled to Cartagena. Offered support to king's newest emissary encountered *en route* to conquer Pizarro, but offer refused. Returned to Cuzco after four-year absence, having gained nothing. Reunited with Indian wife and mestizo daughter (Elvira).

Left for silver town of Potosí but discovered no riches. Joined military expedition heading for Tucumán, but singled out by Potosí's chief magistrate for possessing Indian porters. Sentenced to 100 lashes while strapped to ass's back. Salt rubbed into wounds. Carried off on stretcher, maimed for life. Recovered eventually, but determined on vengeance. Potosí's (now ex-) magistrate was followed to Lima, and then to Cuzco, where justice finally effected three and a half years after humiliating crime. Ex-magistrate affixed to his table with a poniard. After taking sanctuary in Cuzco Cathedral fled to Tucumán with help of friends. Had to be blackened and disguised as Negro servant. At Tucumán took part in rebellion against new laws (those forbidding ownership of Indians). Defeated and sentenced to death but fled to Lake Titicaca.

Stayed in hiding for two years. Emerged when offered amnesty to fight against those protesting over new laws. Served as arquebusier and received two bullets in leg. Rolled downhill into river. Rescued and returned to Cuzco. Worked again as horse-breaker. Joined an expedition to fight Indians; hand maimed. Heard of Ursúa's expedition from Martín de Guzmán, old comrade, and left Cuzco together with him and own daughter Elvira. Martín sacked from expedition but self recruited.

Whether Ursúa knew all or any of these facts is unknown, but he must have seen a hunched, elderly cripple and may or may not have observed the embitterment that partnered this physical damage. Peru's viceroy, the Marquis de Cuñete, was apparently alarmed at the concentration of brigandage around Ursúa, for Aguirre had brought a dozen miscreants with him; but one suspects Cuñete may also have been glad of their departure. Only Martín de Guzmán's services were actually dispensed with, but his brother Fernando de Guzmán stayed with the party (and was to play a damaging role). Before the expedition even began Ursúa received direct and explicit warning that Aguirre might become difficult. 'Where are we going?' Aguirre asked his leader. 'To conquer the Omaguas, find El Dorado and wealth,' answered Ursúa. Aguirre argued that Peru possessed certain wealth which could be obtained rather more easily. 'But that would be a violation of our duty to our king and lord,' replied Ursúa. It is almost possible to hear Aguirre's snort of disgust at such an answer, though this is not recorded. The good, the generous, the sweetly disposed Ursúa may even have believed he had won the argument. The crippled, the twisted and vengeful Aguirre undoubtedly considered that Ursúa had done nothing of the kind.

At all events the scene was set, in that year of 1559 (when Elizabeth of England had been one year on the throne, and almost half a century before Jamestown's founding), for the second major assault upon the Amazon. Clements Markham, with his notion of romance concerning this exploit, concludes his introduction no less enthusiastically. 'The career of Aguirre,' he writes, 'is certainly the most marvellous and extraordinary in the history of South American discovery . . .' It is tempting to believe Markham is describing some other man. Aguirre was extraordinary, perhaps, but marvellous by no stretch of any imagination. Markham had earlier described the expedition as 'the most appalling in the annals of Spanish enterprise'. And so indeed it was.

Pedro de Ursúa was not only foolish in taking along undoubted villains; he also took his love. Doña Inez de Atienza may or may not have been his wife, but she was his lady, having loved him since he first landed in Peru. What kind of lady, whether of good behaviour or otherwise, is unknown, mainly because the different contemporary accounts paint such different pictures.

The portrayal of Doña Inez makes a good example of this historical variance. One longs to know the truth but has to make do with an amalgam of differing accounts. Some of the chroniclers of this expedition interviewed its members, others did not, and all but one condemned the woman. The majority wrote that she was of bad character, with worse manners. They implied or even stated that much of what followed during the expedition was her fault. The one chronicler who hurried to her defence, Castellanos, did so with far greater vigour than the others had decried her, and it is tempting to favour his version. When she died – to leap ahead in this particular story – his rhyming verses were ecstatic in her praise. Was this entirely fanciful on his part or had she been (even partly) worthy of such sentiment?

The birds mourned on the trees, the wild beasts of the forests lamented, the waters ceased to murmur, the fish groaned beneath them, the winds execrated the deed, when Llamoso cut the veins of her white neck. Wretch! Art thou born of woman? What beast brought forth a son so wicked? How is it that thou dost not die in imagining a treason so enormous? Her two women, amidst lamentations and grief, gathered flowers to cover her grave, and cut her epitaph in the bark of a tree: 'These flowers cover one whose faithfulness and beauty were unequalled, whom cruel men slew without a cause.'

It is easy to prefer the Castellanos description and to assume that the good, the loyal, the perfect Ursúa would have loved someone of merit – even if the birds were not actually to grieve when she died. His error lay in taking her, mourning birds or not. Such expeditions did not profit by female company, good or bad.

As with any foray about to embark into the interior, Ursúa had too many practical problems to worry about the rights and wrongs of taking a lady. As always there was a shortage of money and the difficulty of finding sponsorship; but, somehow, he had to purchase equipment for his 300 soldiers. There had to be powder, arms and munitions, horses and cattle, rope and ships' stores, and there had to be the vessels themselves. (Both Gonzalo Pizarro and Orellana had stressed the need for river craft.) Some twenty-five ship-builders plus ten Negro carpenters were sent a few leagues downstream from Lima to start upon this work.

Unfortunately the preparations took time, causing some sponsors to withdraw their money, notably a priest named Pedro Portillo. This man, not as priestly as they come, had amassed some capital. He offered a large slice of it to Ursúa. In return for this outlay he would be vicar to the expedition, and perhaps become bishop of the new lands to be conquered. The preparatory delay then worried him and he withdrew his loan (having possibly discovered better dividends elsewhere). Ursúa told some comrades of his resultant plight, and these men, all 'of elastic consciences', promised to assist. They spun some yarn about a dying man to the recalcitrant priest, seized him as he left church, and forced him to sign an order for the promised loan. Then, having pointed 'fire-arms at his chest', they managed to acquire a further order for the remainder of his wealth. In this manner Pedro Portillo was able to treble his contribution to the expedition.

No sooner was this problem settled than another arose, caused not by one priest but by two soldiers. Francisco Diaz de Arles had been with Ursúa ever since the two of them had left Spain. Diego de Frias had been highly recommended to Ursúa by the viceroy, and had been made treasurer to the expedition. Both Arles and Frias became aggrieved when another man, Pedro Ramiro, was appointed over their heads as Ursúa's lieutenant-general. Such jealousy must have arisen ever since rank was invented, but Arles and Frias were not content to let their unhappiness smoulder quietly. They took violent action. Together with two others they attacked Ramiro at a river crossing, before strangling him. Then they hurried to Ursúa to tell a tale about Ramiro's forthcoming rebellion and how he planned to take command. An independent witness had also rushed to Ursúa with quite a different story. Ursúa reacted wisely, did nothing, and certainly avoided provoking a real rebellion against himself, led by the murderers. They were taken to the town of Santa Cruz, as there had to be an investigation of their deed, if nothing else. At Santa Cruz they were tried, found guilty and condemned to death. These four murderers and all the townspeople assumed Ursúa would now intervene, old comradely ties being stronger than some transitory misdeeds. However, the governor of Santa Cruz thought otherwise. He forbade any form of appeal – by anyone – and strengthened the sentence by ordering the executions to be performed publicly. These were carried out, and Ursúa returned to his task of worrying about guns and powder, horses, cows and boats.

If ill omens are being sought, this expedition was faring none too well even before it had begun. There was Aguirre, with a twisted mind to match his body. There were his comrades, equally accustomed to rebellion. There was Doña Inez, and not everyone had expressed a favourable opinion about her company. Money had been forced from a priest at gun-point, and four men had been executed for killing the second-in-command. If blood is shed at a commencement, said the superstitious, there will be blood at its ending, and fears were expressed in many quarters concerning the expedition's prospects.

Part of the trouble was the considerable postponement. The expedition had left Lima in February 1559. It would not properly begin upon the river until October 1560. There were reasons for delay – the finding of carpenters, the building of boats, the collection of sponsorship, the re-collection of sponsorship, the killing of Ramiro, the execution of his killers, and of course all the relatively humdrum matters connected with any expedition of 300 men likely to last a year.

The boat-building contingent, under García del Arze, had been sent ahead of the main party, with instructions not only to build boats but to wait for a major force commanded by Juan de Vargas. For some reason, presumably impatience, Arze did not bother to wait for Vargas. He sailed downstream for 200 leagues (over 700 miles), lost two men on the way (who merely vanished in the forest) and then built a fortified post against the Indians. His powder was short and, at one critical moment of attack, Arze used a last-ditch measure that proved to be successful. He fired the ramrod from his gun at the leading enemy canoe, whereupon 'nearly the whole team of them fell into the water', according to the major chronicler. The Indians not only retreated but subsequently proposed peace, bringing food and presents. The Spaniards, uncertain of the proposition, invited the peace mission within their stockade and then killed all twenty. This perfidy was entirely successful. Arze and his thirty men were thenceforth untroubled by Indians while they waited three months for Ursúa to catch up with them.

Meanwhile Juan de Vargas had travelled to the meeting place and had failed to find Arze there. He therefore travelled further downstream, again failed to find the boat-builders, and left a group of his own men behind while he and a smaller party went in search of food. He found some, captured many of the Indians whose food it was and returned to his abandoned group before discovering that three had died of hunger, while the remainder were planning a mutiny. Soon afterwards Ursúa and his contingent joined this group, creating (at last) a temporary sense of well-being within the expedition.

This was just as well, as problems were mounting daily. The vessels, made by those twenty-five carpenters with their ten Negroes, proved to be unsatisfactory. They had been constructed of unseasoned wood and sprang leaks when set afloat. To some extent the errors could be rectified – by repairing the better craft and making rafts and canoes to replace the unserviceable units – but the end result was less transport than had been planned. There was only space for a few cattle, for forty of the 300 horses and for much less provisioning than had been anticipated. Many of the men now wished to return to Lima. In effect this was mutiny, however reasonable; and all of Ursúa's charm, admonishment, pleading and threats were necessary to cajole, tease and bully the men to stay with him. In the end not a man did defect, but most of the horses and nearly all of the cattle had to be left to fend for themselves. Soon afterwards the three groups were united, García del Arze and his boat-builders, Juan de Vargas and his party, and the major force under Pedro de Ursúa. It was now early October 1560.

On this expedition, at last unified, there had already been murder, execution, and other loss of life caused by Indians and hunger. There had also been changes of plan as boats were abandoned and cattle and horses forsaken along with important stores; but at least the expedition was under way. Ursúa's thoughts are not recorded, but keeping the expedition together had already proved more than troublesome. If the goals of El Dorado and Omaguan wealth occupied his reflective waking hours, this fact is not anywhere apparent. Instead, reading between the lines of the chronicles, it would seem as if nothing very much occupied his mind. He enjoyed his lady's company, some say excessively. He did not worry about mutiny, some say carelessly. The desperadoes among his company did not trouble him for the time being, not even Lope de Aguirre. Ursúa behaved, or so it would appear, like some elderly gentleman on a not very onerous cruise. Perhaps, at thirty-five, he felt elderly, having been engaged in warfare and turbulence for all his adult years. Perhaps, even more to the point, no woman had ever before been his steadfast companion.

When his first appointed lieutenant, Pedro Ramiro, had been assassinated, this vacant position had been offered to Juan de Vargas, who had done well in leading his contingent. The high post of *alférez-general* was given to Fernando de Guzmán, brother of the other Guzmán who had been forbidden from the expedition. Both appointments were to prove unwise in the light of subsequent events, but the good and generous Ursúa was never at his best in assessing character. After a two-week stay at the final meeting place, where the thirty-seven horses (three having died) were exercised for the first time since their embarkation, the small army of exploration set off eastwards and downstream. Despite the losses, it was still a sizeable venture. There were about a hundred more men than Orellana had possessed, and almost twice as many as Francisco Pizarro had used to conquer the Incas.

Ursúa's expedition initially proceeded with marked similarity to that of Orellana. There was the remorseless search for food, the days of hunger and then others of satiated appetites. There was trouble with the boats as they sprang leaks, became damaged, were repaired and occasionally abandoned. (The largest of Ursúa's craft proved least satisfactory and had to be left behind.) Indians were captured, conversed with (somehow) and were either encouraging or discouraging concerning gold in their general area. Ursúa realized that favourable encounters were more rewarding and gave 'trifling presents, such as glass beads, knives, looking glasses, and other childish toys'. Gradually a better relationship built up between invaders and invaded. Ursúa issued instructions 'to prevent the knaveries which insolent soldiery are in the habit of committing', and the Indians responded with greater friendliness.

It is important to remember the prevailing attitude towards Indians. They were part slave, part beast of burden, part wealth. The Pope may have decreed that they had souls to be saved, but the edict had not been welcomed by the colonials. The new laws, giving certain rights to Indians, were even less warmly received. Almost all the explorers/settlers/conquerors wished to treat Indians as they had since the beginning. A single quotation may give the flavour of those early times, such as a passage by Michele de Cuneo, one of Columbus's officers. In 1494 he had captured a Carib woman and had brought her on board ship:

When I had taken her to my cabin she was naked – as was their custom. I was filled with desire to take my pleasure with her and attempted to satisfy my desire. She was unwilling and so treated me with her nails that I wished I had never begun. But – to cut a long story short – I then took a rope and whipped her soundly, and she let forth such incredible screams that you would not have believed your ears. Eventually we came to such terms, I assure you, that you would have thought she had been brought up in a school of whores.

Ursúa's appeasement of Indians did not inspire universal enthusiasm. It earned even less when he appeared to favour Indians at the expense of his own soldiers. In one village, whose inhabitants were friendly, they offered food but also hid some. Certain Spaniards observed this subterfuge and plundered the concealed provisions. Ursúa responded by taking action – against the Spaniards. He imprisoned those responsible, who included among their number a servant of Fernando de Guzmán, the *alférez-general*. This was construed by some as a deliberate insult to Guzmán. (The men, after all, had only taken food from Indians.) Other alleged wrongdoings by Ursúa were also noted by those eager to observe such things. Alonzo de Montoya, for instance, had seized some canoes, had discovered food, and was all set to return to Peru when he was arrested and imprisoned. By rights he should have been executed for this undoubted mutiny, but he was pardoned and set free to continue with resentful talk. Worst error of all, to those hungry for gain, was Ursúa's apparent lack of enthusiasm and lack of success, thus far, concerning gold. A few Indians had been seen wearing precious metal, hanging it around their necks or from their ears and noses, but for the most part the explorers encountered roots, fruits, grain 'and innumerable quantities of mosquitoes, especially sand-flies'. What was the purpose of suffering if it were not partnered by gain?

There is no evidence that Fletcher Christian planned mutiny from the outset of the *Bounty*'s voyage, or even when the ship left Tahiti *en route* for the West Indies. The mutiny simply happened, or so it would appear, quite unforeseen by either side. With Ursúa's expedition there is every indication that mutiny, rebellion and murder were possibilities from the start, quite apart from the mutinous and murderous acts that preceded it. The various irritations, grievances and insults were not adding fuel to the flames; they were more like flint, ever ready to spark. Aguirre and his accomplices had been in so many rebellions that these had become a way of life. When Montoya was set free after his crime of gross disobedience the chances of mutiny were further increased, punishment having apparently been abolished. The only uncertainties about the inevitable rebellion were when and where.

A further flint was created when Ursúa appointed a vicar-general. This man would be in charge of all matters spiritual, and Alonzo Henão took his job seriously, not to say officiously. He promised to excommunicate all those who did not return stolen goods such as weapons, munitions, equipment, provisions. The resentment that followed, which should have been aimed at the vicar, became deflected towards Ursúa. He was plainly behind these excommunications. Or maybe it was Inez who was behind Ursúa? It was even argued that the army was being governed through him by her. The two of them always had their tent pitched at a distance when he, at least, ought to have rested at the centre of his men. He and she plainly disliked the army. Therefore the army resented and disliked them, or so said a large number of its men.

Chief among these was none other than the recently promoted Fernando de Guzmán. He was well disposed to the soldiers and, in return, was liked by them. Thus, as the chronicler Simon puts it, 'entering by the door of ambition (which is always open) they offered to put his hands into it, up to the elbows, by making him the successor of Pedro de Ursúa'. The mutineers cajoled Guzmán, disclosed their offer and their intentions, and said these 'were founded in a holy zeal'. 'There is no greater crime than that which is done under the mask of religion,' adds Simon, who was plainly against this impending rebellion. 'Don Fernando did not dislike the arguments of the mutineers,' concludes the chronicler, never able to conceal his personal opinions. The when and the where would soon be revealed as the time and the place drew nearer.

Lope de Aguirre was wholly in favour of mutiny, and became ringleader of those relishing a change in command. He and his men thought that New Year's Day would be a suitable occasion. The year 1561 could begin with a clean sheet, as it were. Ursúa had been warned, mainly via his slaves, but he posted no extra guards. The rebels found him lying in his hammock talking to a young page. 'What seek you here at this hour?' asked Ursúa. For answer they stabbed at him, but missed. He had time to reach his sword and buckler before the rest of the party entered. The newcomers were more than a match, and Ursúa barely had time to call upon his creator before being killed. 'Liberty, liberty, long live the king, the tyrant is dead,' shouted the executioners. As the hallowed cliché rang round that clearing in the Amazon forest it reached the ears of Juan de Vargas, lieutenant-general. Putting on his *escaupil*, or suit of cotton armour, and holding sword, shield and rod of office, he hurried towards Ursúa's lodging. The rebels managed to disarm him. Then, when his arms were pinned, one man thrust a sword so savagely at his chest that it emerged to wound another man standing close behind. 'Liberty, *caballeros*, long live the king,' they shouted, stabbing and stabbing again their former leader and his deputy. Ursúa's governorship had been brief. He had embarked from the boatyard on 26 September 1560 and he died, aged thirty-five, on 1 January the following year.

Brother Pedro Simon does not say whether the birds mourned or the beasts lamented, but does append a touching obituary. Ursúa 'was of middle size, slightly formed, but well proportioned, with the manners of a gentleman; light complexion and beard the same, courteous, and affable, fond of his soldiers, and more inclined to mercy than to justice; thus his enemies could not complain of his having done them wrong: he was too confiding and had but little precaution, and his great goodness was the main cause which brought him to so sad an end'. One portion of Markham's 'romance' had been concluded. The 'extraordinary' and 'marvellous' Aguirre was ready to take his stand.

Being, as it were, professional rebels, the killers of Ursúa and Vargas knew what to do in the wake of their insurrection. Firstly they sought and murdered particular friends of the two dead men (the numbers involved are not recorded). They ordered that no man should speak in a low voice, for fear he might be plotting revenge, and no man should leave his quarters at night for the same reason. Both Ursúa and Vargas were buried in Ursúa's house without delay, 'together in death as in life'. Two new leaders were named: Fernando de Guzmán, as governor, and Lope de Aguirre, as *maestro del campo*. These matters concluded, much of Ursúa's personal wine was distributed in a liberal manner. Not only did it taste like immediate gain but it lessened any sense of unease over the traitorous acts in which all were now implicated.

On the following day many more appointments were made. Ursúa had been laggardly (or niggardly) in offering such posts, and the rebels wished for change. Also, or so the leaders thought, such elevations might make those involved less likely to defect. Among the creations were a captain of the guard, several captains of infantry, a captain of horse, a standard-bearer, a chief judge, a high constable, a paymaster-general, a sea captain, a quarter-master (in charge of warlike stores), several knight commanders, and a sea admiral. Most of the appointments were somewhat meaningless – one wonders in particular about the paymaster and the admiral – but those receiving these promotions knew better than to refuse. Diego de Balcasar, the man appointed judge, accepted the staff of office but said: 'I take [it] in the name of King Philip our Lord, and in no other.' For this blatant lack of enthusiasm concerning his new leaders he was closely watched and eventually killed. His loyalties were plainly alien to the enterprise.

Don Fernando de Guzmán, as new leader, called a council of the more important individuals, and stressed the importance of looking for gold. That was the purpose of the expedition. It was the reason why Ursúa had been killed; he seemed to have forgotten his duty to search for El Dorado. Guzmán asked every man to sign his name by way of agreeing with this reaffirmed declaration of intent. He signed first, and passed the document to Aguirre. At this moment one warms – ever so slightly – towards the crippled and undoubted villain of the story. He signed all right, but wrote 'Lope de Aguirre, the traitor'. As the others were busily proclaiming their virtue, and also their absolute correctness in murdering their former leader, there was a general spluttering at such self-condemnation. They called for explanation and received it.

'What madness and gross ignorance is this into which some of us have fallen?' Aguirre began (according to Simon). 'Do those who have killed a king's governor think their act may be excused? Will a paper, replete with signatures, create blamelessness for all?' In his opinion, fostered by years of wrongdoing, nothing but recrimination ever emerged from Spain. To join the losing side was one kind of fault. To instigate and carry out a rebellion was a certain error bringing equally certain retribution for all concerned. Should the land they discover 'be ten times richer than Pirú and more populous than New Spain (Mexico) . . . I tell you it will cost us all our heads'. There was no point, he argued, in even bothering to find new lands or new wealth, for 'our lives will be sacrificed', so it would be better to return to a good land 'which is Pirú'. This, as will be remembered from his initial conversation with Ursúa, was what he had wanted all along.

Once again, Aguirre was overruled. One man in particular, Juan Alonso de la Bandera, spoke for the majority when he reasoned that Ursúa's death had been no crime, that Ursúa had forgotten about gold, that the king would be better served as a result of the governor's death, and that new lands and wealth should be sought without further ado. Aguirre retreated, having lost this further battle. As before, he retired to contemplate revenge in the hope of winning the war. He knew no other way.

It is easy to forget, when submerged in murders and recriminations, that the Ursúa expedition was ostensibly a down-river foray to explore new lands. With Aguirre outspokenly in favour of returning upstream, and others only vaguely intent upon finding El Dorado, the original impetus – such as it was – diminished still further. Not until five days after Ursúa's death did the expedition move once more, and it journeyed for only one day before halting yet again. At an abandoned village, totally lacking in food, the Guzmán–Aguirre flotilla stopped, mainly to discard some boats and make others. Their flat-bottomed craft, suitable for horses, would not meet the expedition's future needs. Brigantines, with higher sides and a more seaworthy form, were ordered by Guzmán, and the carpenters started work again with their Negro assistants.

In the meantime, and apparently caring not a fig for such tedious practicalities, Aguirre proceeded with the more stimulating activity of insurrection. He saw to it that García del Arze was arrested. This long-standing friend of Ursúa's just might become a problem to the new regime, so he was strangled. Diego de Balcasar, the man who spoke out when appointed judge, was also seized. He managed to escape by hurling himself into the river. Guzmán, on hearing what had happened, shouted to the hiding Balcasar that his life was safe. The fugitive decided to return and, as Simon phrases it, 'did not die this time'. Aguirre heard and believed that two other men, the camp mayor and the paymaster-general, were actively conniving at Guzmán's death. Both men were promptly arrested and finally strangled. Their posts were given to others, setting off a chain of envious resentment leading to further killing. If gold and exploration were still on the agenda, they were assuredly taking second place to intrigue, dissension and death.

At least – to give credit where due – Aguirre seemed to be acting on his new governor's behalf. By whittling away possible opposition, and believing every anti-Guzmán rumour to come his way, Aguirre was undoubtedly boosting his leader's status. Unfortunately Guzmán did not appear to realize how his power was being maintained, and his wishes did not always coincide with those of Aguirre. For example, Guzmán named Juan Alonso de la Bandera as his lieutenant-general. This man had turned the tide against Aguirre during the debate on returning to Peru. Aguirre was never a man to forget defeat and two factions now surfaced: those favouring Aguirre and those on Bandera's side. Guzmán realized he had to ally himself with one party or the other. Sensibly he chose Bandera, but idiotically (if that is strong enough a word) he then cancelled Aguirre's appointment as *maestro del campo*. Compounding this error, he gave the post to the resented lieutenant-general himself, Juan Alonso de la Bandera. Aguirre was relegated to captain of horse and, once again, had lost a battle. Revenge fomented within him like some dreadful bacillus biding its time.

Guzmán knew well enough that Aguirre was no friend, and was repeatedly advised to kill the man. Ursúa had also known that Aguirre was more enemy than friend, and had also been warned. It is therefore possible to suspect that Aguirre, for all his evil intent and general dereliction, did possess some form of skilful endearment. How else did he survive when common sense should, at the very least, have caused him to be chained up? Why did Ursúa and Guzmán seem blind to such blatant danger? Guzmán wished apparently to get at the heart of the man, not with a dagger (as would have been most just) but with soft words and kind promises. He even offered a marriage, proposing that Aguirre's half-caste daughter should be betrothed to his brother, Martín de Guzmán. In further peace-making, Guzmán raised Elvira's status by giving her the title Doña. Aguirre apparently smiled at these offerings, but they did little or nothing to assuage his true intent.

Lope de Aguirre

Forgiveness was not a part of him. Revenge was his desire, to be sought and gained whenever feasible.

Juan Alonso de la Bandera became his immediate target. Not only had this man been given Aguirre's appointment but he was leader of the opposing faction. Bandera learned speedily of Aguirre's loathing and, unlike Guzmán, sent friends to kill him. Aguirre always slept armed, and his accomplices were equally alert, so the murder was easier to plan than to effect. Worse still, from the Bandera faction's point of view, the tables were turned against them. A rumour spread that their lieutenant-general, not content with two appointments, wished to have a third, namely expedition governor. Bandera was intending to kill Guzmán, or so this rumour said.

On hearing such falsehood, Guzmán should not only have blocked his ears but killed Aguirre. Instead, after a moment or two of incredulousness, he believed every word he heard, and was soon plotting with Aguirre over ways and means of killing Bandera. The plan they devised was for Guzmán to invite the proposed victim for a game of cards. One wonders (from this distance in time) why anybody ever believed anybody in that deserted village by the Amazon, but the invited man arrived obligingly and unarmed. With the game in mid-play Guzmán sent for Aguirre, and Bandera suffered a 'cruel death'. Aguirre immediately asked for a reward, and received again his old post of *maestro del campo*. With anyone else, this reinstatement might have softened the desire for revenge. In the case of Aguirre it did nothing of the sort.

Part of the trouble was underemployment among the soldiers. The carpenters took several weeks before the brigantines were ready, being given 'no upper works nor decks' but 'strong hulls'. Another problem was hunger. Indians had appeared, bearing food and promising more in exchange for gifts, but some of them had been attacked by the Spaniards. As reprisal, a Spanish food-foraging party was itself attacked and then annihilated by the Indians. Both the hunger and the lack of activity made Aguirre's work all the easier. He steadily promoted the notion of returning to Peru and, cunningly, boosted Guzmán's leadership. Everyone was made to swear that Philip of Spain was no longer his king and lord and to forsake his rights as a Spaniard. As no man could serve two masters, Don Fernando de Guzmán was to be their prince and king. Three men refused to swear this oath and were swiftly put to death.

During the protracted halt, while the boat-building was slowly taking place, the idea of going back to Peru became transformed. Instead of being peaceable it would be warlike. Peru would be attacked and, if all went well for the returning force, would be conquered. Francisco Pizarro had done this when he had subjugated the Incas. Gonzalo Pizarro had also attacked Peru, had won it for a while and had shown what could be achieved. Guzmán and Aguirre could also do it, or so Aguirre argued, but there had to be unanimity of purpose if this third conquest was to succeed. Everyone was made to swear to it, 'by God, and Santa Maria, his most glorious mother, by those holy works of the Evangelists, and by the consecrated host'. A document was drawn up, and all signed. On this occasion there were no dissenters.

If Guzmán still had doubts about forsaking his true king and attacking Peru, these were skilfully annulled by Aguirre. When the signings had been completed the crippled rebel marched to Guzmán and announced: 'All these cavaliers and myself, have elected your Excellency to be our Prince and King; and as such we come to tender you our obedience, and to kiss your hand, supplicating your acquiescence.' Thenceforth the new prince and king, installed in place of the murdered Ursúa, was always called 'Your Excellency'. His decrees began: 'Don Fernando de Guzmán, by the grace of God, Prince of Tierra Firme, and of Peru . . .' Aguirre certainly knew about flattery. He had promoted Guzmán from being an ordinary member of an exploratory foray (and one whose brother had been banned from it) to the titular head of Spain's richest overseas kingdom. Guzmán himself totally welcomed this new status, dined alone, was 'served at table with all ceremonies' and became thoroughly 'puffed up in his presentation of majesty'.

In truth, of course, he was a rebel living with some equally treacherous comrades in a deserted village somewhere along the banks of the Amazon. For all their unity and sworn statements the prospects were not outstanding. Their food was short. The expedition had gained nothing thus far. There had been great blood-letting and Guzmán himself was living precariously. Either Aguirre would be the end of him or Spain would, such traitors being resented at a distance as assuredly as if at home. However, in Guzmán's eyes, as he feasted in royal manner, surveyed his army (still in excess of 200 men) and examined his fleet (of canoes and brigantines), there remained only one hurdle to be overcome, the entering and conquering of Peru. How best, therefore, to go about this task?

From the expedition's Amazon standpoint the forthcoming conquest of Peru seemed remarkably simple. The rebel army would sail down the Amazon from its current refuge, head north-west to the Island of Margarita (as Orellana had done) and then proceed to Nombre de Dios (on the eastern shore of modern Panama). The king's ministers and officials residing there would be killed. Those favourable towards the idea of a new Peruvian conquest would be recruited. The swollen army, after burning Nombre de Dios, would then march to the Pacific coast and Panama. Once again, the king's representatives would be murdered and further recruitment would be encouraged. Not only would runaway slaves be suitable material, but word of the rebellion would surely bring other supporters. The expanded army, under His Excellency Don Fernando de Guzmán, would not only possess all the weapons looted from both cities but would build a galleon or two with which to sail southwards down South America. This sea-borne force to raid Peru would be so vast, or so they reasoned by the Amazon, that the mighty kingdom would soon be forced to yield. In short, the plan was as straightforward as they come. Weeks had been spent in building boats, murdering, and sorting out priorities. It was time to initiate phase one of the grand design, namely to leave the Amazon.

The major mystery of the Aguirre expedition is now encountered. Despite the recording of so much detail – the signings, the affirmations, the manner of each death – there is no certainty about its emergence into the Atlantic. Did the boats proceed steadfastly down the Amazon, as Orellana's had done? Or did they come out via the Orinoco, as some statements seem to indicate? It is easy to assume the Amazon must have been their route, however long it was, however much it flowed determinedly away from Peru. Any other course, such as taking a river to the north, would have involved journeying upstream into a great deal of unknown territory. Against such reasoning is the fact that Aguirre (and therefore Guzmán) was impatient to conquer

Peru. He knew his followers might change their minds if circumstances altered. He must, in consequence, reach Margarita and Panama with minimum delay. To proceed eastwards for months and months might foster disaffection for the Peruvian enterprise. By striking north, somehow, they would be embarking more positively upon their plan.

There is evidence to suit both theories. Simon definitely indicates the northern notion:

It had come to Aguirre's knowledge that there were many soldiers who would rather have remained in any moderately fair province, than go upon the present mutinous expedition. So Aguirre arranged to make a turn out of the direct route, and, having navigated three days and one night in this westerly direction, they came to a few empty huts . . . in a miserable wet country . . . where the air was filled with mosquitoes.

The huts and subsequent miseries are not as important (to us) as the fact of heading west. This supposes that they somehow reached and ascended the Rio Negro. What Aguirre could not have known was that, by going upstream along the Negro, he would be able to meet the waters of the Orinoco. Amazingly, the colossal river networks of the Amazon and the Orinoco are actually united. It is possible to travel from one to the other by the Casiquiare Canal, an entirely natural and wholly improbable union of both rivers. Had Aguirre's party stumbled upon this phenomenon, the event might have found its way into some of the subsequent narratives. Not every day do boats fighting their way upstream find themselves floating downstream without a change in direction, and the happening is presumably memorable. (In fact, many Amazon rivers flow upstream if the nearby major river is in spate. When the Amazon itself is in flood even some of its colossal tributaries can change their flow. The mutineers were not to know this and, one suspects, would have been astonished by Casiquiare, even if they did have other thoughts on their minds, such as the conquest of Peru.)

There is also evidence that, despite Aguirre's turn 'out of the direct route', he was loyal to the Amazon. The time taken by his army to reach the river mouth is about right. The travelling time from that mouth to Margarita is also what one would expect. A further confusion, not helping the evidence either way, is that many early writers called both the Orinoco and the Amazon by the one name, Marañón. In short, no one is precisely sure which river was used by the mutineers. Many of the details, such as who killed whom and where, *are* well recorded, and perhaps that information seemed more critical than the whereabouts of the actual waterway on which these events were taking place. The expedition was not one of geography but of carnage, of Spaniards killing Spaniards.

Doña Inez de Atienza was still with the party. She had been spared when her lover, Pedro de Ursúa, had been killed and later became attached to Lorenzo Salduendo, captain of the guard. Father Simon is no Castellanos when describing this lady. The latter, it will be remembered, told how the birds and wild beasts were saddened at her death. Simon writes that she 'had not left the evil ways she had continued in since she had left Pirú'. Clements Markham, plainly taking his lead from Castellanos, writes that 'the poor broken-hearted girl was utterly helpless' following Ursúa's death, being 'in the hands of incarnate fiends, with hearts harder than nether mill stone'. From this distance one wonders what she could possibly have done except attach herself to another individual and hope for some protection.

Salduendo was rather too protective. When the boats were being loaded, following a further raising and strengthening of their bulwarks, he ordered mattresses for the lady Inez and her mestizo servant. Aguirre countermanded these instructions, claiming insufficient space. Shortly afterwards, ever eager for malevolent gossip, Aguirre heard how Inez had predicted many deaths. She had been burying another servant (who seems to have died naturally) when she exclaimed that the dead girl would soon have others to keep her company. Aguirre immediately assumed that Salduendo was plotting against him. He therefore had Salduendo arrested and reported the matter to Guzmán. Guzmán urged restraint, but this was neither a word nor a policy that Aguirre understood. Salduendo was killed, and Guzmán protested to no avail. Without her new protector Inez was now doomed, and swords were used to murder her. Simon, content to decry her evil ways, was nonetheless shocked at her killing and the manner of it: '. . . even the most hardened men in the camp, at sight of the mangled victim, were broken-hearted, for this was the most cruel act that had been perpetrated.' Afterwards Guzmán 'upbraided' Aguirre, which sounds like a modest scolding.

Don Fernando de Guzmán, for all his titles, must have suspected his days were numbered. With so great a quantity of death, mainly among senior officials, all the highest must have felt a qualm. Certainly Aguirre did so, and strengthened his bodyguard; yet he had instigated most of the killing and, by this yardstick, was more secure than others. However, he rightly assumed that his actions had caused enmity, and could not have been greatly surprised when news reached him of plans for his assassination. Alonzo Montoya was in charge of the new anti-Aguirre faction, but two of his council secretly decided to throw in their lot with Aguirre after the decisive planning meeting. Montoya was therefore a dead man while still thinking he could get the better of Aguirre.

When this further revolution was being planned the boats were being refurbished on a long, narrow and previously uninhabited island. (The fear of Indian attack always existed, though every Spaniard should have been more wary of his fellow countrymen.) At one end of the island Guzmán had his camp. At the other end Montoya was camped with his followers. Aguirre and his men had installed themselves centrally. This separation of his two enemies was a sound move. Aguirre was undoubtedly a professional, while the others were amateurs, hoping there would be no more killing and taking no significant steps to protect themselves. Nor did they seriously attempt to kill Aguirre, whose death had been proved necessary over and over again.

For the benefit of his followers, Aguirre told a tale that Montoya and Miguel Robedo (recently appointed admiral) were both plotting to kill Guzmán. These two were therefore despatched with sword and lance, leaving no one else any the wiser – for the time being. The next problem lay at the other end of the island where His Excellency Don Fernando was sleeping. Aguirre waited until dawn, collected more men *en route*, told a similar tale that their leader was about to be attacked, and insisted everyone should take particular care not to harm Guzmán. The first to die was Padre Alonso Henão, who had taken the oaths favouring Guzmán against the true king. Three of Guzmán's close associates were also killed, and then followed a cosy interchange between Aguirre and his leader. 'What is all this, my father?' asked Guzmán, using the form he adopted when speaking to the crippled rebel. 'Do not be alarmed, Your Excellency,' replied Aguirre before proceeding with the slaughter. Guzmán did not have much time to be alarmed. Two men in Aguirre's party knew that Guzmán was also to be killed, but only two. Aguirre had been concerned that others might wish to save their leader. The two men set about their task in a straightforward manner, despatching Guzmán by firing their arquebuses straight at him.

Thus died the most casual rebel, Don Fernando, by the grace of God, Prince of Tierra Firme, and of Peru . . . Dates are uncertain but he held his royal post, however fictionally, for a very few weeks. As with Ursúa, Padre Simon appended a touching obituary for Don Fernando: 'He was scarcely twenty-six years of age, of good stature, well formed and strong of limb, with the manners of a gentleman, fine face and beard, slow to action, more kind than otherwise, and born in the city of Seville.' He might have lived longer had he been quicker to action and with the manners of a rattlesnake. It was no good being more kind than otherwise in Aguirre's company. It was no good being anything save wholeheartedly intent upon Aguirre's end.

Once again, as after Ursúa's murder, Aguirre knew what to do. He addressed the remaining men, spoke of Guzmán's failure as a leader, affirmed that the killings had been necessary and everyone should now proceed with renewed vigour. And this, more or less, is what they did. Aguirre was generous with promotions, raising his friends to all sorts of ranks. He himself became general and 'powerful chief'. The men reportedly called themselves *marañones*, on account of the plots, the *marañas*, that had been so paramount. (Maybe they did, and for that reason, but the river Amazon had already been given the name Marañón for other possible reasons: because Marañón was the name of the first sailor to see it; as a derivation from the query *mare an non?* [sea or not?]; or because the river itself, certainly at its mouth, resembled an entanglement or plot. The Aguirre party may not have been on the Marañón at all, but heading up the Rio Negro instead. Such a minor point would not have troubled this particular expedition. Most of its members could not have known, or greatly cared, about the actual waterway, but they certainly knew of the plots and were therefore *marañones*.)

The murdering did not cease now that all immediate rivals for the leadership had been annihilated. After the expedition had left the Town of Butchery, its name for that long, narrow and previously uninhabited island, eight more Spaniards were killed within a week, some because Aguirre feared their disloyalty and one because he was just an *amotinadorcillo*, a poor little mutineer. Three Spaniards and some Indians died when their small craft was overturned, an accidental and unaccustomed form of demise under Aguirre's command. One Indian died in an experiment to determine whether the local brand of arrow was poison-tipped. He was duly scratched with it and perished on the following day. Padre Simon describes these killings most casually, but is outraged when Aguirre later commits 'one of his greatest cruelties'. The 'powerful chief' decided to abandon all Indians in the party, whether male or female, who had become Christians during the journey. Indian slaves/servants/paddlers had been brought from Peru and also gathered along the way. Those who now professed Christianity, either through faith or their appraisal of the situation, were put ashore in the territory of a quite different Indian group. Maybe the new arrivals were not killed, and the change in climate was not lethal to these Indians from elsewhere, but Padre Simon had no such doubts: 'It was certain that these poor creatures would soon perish.'

Aguirre's reason for this action was a lack of space within the brigantines. At least the individuals had not been slaughtered, or not directly, and there was some validity to his argument. The expedition, wherever it was, knew it would be meeting the rougher waters of an estuary and then the open sea. Tidal signs were being increasingly detected and a rocking, lurching boat, perhaps shipping water from time to time, made space and payload more crucial issues than when floating down-river. It is not recorded how many Indians were forcibly expelled by Aguirre, or how much freeboard and general seaworthiness he gained in the process, but life afloat must have been easier thereafter. Further Indians were lost on fishing and food-finding forays. Unused as they were to major waves or oceanic swell coming up-river, they either drowned or were swamped while paddling after the much larger brigantines. It was therefore with more space and buoyancy than ever before that Aguirre and his party sailed into the Northern Sea, the Atlantic, on the first day of July 1561.

The sudden emergence of a date adds a touch of reality to this blood-letting nightmare. The texts recording the journey are extremely short on practical details such as dates and whereabouts, but they do agree on 1 July and the open sea. It had been February 1559 when the expedition had left Lima, and October 1560 when it had embarked upon the river. Pedro de Ursúa's governorship had lasted for three months and six days until his murder on 1 January 1561. Lope de Aguirre's governorship, if combined with the period when he operated through Guzmán, had therefore lasted almost twice as long by the time its survivors reached the Atlantic. As for the number who accompanied him that day, of that there is no record. 'About' 300 soldiers and a quite unknown assortment of Indians and half-castes had left Lima. Only the major Spanish deaths were recorded, and this particular account has so far listed forty-three, whether by Spanish hands, Indian hands or mere accident. There must have been more deaths because some are mentioned casually, being incidental to some other story, as when Doña Inez is overheard while burying a mestizo servant. There is talk of starvation and the possibility of disease, but little attention was accorded to these more natural hardships, inter-necine death being much more interesting. The army to conquer Peru had certainly been whittled from its earlier strength, but Lope de Aguirre was now fully in charge of his vengeful mission. If born in 1509 he was now fifty-two. He had spent twenty-seven of those years in the New World, losing at most encounters but always adding to his tortured sense of grievance.

It took the two brigantines seventeen days to reach the island of Margarita. (This fact does not confirm or contradict the Orinoco story. From the Amazon's mouth to Margarita is considerably further, but it would have been possible in seventeen days. Similarly the shorter journey could have taken that time, had wind and weather been unfavourable.) Aguirre had removed all navigational aids, such as compass and cross-staff, from the second vessel, since he wished it to follow him precisely – by night with the aid of a lantern. As ever, the professional rebel was afraid of rebellion by others. In this case he was fearful that his *maestro del campo*, in charge of the second brigantine, might hurry off to Spain and summon retribution upon his head. Both vessels therefore did stay together until, on reaching Margarita, they were forced into different ports by a contrary wind. Aguirre tied up in Paraguache, still known as the Tyrant's Port, and his *maestro* put in two leagues further north. Both were a short distance from the principal city of the island, the seat of government.

Somehow Aguirre had to capture this city. He wanted to equip himself suitably for heading further west, to Nombre de Dios and Panama. On the morning of 20 July he therefore disembarked, having slaughtered two more soldiers who had incurred his suspicions. Aware that his arrival would prompt questions on the island, Aguirre spread the word that he had arrived from Peru *en route* to quell some disturbances on the Marañón. (If you have to lie, incorporate truth wherever possible.) He let it be known that he wished for provisions and would pay for them. As earnest of his professed intentions he gave handsome presents, including a magnificent scarlet cloak, trimmed with gold lace, and a silver-gilt cup, in return for two bullocks slaughtered on his behalf by a friendly islander.

The governor of Margarita heard of the newcomers, their arrival from Peru, their generous payment for provisions, and ordered that food should be sent to the ships forthwith. He himself, with half a dozen officials, then set off to meet Aguirre and his men. Aguirre was extremely affable at the encounter and asked permission for more of his men to disembark, not only in full armour but fully armed. They had, he explained, considerable military zeal and wished to exercise their skills. This they did, most speedily. The governor and his party were relieved of their weapons and made prisoner. So too was everyone else met by Aguirre and his little army as they marched the dozen miles to the island's capital.

An advance party, under Martín Pérez, entered the Margarita fort, still conveniently open. 'Long live Aguirre! Liberty! Liberty!' they shouted, while disarming the general populace. Aguirre, upon his arrival, went straight for the royal treasury. Without waiting for such minutiae as keys he battered down its doors and removed all the gold and pearls. He then found the wine and distributed it freely among his men. Next he just looted the place, of clothing, of merchandise in general, of money. Houses were burned, women abused, cattle killed, and so ended day one of Aguirre's stay on Margarita. It was not yet Peru, but he was on his way.

The number of men in Aguirre's army is now even more difficult to ascertain. On the one hand he is still killing followers accused of possible perfidy, while on the other he is raising recruits from the island. Among those killed was his captain of ammunition, whose post was then given to Antón Llamoso, a faithful follower if ever there was one (and the killer of Doña Inez). This man was subsequently accused through the same heady mixture of rumour and gullibility. Llamoso protested his innocence. Aguirre, as ever, preferred the rumour. Realizing that a more drastic form of affirmation was necessary, Llamoso threw himself upon the body of one recently deceased, another alleged traitor to Aguirre's cause. 'Curse this man', said Llamoso, who 'wished to commit so great a crime; I will drink his blood.' He then sucked at the fluid issuing from the corpse and swallowed what he sucked. The observers were battle-hardened, with dead men and oozing wounds commonplace in their combined experience, but all were impressed by Llamoso's desperate gesture. Along the way Llamoso had learned a thing or two about his chief; those lessons saved his life.

The man whose congealing blood had preserved Llamoso was Martín Pérez. He had been placed by Aguirre in charge of the Margarita fort. It was an important honour, causing some soldiers to speculate that Pérez might become their chief should disaster overtake Aguirre. Their remarks were overheard, making the man's death inevitable. A certain 'bearded little monkey' (as Simon calls him) was given the task of assassinating Pérez, and tried to do so with an arquebus. Others then assisted with daggers and knives, but the unfortunate Pérez was still able to stagger about the fort, his bowels and brains most visible. He begged confession loudly, continuing until the bearded monkey finished him by slicing his throat. Had Pérez been killed more cleanly there would have been no mangled body for Llamoso to exploit so horrendously and so effectively.

Perhaps all tyrants are clear-cut in their wishes and intentions. Aguirre was quite straightforward about whom to kill: namely, anyone he or others suspected of the smallest treachery towards him, as in whispering, meeting in suspicious circumstances, or doing anything to be construed as connivance. He even listed groups deemed worthy of execution: every monk (save the Mercedarios), all bishops, viceroys, presidents, *oidores* (auditors), governors, lawyers, *procuradores*, every *caballero* of noble blood, all public women, and of course every enemy of his cause. He was as good as his word in that he did indeed kill representatives from each of these categories, and he should have been listened to with extreme care. It was with similar truthfulness that he had signed himself 'Lope de Aguirre, the traitor'. He still persisted in that vein, placing on the bodies of two Margarita victims the inscription: 'These men have been executed, because they were faithful vassals of the king of Castille.' This example of candour was followed by a mocking sneer towards the corpses: 'Let us now see if the king of Castille will raise you again.'

During the killing, the looting, the general consolidation of power, word reached Aguirre of a large and well-armed vessel at anchor in the nearby port of Maracapana. It would serve his needs precisely for the voyage to Nombre de Dios, being an immense improvement over his two Amazon-built brigantines. He immediately despatched a force of eighteen men in one of the brigantines to capture the ship. On the way some of them thought it might be preferable to switch sides. They seem to have formed the majority, or at least the more powerful element. At Maracapana the ship's captain welcomed all aboard, heard their news, heard all about Aguirre and listened to their proposal to defect. He then promptly disarmed all eighteen of his guests. There were protests, but he was entirely right in exercising all possible caution – as right as Ursúa and Guzmán had been wrong in failing to do so.

In charge of the vessel was Brother Francisco Montesinos of the Order of Santo Domingo. He was on a missionary exercise, converting the Indians to Christianity, but he abandoned that work on hearing of Aguirre. With all possible speed he sailed for Puerto de Piedras, the nearest harbour to the capital city of Margarita. Aguirre learned of his party's defection only after first assuming that the vessel he saw entering port was arriving as his prize. Needless to say he was enraged at the news, all pious Catholic ears (as Simon phrases it) being 'horrified at his blasphemous and heretical words'. His first act was one of simple revenge. He ordered the captured governor and three of his aides to be killed. Aguirre used their deaths not so much to stiffen his men's resolve as to clarify the depth of their rebellious involvement:

Do you see, O *marañones*, in the bodies now before your eyes that, independently of the crimes you committed in the river Marañón by slaying your governor Pedro de Ursúa, and his lieutenant Don Juan de Vargas, by making a prince of Don Fernando, and giving your oath of allegiance to him as such, you have divested yourselves of all rights in the kingdom of Castille, you have forsworn allegiance to the king Don Philip . . . You afterwards added crime to crime; you executed your own prince and lord, many captains and soldiers, a priest, and a noble lady and, having arrived at this island, you have forcibly taken possession of it, dividing the property found in it amongst yourselves . . . You have destroyed the books of the treasury and committed sundry and diverse wickednesses. Now you have killed another governor, an *alcalde*, a *regidor*, an *alguazil mayor*, as well as other persons, whose bodies you now have before your eyes . . .

The recapitulation must have emboldened some and terrified others, particularly when Aguirre explained that criminals such as they were would not be safe in any part of the world. They should therefore not leave him. They should sell their lives dearly when the occasion offered, and all should be of one mind. 'Against such a union, all the force that may be sent against you will be of little avail . . . Mark well what I have said, for it is a question of life and death.'

The battle between the land forces under Aguirre and the ship under Brother Francisco started as a war of written words. (The vessel stayed irritatingly out of range, although plainly ready for action.) If Aguirre really did compose the letters ascribed to him he was not just a simple, twisted rebel. His opening salvo to the friar is rich with aggrieved cunning.

Magnificent and Reverend Sir, – It would give us much greater pleasure to celebrate your paternity's reception with boughs and flowers, than with arquebuses and discharges of artillery, because it has been told to us, by many persons, that such would be more generous; and, if we are to judge by the proceedings we have this day observed, which are greater than we had been led to expect; it would seem that your paternity is a lover of arms and military exploits; and thus we see that you imitate the honour, virtue, and nobility, which our forefathers attained sword in hand . . . [and on for a couple of pages in similar taunting, self-effacing yet self-excusing style, before he reaches his conclusion] . . . In your reply, I beseech your paternity that you will write to me, and let us treat one another well in this war. God will bring trouble on all traitors, and the king will restore the loyal to life, although up to this time we have seen no one resuscitated by a king; he cures no wounds, he restores no one to life. May the most magnificent and reverend person of your paternity, be in great and increasing dignity. From this fortress of Margarita, I kiss the hands of your paternity. Your servant, LOPE DE AGUIRRE.

This letter was despatched to the ship via Indians in a dug-out canoe. On board the missionary's ship it was received with a mixture of astonishment and ridicule. The captain/friar replied in straight-forward and expected fashion. He advised Aguirre to abandon his road of errors, to return to loyalty, to stop shedding blood and, as a Christian, to have reverence for churches and the honour of women. Even while the Indians had been paddling seaward with his letter, and then landward with its reply, Aguirre had continued with his blood-letting. Two soldiers had been seen on the beach, an obvious prelude to desertion. They were hung at the *rollo*, the column (of hardwood at Margarita) symbolizing governmental authority, always useful as gal-lows or garrotting post. Having then received the blunt reply to his aggressive, fawning letter, Aguirre could only watch the ship up-anchor and sail away. Brother Francisco had decided to refrain from battle. Instead he would visit the South American mainland, inform higher authority of the Margarita situation and obtain assistance. Considering that almost everyone on the island would have rallied to his aid, and that many of Aguirre's men would have done so given opportunity, his retreat probably prolonged Aguirre's rule longer than had he taken immediate action. However, he did sail away, and Aguirre had to watch the chance of acquiring this prime vessel slip from his grasp.

By this time both Amazon brigantines had been sunk, for fear that men might abscond in them. The only ship now available that was fit for the major voyage west was still being built in the dockyard. Aguirre therefore sought out carpenters who could complete the work. They fully appreciated the danger of employment by Aguirre, but realized he would leave their island only if the ship was finished. While they warily set about this task Aguirre gave his soldiers permission to do as they pleased. They could kill, loot, fight, destroy, feast, drink and be merry, but they had to respect the churches and female honour. All were 'joyous' at the news, hurrying to exercise this sudden liberty.

Aguirre, apart from urging haste at the dockyard, continued with killing. A certain Villena was suspected of treachery, but escaped before the inevitable retribution came his way. Villena's friends were therefore suspect, and two were quickly murdered. Their landlady was then killed by being hung on the *rollo*. Her husband, although old, crippled and away on his farm, was also sought and killed. A friar remonstrated, so he too was executed. Aguirre remembered that he had confessed to another friar of the same order ('more out of form than for the health of his soul', says Simon), and so ordered death for him as well. This killing was performed 'without loss of time'. The man's jaw was first broken by strangulation, and the same rope was then lowered to his neck. An old man in Aguirre's party, no doubt exhausted by the journey thus far, begged to be excused from further travel. Aguirre granted his request, telling soldiers to 'go and see that he is safe'. They comprehended the command and quickly added the old man's body to those dangling from the *rollo*. A woman was the final victim of this particular series. She had billeted a soldier who had absconded, and her crime was not knowing where he had gone. (Or not telling; it did not matter which.)

Aguirre departed from Margarita on the last Sunday of August 1561. His sailing might have been one day earlier had not a flotilla of dug-outs arrived from the mainland. In charge of them was Francisco Taxardo who was normally occupied with conquering and colonizing some of modern Venezuela. He had heard about Aguirre and had arrived to see what could be done. Unfortunately for the success of his mission, he reached the island when the rebels were at their most organized, being all together, fully armed, and more united than on earlier days. Taxardo hailed Aguirre from the security of a little forest, and Aguirre shouted back from within the fortress. Neither felt capable of defeating the other, and Aguirre saw little point in a delaying engagement. Therefore he and his men climbed down a single ladder on the far side of the fortress, out of sight of Taxardo, and took ship. About 150 embarked in the three vessels (two small, but one the brand-new ship from the dockyard) that now made up his fleet.

The man who had been named admiral lost his arm during the embarkation, an improbable event in normal circumstances. Apparently Aguirre was getting his feet wet while attempting to board. The admiral, Alonso Rodrígues, tactlessly offered assistance. Aguirre was offended and, drawing his sword, cut off the arm put out to help him. For a moment he was contrite at this unnecessary wounding, but the impulse did not last. The admiral, already armless, was soon lifeless, having not only offered aid but then having the temerity, despite his wound, to object to the loading of three horses and one mule. A single error was sufficient to bring death; two were more than adequate.

Aguirre had spent forty days upon the island of Margarita. He had lost about fifty men, some through desertion, and had not gained as many as he had hoped. He had certainly improved his fighting power with stolen crossbows, swords, lances. He had the three disputed horses that would help him to capture others, and had taken ample trappings. Instead of voyaging to Nombre de Dios and then crossing to Panama, as had been his original plan, he decided to head for Burburuta, just two days' sailing south-west from Margarita. In fact, owing to calms, they did not arrive until 7 September, and Aguirre's pilots – captured on the island – were therefore lucky to survive.

His first act upon the mainland was to set fire to a merchantman that had been scuttled with its provisions before his arrival, but was still partly above water. His second was to burn his own boats, the dockyard vessel and the two lesser craft (which had been forced, as before, to keep in sight of the flagship). The small town and port of Burburuta had been abandoned at his approach, save for one old Aguirre soldier, Francisco Martín. He had been with the brigantine sent to capture Brother Francisco's vessel and had, so he said, been forcibly detained. He had gained his freedom at the first opportunity and was happy to greet his old chief again. Aguirre, more familiar with disloyalty and defection, was overjoyed at such compliance. The two rebels embraced each other enthusiastically.

Francisco Martín appears to have been the only man on that northern shoreline of South America in favour of the newcomers. All the governors, generals and ordinary citizens of the towns and villages ranged along the coast were, like so many disturbed wasps, in a flurry of urgency. How strong was Aguirre's force? How strong a force was needed to conquer him? How many men could each town raise, and where and when should they gather? In the meantime, Aguirre and his men were busy accumulating horses and other necessities. After considerable effort they had captured thirty plus an assortment of unbroken mares. Suddenly Aguirre was back to his old profession of horse-breaking, and no doubt felt pleasure at exercising his ancient skill. (One also suspects, knowing the short rein on which his own temper was held, that horses yielded speedily. A soldier from Margarita learned – too late – of this fickle temperament by carelessly asking, on stepping ashore at Burburuta, if they had reached mainland or another island. His death was near immediate.)

The new plan, now that Panama and the Pacific had been abandoned, was to march via New Granada (essentially Venezuela) to the kingdom of Peru. This was a considerable undertaking, quite apart from the conquest at its end. From his disembarkation point in South America to Quito (then in Peru), the straight-line distance was 1,250 miles. The intervening country was only half-explored, mountainous or forested (or both), and largely populated by (largely) hostile Indians. To some observers Aguirre must appear solely as a psychopathic horse-breaker who should have been incarcerated at least a quarter of a century earlier. However, he did possess a lunatic vision and much awesome courage. In other circumstances this fearful combination might have made him hero. As it was he became undoubted villain, and he added to his villainy almost each and every day.

The immediate plan, which would bring Aguirre no nearer to Peru, was to march upon Valencia. This small town, a short distance from the disembarkation point of Burburuta, had refused horses to the rebels. It therefore deserved to be punished. More desertions and more killings preceded Aguirre's departure – one man being killed because he was sick – but the rabble rebel army eventually sought out the awkward, slippery, mountainous path that led towards Valencia. The horses had such difficulties with their loads that soldiers were forced to carry some baggage. Even the captains had to take a share, Aguirre showing powerful example by burdening himself with more than his due. The journey took eight days and, by the end of it, Aguirre was himself a sick man. 'Kill me, *marañones*! Kill me!' he cried. They might easily have done so, but did not, and the rebellion continued on its way.

The inhabitants of Valencia had long since fled by the time Aguirre arrived, transported in a hammock. They had vanished to an island, as good and inaccessible a hiding place as any. This did not stop the destruction of their town, which proceeded apace while Aguirre first worsened and then steadily improved. Those who had broken rules while their leader lay ill, for instance by leaving town without his permission, were forced to pay the penalty on his recovery. The paymaster died this way (and no longer had the problem of no pay for anyone, the only payment – as Simon points out – being what each man purloined for himself). At Valencia, having fully returned to his former spirit, Aguirre wrote a considerable letter to King Philip of Spain. It helps to explain the crippled traitor and will, therefore, be quoted as an obituary, more honest than most, more revealing than most, when his life is at its end.

About 140 men, together with ninety horses, left Valencia after a stay of fifteen days. Once again they were on a mountainous track. Desertions became more regular, with ten men vanishing, each independently, during the first three days of travel. Heavy rain began to fall. The horses slipped, collapsed, and even rolled backwards on occasion ('to the great inconvenience of the soldiers,' states – or rather understates – Padre Simon). Aguirre, now with all his old vigour renewed, not only utters 'a thousand blasphemies' but shouts: 'Does God think that because it rains in torrents I am not to go to Pirú, and destroy the world? He is mistaken in me.'

The delays at Burburuta and Valencia, and those enforced by travel in this difficult area, had given the royalist forces opportunity to prepare themselves for an encounter. Considerable support had been given to Aguirre's enemies by the desertion of Pedro Alonzo Galeas. This man had been encouraged to leave by Aguirre's request for a drum. On hearing from Galeas that no such instrument was available, there being no parchment, Aguirre had replied that Galeas's own skin would serve very well. The suggestion was not immediately followed by the act, and Galeas did not wait to provide a second opportunity. In the royalist camp they initially suspected him of spying, but he managed to convince these former enemies of his sudden loyalty to them. Galeas was also able to detail Aguirre's strength in men and materials, even asserting that only fifty men accompanied their leader out of choice; the remainder would flee at the earliest opportunity. Galeas now recommended how best to defeat the tyrant. A pitched battle was not the way; it would be better to retreat and retreat. Aguirre would then be exhausted without a fight.

In fact both sides retreated at the first meeting. Neither was aware of the other's approach, as both slithered in the rain along the same mountain pathway. Suddenly they were confronting each other in a

A portrait by Titian of Philip II of Spain, to whom Lope de Aguirre wrote forthright, bombastic and extremely honest letters.

particularly narrow section. The royalist forces, less seasoned and less well armed, seem to have been the speedier to retire. Some helmets and lances were even knocked from them as the men whirled around, and these they abandoned on the path. Aguirre made great play of the forsaken objects, and of the kind of men to lose them. His own force laughed and rested, resuming their march by moonlight at three in the morning.

The governor of the area, extremely keen to conquer without a fight, decided to announce a full (and remarkable) pardon for any of Aguirre's men who left him to join the king's side. A similar amnesty would even be granted to Aguirre himself, should he forsake his rebellion. All would be forgiven in the name of the king of Spain. However, if such an offer did not appeal, the governor was prepared to meet Aguirre in single combat. The two of them could settle the issue without unnecessary loss of life.

Copies of these pardons and offers were placed around the town of Barquisimeto. Aguirre was about to invade this place but, as a preliminary, also did some writing. By letter he informed the town's inhabitants that they would come to no harm. He only wanted horses and some provisions, all of which would be bought with money. If they refused this simple request he would burn their town, destroy its plantations and tear to pieces any inhabitants he encountered. The threat was hardly to be welcomed, but the people did not set much store by the initial promise. The peaceful purchase of required items did not accord with the stories they had heard of Aguirre's methods. He waited for their reply and rested his men. No reply forthcoming, Aguirre's army prepared to march into the town on Wednesday 22 October 1561. As it marched, so did a royalist force. This was entering Barquisimeto from the other side.

Once again there was retreat. The king's men knew they were less well armed and soon retired to a nearby hill. Aguirre took possession of the deserted town and installed himself in its most prominent and defensible part. The rest of the place he burned, including – inadvertently – the church. Hastily he ordered that its altar-pieces should be saved. In the meantime his men had found the pardons, including the letter specifically addressed to Aguirre. He was quick to denounce the opposition:

Put no trust in governors, nor in their papers or signatures . . . Though the king in person wished to pardon you, I do not believe he would be allowed to do so . . . the relations and friends of those you have slain would hunt you to the death and kill you . . . as I have often said, nowhere are you so safe as in my company . . . if we have some difficulties before we get to Pirú, there we shall find abundance and happiness . . .

Perhaps it was right not to put too much trust in princes, but his listeners must also have known how much or how little to put in rebel leaders.

The governor, having issued his pardons, having challenged Aguirre to single combat, and having attempted to avoid a more general fight, now abdicated from any further leadership. Claiming ill-health (which had sent him to the New World in the first place), he donated command to a Captain Pedro Bravo. The first task of Bravo, not easy, was to persuade his governor to remain with his troops, to which he eventually acquiesced. It was while he, Bravo and the rest were waiting for further reinforcements that they received another letter from Aguirre's busy pen.

Most magnificent Señor, Amongst other papers from you, found in this town, was a letter of yours directed to me, with more promises and preambles than there are stars in heaven . . . it was unnecessary for you to have taken so much trouble, for I well know to what point your power extends . . . Most superfluous are your offers . . . I have nothing to do with affairs in this part of the country; I wish to pay well with my own money, for the cost of some horses and other things . . . I and my companions are only doing what our predecessors did, which is not against the king . . . And in conclusion I say, that according to the sort of behaviour you and yours adopt in our vicinity, so will we treat you . . . Our Lord preserve the most magnificent person of your worship, etc. Your servant, LOPE DE AGUIRRE.

The letter was a statement; it did not expect an answer; but it made the governor wring his hands, wishing again for single combat. (It is easy to suspect that the experienced man of military action would have trounced the peace-loving sick administrator, but the duel never occurred.) He and Bravo met their reinforcements, and word of this union soon reached Aguirre. The rebel chief was unmoved, but not so many of his men. They wished to defect even more urgently than before, spurred on by the pardons and the situation's hopelessness. Captain Bravo strengthened their doubts by approaching close to Aguirre's force and telling them they should forget their dream of victory. Even the traitor, writes Simon, 'was beginning to have some fears of his ultimate success'. These do seem justified.

Considering the violence of previous months, the *dénouement* continued to be most pacific, with more posturing than bloodshed. Lope de Aguirre looked well on a jet-black horse, his silken flag – two blood-red swords on a black background – fluttering beside him. He and some picked men took up a good position, ravines in front and thick growth behind, but were foolishly tempted from it by a royalist retreat. The royalists then occupied the place, while skirmishes back and forth made sound and fury but no casualties. The first to fall was Aguirre's splendid horse, but still no man had died on either side. A prominent rebel, Diego Tirado, then deserted. He was warmly acclaimed by the governor's forces, given the governor's horse, and encouraged to show his former friends that no harm had come to him. Aguirre was incensed: '*Marañones*, is it possible that a few herdsmen, with sheepskin jackets and hide bucklers, thus show themselves amongst us, and you do not bring them to the earth?' It was extremely possible, as all saw all too clearly.

With disarming simplicity Padre Simon now tells us that Aguirre 'began to reflect' upon his projected conquest of Peru. The idea 'flitted before him' that he was not to be victorious. He was therefore now considering it best to return to the coast, find vessels, and sail with his men to some place where he could abandon his way of life. However, his men were abandoning him too speedily for this most reasonable assessment to be put into practice. Even his confidential guards, posted to keep others from defecting, were leaving for the other side.

Nevertheless he did commence his retreat. The date was 27 October 1561. He disarmed many of his men to prevent them from absconding, but the distrust back-fired. How were they to defend themselves against the king's men if they had no weapons? Aguirre relented, and actually apologized. It was the only error, he said, that he had made during the entire expedition. Would they please take their weapons back? Some of his men refused to do so for a time. They had been mortified by his act, and only with considerable persuasion from their

leader did they agree to carry arms again. As they marched, with the
idea surely flitting through all their minds that victory was beyond their
grasp, they were verbally harried by Bravo and his men. Why not
desert? Where was Aguirre leading them? What was the point of
carrying on? The war had become one of persuasion and words, with
arquebuses mere background noise to all the argument.

The *marañones* found it easiest to defect by charging at the enemy
and then shouting, 'Long live the king!' They were not killed during
their mock charges, partly because the royalist army only possessed five
arquebuses all told. One suspects Aguirre's force could easily have won
the day had it had stomach for the fight. As it was, his men wished to
take advantage of that most generous pardon and change sides. The
more men who did go over, the greater the urge for others to follow.
Eventually only one of the soldiers remained with Aguirre. He was
Antón Llamoso, the man whose life had been spared when he had
sucked blood to assert his loyalty. Aguirre asked why he had not taken
advantage of the governor's amnesty. 'We have been friends for life,'
said the ever faithful Llamoso, 'and we will die as friends.'

However, Aguirre left him to attend to a more serious matter. His
mestizo daughter, Elvira, was still in his company, together with a
younger girl named Torralva. Elvira's thoughts about the expedition,
her father, the killings, the rebellion, are nowhere expressed. Nothing
is even recorded from her lips when it became her time to die. Aguirre
picked up an arquebus and said: 'Commend thyself to God, my
daughter, for I am about to kill thee; that thou mayest not be pointed at
with scorn, nor be in the power of any one who may call thee the
daughter of a traitor.' Torralva rushed upon him, managing to grab the
gun. It was of no consequence. Aguirre took his poniard and killed his
child with that.

By this time he was surrounded. He rushed to the doorway, loaded
arquebus in hand, but could not make it fire. In 'the most dejected
manner' he then threw all his weapons to the ground and retreated
indoors. He was still prepared to bandy words and objected to the lowly
status of the man about to kill him. He then addressed a *caballero*,
saying he had important things to tell. The attackers hesitated,
wondering if they should wait for the governor. Others thought it best
to sever the man's head without delay. In the end two of his own

marañones did the deed, shooting with their arquebuses. Then his head was severed to be taken outside as a form of welcome for the approaching governor.

Elvira's body was buried in the nearby church. Aguirre's remains were quartered and thrown into the road. The victors wanted spoils as evidence of their work, in particular the black flags with crossed swords. The governor did not agree and offered Aguirre's hands. Valencia and Mérida, the two towns principally involved with the traitor's overthrow, would have a hand each. These were to be fixed to the *rollo*, the left hand for Valencia and the right for Mérida. Aguirre's head was to be taken to the more important community of Tocuyo. There it would be displayed in an iron cage, a warning to all wrongdoers. And there it was displayed, long after it had become a skull. The hands received much shorter shrift. The men of Valencia threw their trophy to some dogs before reaching home. Those from Mérida acted similarly, tossing theirs into a river; its smell had begun to offend them.

Thus ended the second Amazon journey. It had been transformed along the way into an attempted conquest of Peru, but it was undoubtedly the second journey from the Andes to the Atlantic, whichever route it took. The geographical aspect of this voyage became submerged beneath all the killing and rebellion; the cruise had been, to repeat Clements Markham's words, the 'wildest, most romantic, most desperate, most appalling in the annals of Spanish enterprise'. Its original and forgotten purpose had been to search for the lands of El Dorado and the wealth of the Omaguas. Its second intent, once the initial leadership had been deposed, had been to sail to Panama *en route* for Peru. That journey had been two-thirds accomplished, namely the river section and the Atlantic voyage up to Margarita. The feat is difficult to observe amidst the carnage, but it was achieved nonetheless. Orellana's exploit of Andes to Atlantic had thus been repeated a couple of decades afterwards, and Aguirre was its undoubted leader for almost all the way.

Nevertheless it is the personality of this twisted individual that sticks in the memory, rather than his considerable journey. The letter he wrote to his king when resting briefly in Valencia will serve better as epitaph than the indictments written by others at the time. In it he reveals himself, his contradictions, his disloyal servitude, his aggressive humility. If he had had more fortune in his life he might have been a better man:

King Philip, a Spaniard, son of Charles the Invincible! I, Lope de Aguirre, thy vassal, am an old Christian, of poor but noble parents, and native in the town of Oñate, in Biscay. In my youth I crossed the ocean to the land of Peru, lance in hand, to perform what is due from an honest man, and, during 54 years, I have done thee great service in Peru, in the conquest of the Indians, in forming settlements, and especially in battles and encounters which I have fought in thy name, always to the best of my power and ability, without asking thy officers for payment, as will appear by the royal books.

I firmly believe that thou, O Christian king and lord, hast been very cruel and ungrateful to me and my companions for such good service, and that all those who write to thee from this land deceive thee much, because thou seest things from too far off. I, and my companions, no longer able to suffer the cruelties which thy judges and governors exercise in thy name, are resolved to obey thee no longer. We regard ourselves no longer as Spaniards. We make a cruel war on thee, because we will not endure the oppression of thy ministers, who, to give places to their nephews and their children, dispose of our lives, our reputations, and our fortunes. I am lame in the left foot, from two shots of an arquebus, which I received in the battle of Chucuinga, fighting under the orders of the marshal Alonzo de Alvarado, against Francisco Hernandez Girón, a rebel, as I and my companions are now, and will be unto death: for we know, in this country, how cruel thou art, that thou art a breaker of thy faith and word; therefore, even if we received thy pardon, we should give less credence to it, than to the books of Martin Luther . . .

Hear me! O hear me! thou king of Spain. Be not cruel to thy vassals, for it was while thy father, the emperor Charles, remained quietly in Spain, that they procured for thee so many kingdoms and vast countries. Remember, king Philip, that thou hast no right to draw revenues from these provinces, since their conquest has been without danger to thee. I take it for certain that few kings go to hell, only because they are few in number; but that if there were many, none of them would go to heaven. For I believe that you are all worse than Lucifer, and that you hunger and thirst after human blood; and further, I think little of you, and despise you all, nor do I look upon your government as more than an air bubble. Know that I, and my 200 arquebus-bearing *marañones*, have taken a solemn oath to God, that we will not leave one of thy ministers alive. We consider ourselves, at this moment, the happiest men on earth, because, in this land of the Indians, we preserve the faith and the commandments of God in their purity, and we maintain all that is preached by the Church of Rome. We expect, though sinners in this life, to enjoy martyrdom for the laws of God.

On leaving the river of Amazons, which is called Marañón, we came to an island inhabited by Christians, called Margarita, where we received news from Spain of the great conspiracy of the Lutherans, which caused us much terror and alarm. In our company there was one of these Lutherans, named Monteverde, and I ordered him to be cut to pieces. Believe me, O most excellent king, that I will force all men to live perfectly in the faith of Christ . . .

In the year 1559, the marquis of Cañete entrusted the expedition of the river of Amazons to Pedro de Ursúa, a Navarrese, or rather a Frenchman, who delayed the building of his vessels until 1560. These vessels were built in the province of the Motilones, which is a wet country, and, as they were built in the rainy season, they came to pieces, and we therefore made canoes, and descended the river. We navigated the most powerful river in Peru and it seemed to us that we were in a sea of fresh water. We descended the river for 300 leagues. This bad governor was capricious, vain and inefficient, so that we could not suffer it, and we gave him a quick and certain death. We then raised a young gentleman of Seville, named Don Fernando de Guzmán, to be our king, and we took the same oaths to him as are taken to thy royal person, as may be seen by the signatures of all those who are with me. They named me *maestro del campo*; and, because I did not consent to their evil deeds, they desired to murder me. I therefore killed this new king, the captain of his guard, his lieutenant-general, four captains, his major-domo, his chaplain, who said mass, a woman, a knight of the Order of Rhodes, an admiral, two ensigns, and five or six of his servants. It was my intention to carry on the war, on account of the many cruelties thy ministers had committed. I named captains and sergeants; but these men also wanted to kill me, and I hung them. We continued our course while all this evil fortune was befalling us; and it was eleven months and a half before we reached the mouths of the river, having travelled for more than a hundred days, over more than fifteen hundred leagues. This river has a course of two thousand leagues of fresh water, the greater part of the shores being uninhabited; and God only knows how we ever escaped out of that fearful lake. I advise thee not to send any Spanish fleet up this ill-omened river; for, on the faith of a Christian, I swear to thee, O king and lord, that if a hundred thousand men should go up, not one would escape, and there is nothing else to expect, especially for the adventurers from Spain.

The captains and officers who are now under my command in this enterprise, and who promise to die in it, are Juan Jeronimo de Espindola, a Genoese, captain of infantry, admiral Juan Gomez, a Spaniard [a long list follows], and many other gentlemen. They pray to God that thy strength may

Lope de Aguirre

ever be increased against the Turk and the Frenchman, and all others who desire to make war against thee; and we shall give God thanks if, by our arms, we attain the rewards which are due to us, but which thou hast denied us; and, because of thine ingratitude, I am a rebel against thee until death.

LOPE DE AGUIRRE, THE WANDERER

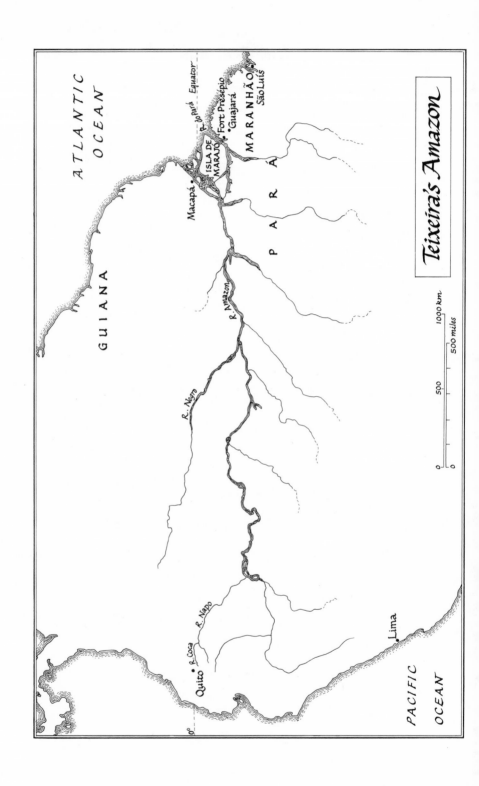

Teixeira's Amazon

IV

Pedro de Teixeira
MAKING THE AMAZON PORTUGUESE

The city of Belém lies a short distance from the mouth of the Rio do Pará. It is also near the mouth of the Amazon. Both statements are correct because the mightiest of all rivers concludes its journey by creating quite the mightiest delta, and breaking into two main streams. The division starts shortly after the Xingu has poured its water into the Amazon, and thenceforth the major stream becomes a confusion of lesser rivers as these circumnavigate the various islands fashioned in the past. When Amazon water finally reaches the Atlantic it does so over a span of some 200 miles. The flow issuing from the most southerly portion of this tremendous delta has been given the name of Rio do Pará, and ninety miles up that particular channel, on its southern bank, lies Belém, the largest city upon the Amazon.

It was founded in January 1616, and was therefore not in existence when either Orellana or Aguirre passed this way – if indeed either explorer did take the Pará route to the Atlantic. The picturesque port, a haven for ferries and fishing vessels, is much affected by tidal heavings from the Atlantic, those ninety miles away. Given the right (or wrong) conditions the harbour area, including the old fish market, can be partially submerged by the brown, warm water of the Amazon. Most of the city is in no such danger, with its mango-lined *avenidas* leading uphill, away from the river and towards the vastness of Pará state. Although Belém has now been in existence for almost four centuries, there is still a feel of the old days. The colour and urgency of the river is as it ever was. The opposite bank, many miles away, is still no more than a smudge of green. And there exists a sense of isolation, despite the airport and the new strand of road leading 1,300 miles south to

Brasilia. Consequently it is not difficult to imagine the day in 1616 when a Portuguese force first sailed into Guajará Bay. Its soldiers built a fort where they landed, naming it Presépio, 'the crib'. Later this encampment became the town of Santa Maria de Belém. Later still this title was shortened to its present form, and, confusingly, the place also came to be known as Pará.

The two preceding chapters, dealing with the exploratory voyages down the great river, were of Spanish exploits. The initial chapter, describing the accidental discovery of Brazil, was a Portuguese matter, but since that year of 1500 the Portuguese voice on the Amazon had been quiet. In theory, and according to the Treaty of Tordesillas, the entire river lay in Spanish territory, with only South America's eastern-most portion allocated to the Portuguese. Also in theory, this delinea-tion should not have been important, because for the last two decades of the sixteenth century and the first four of the seventeenth, the Spanish king was also the king of Portugal. Nevertheless the Spanish and Portuguese did think of themselves as different peoples, with (moderately) different languages, separate histories, and two distinct slices of the New World that were their due.

Quite the most extraordinary consequence of the gentle rivalry between these two powers lay in the smaller, weaker, poorer nation eventually acquiring almost all of the Amazon basin. There were reasons, such as the Spanish obsession with its rich Indian empires, but it is a remarkable fact that Portugal finally managed to possess half of the South American continent. Crucial to this success were the events on 12 January 1616, when Fort Presépio was founded. The men at work on its construction could not have imagined the importance of their labour. To them it must have seemed one more unrewarding task in that unending wilderness of brown rivers and green trees. The insects were demanding. The Equator was not far distant and the heat was intense (Belém's average temperature being 78°F). Perhaps there was a smirk or two of disbelief as they named the general region Feliz Lusitânia.

What had caused the Portuguese to land a force of 150 men, to build the fort, and to make their national presence felt, was not a suspicion that Spain was gaining the upper hand – though it might have been, as Orellana's and Aguirre's exploits were now embedded in history.

Pedro de Teixeira

Instead it was a threat far more unwelcome even than any Spanish influence, namely the existence of English, Irish, Dutch and French forts and trading posts within the area. These other nations were trespassers upon an Iberian entitlement. They had not discovered the New World, nor were they entitled to a piece. Besides, they were ancient enemies. Queen Elizabeth's victory over the Armada had occurred only twenty-eight years earlier. Spain and France, as Aguirre had underlined in his letter, were unhappy neighbours. Ireland and the Netherlands were more distant, but also had no rights around the Amazon. Spain and Portugal did not see eye to eye on every issue, and regarded each other's aspirations jealously, but they were united against a common enemy. Their fury was particularly intense against a host of common enemies making settlements here and there, affronting the Castilian crown, doing as they pleased. It was time for action, for joint Iberian action.

As Spain was the more powerful nation, with riches pouring in from the new kingdoms, it was mainly up to Spain to evict all intruders. This task proved formidable, the new lands being so vast, so difficult to control. The oceans were the scene of an even greater free-for-all, with the distinction between piracy and national endeavour either slender or quite invisible. For the Spanish it was like swatting mosquitoes, with others all ready to pounce should any guard be taken down. Northern Europeans were gaining in the West Indies, and strongly along Guiana. The French had settled near Rio de Janeiro in 1555 and had had to be expelled. They had then moved north, from 'Antarctic France' to 'Equinoctial France', and their important post at São Luís (on the coast to the south of Belém) was not razed until 1615. Flushed with the success of this action, the Portuguese attackers then turned their attention towards the Amazon. Hence Fort Presépio, and that small enclave upon one piece of the enormous river.

São Luís and Rio de Janeiro were, in the main, settled by Portuguese, but it was generally considered that all the Amazon lay within Spain's domain. Its mouth was well to the west of both these Portuguese cities, and the bulk of the river was even further into Spanish territory by any interpretation of Tordesillas. The river's principal merit for Spain lay in the access it could provide to and from the Andes and their precious kingdoms in the west. It was therefore a Spanish waterway, by right of papal edict, by right of discovery and, rather more obliquely, by right of purpose.

However, if the New World is viewed through the eyes of some Spanish controller, desperate to keep track of areas his fellow countrymen either had invaded or would soon invade, his task does appear monumental. South America, then either firmly settled (as in Peru) or being nibbled from top to toe, covers six million square miles. Central America may be smaller but is more complex with all its islands. North America is bigger even than the southern continent, and Spaniards were pushing northwards everywhere, up the east and west coasts and also north from Mexico. Spain itself, covering less than 200,000 square miles, was dwarfed by these new dominions. Small wonder, therefore, that assistance would be welcomed in this gigantic act of acquisition. Hence, in Madrid on 4 November 1621, the decision was made to withdraw some of the restrictions formerly placed on Portugal. In future Portuguese forces would be permitted to safeguard at least the lower Amazon on behalf of the king of Spain and Portugal. Spain did not like yielding anything, anywhere; but, if enemies were encroaching, who better to ask for help than Portugal?

There were supporting reasons for this Spanish decision. The lower Amazon was nearest to the Portuguese settlement. The fort of Presépio had now been founded and there were reports that the Portuguese intended sending an exploratory party further up-river. It was best to give approval to such a move before it occurred. Portuguese influence along the initial reaches of the Amazon would help to repel further probings from the strong foreign presence along Guiana, notably the French and Dutch. Spain was a child with too many toys to hold. It was wiser to enlist the aid of a friend than lose any more. The friend might even be able to retrieve some of those already stolen.

This relaxation by Spain, a short-term expedient – or so it was assumed – to rid the Amazon region of foreign transgressors, was to have far-reaching consequences. In a most casual manner the Portuguese were to exert increasingly strong influence upon the river, mainly for the elementary reason that no Spanish were in the area. Of considerable relevance was the continent's geography. The Andes do form a barrier. Anyone by the Pacific coast of South America thinks twice before travelling eastwards over that tremendous mountain range. Conversely, anyone on the Amazon thinks little of moving further upstream, either on the main course or by some tributary. Therefore the west coast settlements would not readily expand eastwards, while those along the Amazon would move steadily westwards. In a relaxed and unconquering fashion the Portuguese would find themselves consuming almost all the Amazon basin while the Spaniards were busily taking possession of everywhere else. It just so happens, which no one could have known at the time, that the single Amazon river drains more than half of the South American continent, and therefore whoever controlled the river would control a major portion of South America.

Fort Presépio, so small a settlement on one bank of the Pará, was the first important step in this huge advance. Six years after its founding (and only one after that decision in Madrid), Luís Aranha de Vasconcelos sailed over a thousand miles up-river. This Portuguese adventurer was first to map the lower Amazon. He discovered that the descending river separated into two major branches when about 300 miles from the sea. Vasconcelos also attempted to appease the Indians by giving them presents. With their aid it would be easier to defeat any foreign incursions. Indeed, even on this exploratory, Indian-befriending, map-making mission, two Dutch forts were destroyed as well as one English ship. On board this vessel had been six *hidalgos*, as well as a far greater number of ordinary seamen.

Madrid had reason to be alarmed about the north European activities on the river. The first English expedition specifically directed towards the Amazon had sailed in 1610, half a dozen years before Presépio's founding. It explored many tributaries, went 300 miles upstream, deposited twenty individuals to make a settlement, and returned full of praise for the area's potential. In 1620 another ship left England, even more intent upon Amazonian settlement. (As this was the very year of the Pilgrim Fathers it is easy to wonder whether both sailings were considered equally exciting.) Roger North, who commanded the South American expedition, had been one of Sir Walter Raleigh's captains in the previous century. He therefore knew a little about the continent and its difficulties, but also of its prospects. The settlement he initiated was built about 300 miles up-river, with local Indians helping the foreigners to clear the forest for plantations of tobacco.

In this party was an Irishman, Bernard O'Brien. He learned the Indian language and helped to fight their battles for them. The presence of musketry must always have been decisive against stone-age enemies. O'Brien went up-river for hundreds of miles until a particularly fierce tribe stopped further progress. Upon his return he found that some Dutch were preparing to build their own fort near North's settlement. O'Brien was able to recruit 4,000 Indians and forced the Dutch to move elsewhere. That eviction did not stop him getting a passage on a Dutch ship when, in 1624, he finally returned to Europe. The promised reinforcements had not arrived, but the fort was left occupied as a going concern.

With all this English/Irish/Dutch exploration, trading, farming and consorting with the Indians along the Amazon it is understandable that the Spanish were resentful. Whose river was it? Why were these northerners upon Spanish territory? Of course the Portuguese must be encouraged to exert authority, and no individual rallied to this task more enthusiastically than Captain Pedro Teixeira. Even before the mandate from Madrid he had been active, helping to evict the French from São Luís and to establish Presépio. He had voyaged with Vasconcelos on that mapping, exploring and attacking foray which had finished the prospects of two Dutch forts and one English ship. A couple of years later, along with Pedro da Costa Favela and Jerônimo de Albuquerque, he was again destroying foreign posts, including Dutch and English settlements on the Xingu (a tributary leading into the Amazon from the south) and others near modern Macapá, on the most northerly bank of the Amazon delta. The mosquito-swatting was proving troublesome but effective. The forts were being given a difficult time and the news must have been spreading in northern Europe that easier pickings for settlement or trading might be found elsewhere. In 1629, after yet another voyage to establish Portuguese influence in the area, Teixeira and his fellow countrymen returned to Presépio, now expanding in size and power. There were one or two further engagements, notably against another English expedition, but in the early 1630s the Portuguese could claim to have cleared the Amazon of rival foreign influence.

The fragile alliance between Spain and Portugal no longer had the threat of a common enemy to bind it together. For a few more years

Following their period of exploration the Portuguese became considerable traders in their new-found lands.

there would be a single king for both countries; but, despite this union, there was never unity. Portugal and Spain did not resemble Castile and Aragon, two entities waiting to be fused as part of a single nation. Instead they were two nations, closer than most but always distinct. No man ever claimed to be Iberian. He was either a Spaniard or a Portuguese – like cousins perhaps, or brothers, but never twins. Consequently it must have been more than a little alarming when, one day in 1637, a group of Spanish suddenly paddled into the thriving Portuguese colony on the southern bank of the Rio do Pará.

It had been twenty-one years since Fort Presépio had been founded. Feliz Lusitânia, now part of the state of Pará, had witnessed a steadily increasing Portuguese influence. There had been action concerning more northerly European powers, but no thought or mention of Spaniards. Indeed King Felipe IV (of both nations) had made a

Portuguese the governor of Maranhão, the region lying east and south of Presépio. This lay within Spanish territory if Tordesillas was being followed to the letter, which plainly it was not. The Portuguese had not only expelled foreigners but had successfully, and officially, encroached upon a piece of Spain. With each year that passed the intruders must have felt increasingly confident as they proceeded further upstream, further inland. Like mice emboldened by the continuing absence of the cat, their growing sense of security must have affirmed that the land and rivers all about them were firmly Portuguese. Hence the shock which must surely have prevailed when two Spanish friars with six Spanish soldiers quietly paddled into the harbour at Presépio/Pará/Belém.

Orellana's voyage from Spanish Peru had reached the mouth of the Amazon in 1542. His disastrous return to the area had taken place in 1545. Aguirre's time upon the Amazon had been in 1561, when he may or may not have actually made use of the Amazon's mouth in reaching the Atlantic. In the seventy-six years since that second enterprise there had been no further Spanish expeditions upon the central or eastern portions of the great river, so far as was known to those living at its mouth. So if eight Spaniards suddenly arrived at the Portuguese settlement, what did this say about events upstream? What were the Spanish intentions? And was the river becoming Spanish at its other end? Worse still, were the Spanish now thinking of claiming the entire waterway, as was their Tordesillas right? There were only eight men in the single canoe, but they were Spaniards every one. They posed a threat even more alarming than all those foreign forts.

Inevitably the Portuguese questioned the new arrivals. They learned that the friars, both Franciscans, had been living in a mission on the Rio Napo, the river used by Orellana before he and his party had reached the Amazon. When the local Indians had objected to their presence most of the friars had returned upstream to Quito. However two, claiming divine inspiration, had decided to travel downstream. Although Orellana had already proved the feasibility of the journey, their decision demanded, in many ways, even more courage. He did not know the extent of the river, but they did. He had over fifty men with him; they took six. He built two large vessels; they used a single canoe. The accounts of his undertaking, emphasizing Indian hostility, food shortage and relentless warfare, had undoubtedly discouraged many successors; but they did not discourage the two Franciscans, Domingos Brieva and Andrés de Toledo.

The monks realized that friendliness with the Indians was the key. If the tribes could be persuaded that their visitors were peaceful, most problems would be solved. There would be no hostility, no warfare, and plenty of food. Perhaps also a single canoe would be a less frightening sight than a couple of barquentines, laden with crossbow-men and arquebusiers. And maybe sufficient time had passed since Orellana and Aguirre had passed that way, shooting, stealing, killing, for the Indians to have regained some confidence in passing travellers. At all events the small Spanish contingent with its two friars encountered no real difficulty. They were not attacked, and neither did they run short of food. Someone must also have told them on which branch of the dividing Amazon to find Belém. All eight men were in good physical condition upon their arrival.

Emotionally the Spaniards were welcomed. They plainly had good tales to tell, and any isolated settlement is always eager for news. Politically the new arrivals were an embarrassment. They were moved fairly speedily from their point of arrival to São Luís, the former French settlement down the coast. There they were detained by the governor, mainly because he did not wish news of their successful voyage to be received in Peru. One of the friars, Andrés de Toledo, was then despatched to Lisbon to inform the Portuguese authorities personally of the Spanish venture. There may have been a single king for the two nations, but Portugal was now growing restless with the union. There were demands for a Portuguese king, and an undoubted reluctance to hand any portion of the Amazon to the Spaniards. The sooner the river was firmly established as Portuguese the sooner every foreign power, including Spain, would have to accept the fact. Spaniards could not be permitted to paddle down it as if it were a portion of the open sea.

In retaliation, and without more ado, a huge expedition was prepared by the Portuguese. Its primary aim was to achieve in reverse what the Spanish had just done. However, instead of one canoe containing eight individuals, it would be far and away the largest European force ever to sail upon the Amazon. There would be forty-seven canoes, powered by some 1,200 Indians and Negroes, to transport seventy Portuguese soldiers. This small army would be well equipped, with guns, ammunition, bows, food, and also goods for barter along the way. The expedition was planned on the initiative of Jacomé Raimundo de Noronha, the São Luís governor who had detained the Spaniards. He did not ask permission from home, presumably suspecting it might not be given. In any case he was all for speed, and the huge contingent left Belém on 28 October 1637. In charge was Captain Pedro de Teixeira, veteran of the Amazon.

Teixeira had not only seen much action, against French, Dutch, English, Irish, but he had grown in military prowess entirely in tune with Portugal's growing wish for independence. He had explored many hundreds of miles of what, by Tordesillas, should have been a Spanish river. The more exploration he and his comrades achieved, the more they evicted northern Europeans, and the more they did Spain's work, the less inclined they felt to let Spain benefit from their Portuguese endeavour. At first, based on Presépio, Teixeira and his compatriots might have been content with the Amazon delta area. However, as the years progressed and their familiarity with the river grew, they were hungry for more and more of it. By 1637, when the Portuguese force set sail upstream, the soldiers on board saw every reason for the entire river to become Portuguese. They intended to ravage the Tordesillas treaty by hundreds of miles; in fact by as many hundreds as they could possibly contrive.

Jacomé Raimundo had known exactly what he was doing when he despatched Teixeira. He also knew why haste was important. Not long after the forty-seven canoes had started upon their formidable journey this governor of São Luís was arrested, ordered back to Portugal, tried for his act of transgression and found guilty. Shortly afterwards, with independence coming nearer all the while, he was acquitted by superior authority. His act may have been anti-Spain but it was undoubtedly pro-Portugal; hence his successful appeal to a court containing several in favour of Portuguese independence. The impending break between the two nations became real in 1640, less than three years after Teixeira's up-river departure. The Duke of Bragança was then proclaimed King João IV of Portugal. Thereafter the two countries could behave as two countries, closer than most but rivals nonetheless. Nowhere would their rivalry become more manifest than in the partitioning of South America, and no act was more important in unsettling the agreed percentage than Jacomé Raimundo's despatch of the Amazon armada.

It had been almost a century since Orellana had been the first European to navigate the Amazon river. His journey had ended ninety-five years before Pedro de Teixeira started on his attempt to reverse that achievement, to proceed upstream against the current and finish, if this were possible, where Orellana had begun. Every other major expedition upon the river had been Spanish and downstream. Teixeira's foray was not only the first to attempt the far harder task but was, as a significant shift in power, entirely Portuguese. Or almost entirely – there was one Spaniard, Domingos Brieva. Whether as hostage or pilot, it was thought advisable to transport the remaining Franciscan back whence he had come. Like a rejected article he would be returned to Spanish Peru, safe and sound but definitely returned.

Teixeira's journey upstream was an astonishing endeavour. The Amazon's flow shifts its strength according to each season but can reach six knots. For Teixeira, whether the current was slow or fast, there was nothing to overcome it save muscle-power, mainly from the Indians who were most familiar with this form of travel. Also, whereas the single Spanish canoe, floating casually downstream, had only eight mouths to feed, the forty-seven canoes held 1,200 demanding appetites. Food was therefore a tremendous problem. The feeding of 1,200, or – worse still – the provisioning of 1,200 for several days, was beyond the capabilities of Indian villages, however friendly. The huge force had, in the main, to fend for itself – to catch fish, shoot game, collect fruit, and gather what it could. Navigation upstream, apart from being harder work, also presents greater problems than coming down-river. Which is the correct fork? Is this the main stream or some equally large but irrelevant tributary? Perhaps the Spanish friar was of some assistance, but he had not known he would be making the return journey. Much of the river can look irritatingly similar, even if earlier notes of its appearance have been written down. Teixeira and the bulk of his canoes had to wait, again and again, while exploratory parties checked the way ahead. It must have been an exasperating, as well as exhausting, way to travel.

The greatest problem lay in persuading the paddling Indians to continue with their labour. Not only was it tiring work, day after day, but they were growing homesick. Each day's struggle took them even further from their families. Like parents who fail to impart the entire truth to restless offspring already tired from travel, so did Teixeira assert that the journey was almost finished when it was in fact half done. At the end of each day the Indians would congratulate themselves that their travail had finally ended, but on each new morning they were told of one more effort to reach their goal. Every particle of Teixeira's tact, diplomacy, cunning and persuasive power must have been needed to maintain progress remorselessly up-river, for month after month.

After eight months of paddling, and cajoling, and entreating, and bullying, Teixeira's small fleet reached its first Spanish settlement. Instead of proceeding from there with his entire force he sent ahead a small party of eight canoe-loads. The remainder were to wait until the return journey could begin. When this larger contingent had been comfortably settled Teixeira departed to follow and catch up the advance guard. The current grew swifter and swifter, and eventually the river (Quijos) had to be abandoned completely and the rest of the journey completed on foot. After almost a year of travel Teixeira reached Quito, the starting place of many an expedition to the east, including those of Orellana and Aguirre. For the first time in that city's existence it was now the reception point for an expedition *from* the east. The year was 1638.

The fact that the first up-river journey had been completed by a Portuguese was as disconcerting to the Spaniards, if not more so, as that arrival at Belém of a Spanish canoe had been to the Portuguese. In Lima the Spanish viceroy pondered what best to do about the Portuguese and their accomplishment. He wrote to the king of Spain, Felipe IV (still also the king of Portugal), informing him of this amazing infringement of Spanish territory and asking how best to take advantage of it. Some advisers argued that the Amazon might provide a better, and safer, passage for the silver and gold being transported to Spain. Not every galleon survived either the free-for-all piracy of the Spanish Main or the terrible storms that could be an even greater threat. In the end the governor decided against altering the well-known shipping route to Spain and advocated precisely the same policy as the

Pedro de Teixeira

Portuguese had adopted in Belém and São Luís. He would encourage Teixeira to leave, but send Spaniards with him to take note of the river, map its convolutions, spy out the land and observe Portuguese involvement in the area. Teixeira had noted how far the Spanish had progressed eastwards along the river. The Spanish would now carry out the same exercise in relation to the Portuguese, and rather more determinedly than the two friars could do, with their half-dozen soldiers in a solitary canoe.

In the meantime Pedro de Teixeira and his party were being given a tremendous welcome. As with the Spanish arrival at Belém there was a longing to offer hospitality, however awkward the situation politically. There were speeches, banquets, ceremonies, fireworks, bull-fights. Teixeira's Indians were allowed to fight some of the bulls with arrows, much to the appreciation of the crowd. The Portuguese party was not being forcibly detained. Rather it was not allowed to leave, at least not for many weeks.

There was no shortage of volunteers among the Spanish for the proposed journey downstream. It was over a century since Pizarro's conquest of Peru and there was still plenty of enthusiasm for adventurous exploits. Besides, now that the river had been vanquished in both directions, the journey held all the promise of excitement without the risk of perishing *en route*. Quite the most spirited candidate was the governor of Quito, Don Juan Vasques de Acuña, a knight and servant of the king for thirty years. He offered soldiers for the journey, to be paid from his own pocket. The viceroy in Lima had other ideas, being unwilling to lose such a valued *corregidor*. Compromise was effected when permission was given to the governor's brother, a Jesuit priest named Cristóbal de Acuña. His sailing orders were not outstandingly priestly, being 'to take particular care to describe, with clearness, the distance in leagues, the provinces, tribes of Indians, rivers and districts which exist from the first embarkation, to the said city of Pará (Belém); informing yourself with all possible precision, of all things, that you may report upon them, as an eye-witness, to the Royal Council of the Indies'.

Whether this was spying or merely taking sensible note of the passing scene is not the issue. Whichever it was, the Spanish would at long last be able to acquire a decent description of the river Amazon, their river Amazon, the greatest river anyone had ever discovered. Orellana had been too involved with survival to take precise or detailed note of the environment. His recording friar had reflected this pre-occupation with food, hostile Indians and general hazard. Aguirre was even less interested in the land he encountered; it was not Peru and therefore worthless by comparison. As for the two Franciscan friars, they had simply been escaping from an unfriendly tribe. The divine impulse did not demand they should make notes upon their journey. No wonder the Spanish authorities instructed Friar Cristóbal to look well about him, to record, to list, to examine and to measure. Not only would Spain acquire a proper description of the river, but it would cost nothing. Teixeira already possessed the boats, the weapons and the manpower to make the journey possible. The Spanish under Acuña could just relax, enjoy the ride and observe everything.

This Portuguese/Spanish venture departed from Quito on 16 February 1639, one year and sixteen weeks after its Portuguese element had left Belém. The Amazon river was suddenly being subjected to a see-saw of different expeditions, down by the Spanish, up by the Portuguese, and now down again by the Portuguese, all in the space of three years. Quito had witnessed the departure of the first-ever Amazon expedition ninety-nine years earlier when the Pizarro/Orellana cohort had marched proudly through its gates. Friar Gaspar de Carvajal had been of its number and had chronicled the outcome. Now another priest would fulfil a similar role, while following in the footsteps of his distinguished predecessor; but one would think, judging by their two accounts, that they had proceeded down entirely different rivers.

Carvajal had undoubtedly had a difficult time. He may have exaggerated the problems and dangers but he made it abundantly clear that an Amazon voyage was no casual cruise. Cristóbal de Acuña either did see the river differently or was determined that others should view it in a wholly favourable light. After pointing out (on what authority?) that the river supports more people than the Ganges, Tigris or Nile, he asserted that 'it only wants, in order to surpass them, that its source should be in paradise'. Instead of worrying about the Omaguas, the powerful Amazonian tribe perfectly able to halt any invader, Acuña calls them 'the most intelligent, the best governed on the river', and mentions that they are 'decently clothed'. He disapproves of their custom of deforming the growing skull, but still attempts not to be derogatory: it 'causes ugliness in the men, but the women conceal it better with their abundant tresses'. The eye of this particular beholder was for observing the best in everything, and he worded his descriptions accordingly.

Certainly he manages what, in modern terms, would be called a public relations exercise. On climate, he observes that 'the heat does not molest and the cold does not fatigue, neither is there a continual change of weather to annoy'. (His comments do not make complete sense – unfatiguing cold and unmolesting heat? – but the flavour of them is wholly approving.) He is enchanted by the Indians' form of life – the ease with which they find game and fish to eat, the simplicity of their agriculture, their collection of salt from burned palm leaves, their gathering of many forms of fruit, their husbanding of turtles. Orellana and Aguirre had merely raided these stores, but Acuña is delighted by the whole turtle business – how they are captured when laying eggs, have holes drilled in their carapaces so they can be towed back home, are then penned in wooden palisades, fattened on a diet of foliage, killed as needed. 'These barbarians never know what hunger is,' he exclaims. As for turtle eggs, they are 'almost' as good as hens' eggs, though 'harder of digestion'.

Acuña enthused over the Garden of Eden quality of life on the river. To make dug-out canoes, the Indians did not trouble to cut down trees. Instead they waited for some suitable trunk to come downstream. This they captured with ropes before towing it ashore. The stranded trunk would be left to wait until the river level fell, and only then would the Indians set to work, hacking at the wood with stone and turtleshell. Nor was Acuña against their obvious affection for alcohol. Aided by wine, 'they celebrate their feasts, mourn their dead, receive their visitors, sow and reap their crops; indeed on any occasion on which they meet, this liquor is the mercury that attracts them and the riband that detains them'. In short, 'the river is full of fish, the forests of game, the air of birds, the trees are covered with fruit, the plains with corn, the earth is rich in mines, and the natives have such skill and ability'. Even if the source of the river was not in paradise, the length and breadth of it could compete for that description.

Modern visitors tend to be impressed by the sight of the Rio Negro's black water not immediately mixing with the greater and browner flow of the Amazon itself. On reaching this point Father Cristóbal, already excited and stimulated by lesser happenings, is ecstatic over the disunited unity, the meeting of black and brown:

Though the Amazon opens its arms with all its force, the new river does not wish to become subject to it, without receiving some marks of respect, and it thus masters one half of the whole Amazon, accompanying it for more than twelve leagues, so that the waters of the two can be clearly distinguished from each other. At last the Amazon, not permitting so much superiority, forces it to mingle with its own turbulent waves, and recognize for a master the river which it desired to make a vassal.

Equally impressive, although earning less excited prose, was his encounter with an electric eel. The fish has 'the peculiarity that, while alive, whoever touches it, trembles all over his body, while closer contact produces a feeling like the cold shivering of ague, which ceases the moment he withdraws his hand'. Acuña's description of the fish was the first ever received in a bewildered Europe. Not for another century did scientists begin to get to grips with the phenomenon of electricity.

At the mouth of the Rio Negro this halcyon expedition experienced its first cloud of disagreement. The date was 15 October 1639 and the Portuguese from Belém had been travelling and labouring for two weeks short of two years. Somewhat reasonably, they wished for reward. What better way of gaining instant wealth, or so they argued, than going up the Negro on a slaving expedition? Acuña and his fellow Jesuits – the Spanish did not send him on his own – had already seen signs of Portuguese slaving practices, such as the erection of crosses in Indian villages. If any of the crosses fell into neglect, or disappeared, this disrespect provided sufficient cause for war, for raiding the village, for capturing Indian slaves.

Initially Teixeira was in favour of the Rio Negro proposal, but the Jesuits were against it on several counts. At Quito they had been assured the down-river journey would take two and a half months; it had already taken eight. Further delay would surely irritate the king of Spain, who wished to fortify the river following the Jesuit recommendations. Additionally the priests objected to the taking of slaves and considered that the Portuguese should refrain from doing so. If the soldiers nevertheless persisted with the slaving expedition, they added, then the priests should be given arms and ammunition so that they could proceed on their own to Belém. Whether Teixeira disliked the idea of permitting a Spanish contingent to travel on its own through what had become Portuguese territory, or had a change of heart concerning slaves, or merely wished to have done with the journey, he cancelled the Negro enterprise. The men persisted that 'they would be held very cheap for having passed so many different nations and so many [potential] slaves, and yet come back empty-handed'; but their leader was adamant. The expedition would continue down the Amazon.

A hundred miles downstream they encountered the huge island now known as Tupinambarana. On it were many families of Indians who had fled when the Portuguese were invading their original territory in Pernambuco, to the west of Recife. Their astonishing migration took them first to the northern part of the state of Mato Grosso and then to the headwaters of the river Madeira. Their journey took years, as they gained the friendship of the local tribes, grew crops, built homes, and then moved on once more. No sooner had they settled on the Madeira than they encountered more white men, Spaniards moving eastwards from the Andes. They therefore moved again, floating down the Madeira before reaching the Amazon island where Teixeira and his party found them. Having travelled some 3,500 miles in their efforts to escape the European invaders, they must have been desolated on realizing there was no escape. There had been 60,000 of them at the start of their epic journey, but only a small fraction of that number had reached the Amazon. They were the Tupinambá tribe and their sole reward was the naming of the land where they eventually settled, not only one of the largest but the most beautiful of Amazonian islands.

Cristóbal Acuña continued with his patient observation and note-taking. The Tupinambá, perhaps eager to tell the travellers what the travellers wished to know, confirmed the story of the Amazon women and even gave a location for them, up in the north towards Guiana. They also produced two new legends which, in various similar forms for different peoples of South America, have lasted into this twentieth century. The first was of a tribe of dwarfs, and the second of people with their feet back to front, whose pursuers would therefore track them in the wrong direction. (The Xavante, who were not subdued until the 1940s, were said to have had the facility of running backwards to mislead those coming after them, and there are many tales of dwarfs.) Acuña wrote it all down, before adding that 'time will discover the truth' in these stories. Time, alas, has not revealed either the Amazons, or the little people, or those with backward-facing feet.

Acuña noted where the tides were first discernible – near the river's union with the Tapajós, some 300 miles from the open sea. He told of gold which, according to the Indians, rivalled in quality that of Peru. And he finished as he had started, by praising the land and its people. It was a region abundant in riches. There were healing drugs within the forest. The huge trees meant that ships could be built more cheaply than elsewhere. There was tobacco, cotton and cacao, all of excellent quality. Sugar could be grown with ease. So too maize, manioc, plantains, pineapples, guavas, coconuts. The skin of the manatee was good for shields, and its flesh for eating. Above all the Amazon river, by invading and draining such a tremendous area, was 'chief master' of this wealth. Possibly more important than all such riches were the Amazon Indians. Mild and generous, they would assuredly 'make good Christians'.

Eventually, more than two years after its departure and on 12 December 1639, the Belém expedition returned home. Pedro de Teixeira was given a tremendous welcome. Father Acuña, meticulous and probing to the end, considered that Fort Presépio had been constructed on the wrong site. It should have been another fourteen leagues nearer the sea, where there existed a better location with a good harbour. He wrote that he was not optimistic concerning the pillaging of Indians for slaves, and solemnly warned his king that the practice would continue. Above all he recommended that Spain should lose no time in occupying Amazonia. This would be easier to achieve from the Amazon's mouth than from Quito and Peru. The river belonged to Spain, and Spain would benefit from it, both as a highway to the Andes and as a future source of riches in its own right.

His advice came too late. He formalized it in *New Discovery of the Great River of the Amazons*, printed in 1641, but the split between Spain and Portugal occurred the year before this publication. King João IV

NVEVO

DESCVBRIMIENTO

DEL GRAN RIO DE LAS AMAZONAS.

POR EL PADRE CHRSTOVAL de Acuña, Religiofo de la Compañia de Iefus, y Calificador de la Suprema General Inquificion.

AL QVAL FVE, Y SE HIZO POR ORDEN de fu Mageftad, el año de 1639.

POR LA PROVINCIA DE QVITO en los Reynos del Perù.

AL EXCELENTISSIMO SEÑOR CONDE Duque de Oliuares.

Con licencia; En Madrid, en la Imprenta del Reyno, año de 1641.

Acuña's book might have restored the Amazon to the Spanish, but came too late for such a reversal.

was not only proclaimed king of Portugal but, on 3 April 1641, king of Brazil as well. Instead of owning about a tenth of South America, as Tordesillas had ordained, the Portuguese had pushed steadily up-river and were on their way to acquiring half the continent. (Brazil is now the fifth largest country in the world, after the Soviet Union, Canada, China and the United States.) No journey was more important in providing this expansion than that of Pedro de Teixeira. The Spanish in Quito had been correct to be alarmed at his sudden presence in their midst. They were right to equip him with Spaniards for his return voyage, and could not have chosen a better representative for their cause than Father Acuña; but this wisdom came too late for Spain. Jacomé Raimundo, São Luís' governor, had been perfect in his timing when he had despatched Teixeira, but Acuña's recommendations were, in the main, ignored. His book was poorly received, being an account in Spanish of a matter that, to all realists, only involved the Portuguese. Henceforth it was their river, Pedro de Teixeira having firmly proved the point.

What is not proven, to any degree whatsoever, is the character of Teixeira. To say he ends up a shadowy figure is both understatement and unhelpful. Acuña, so assiduous in describing everything he sees, makes no description of the Portuguese leader. It was not his brief to do so, but some comment might have been expected as the journey proceeded and decisions were made either rightly or wrongly in Acuña's eyes. The Spanish chronicler does not seem to have noticed the leader. There was not even comment when Teixeira obeyed earlier instructions by taking possession, in the name of Portugal, of a place he called Franciscana. It lay opposite the Rio de Oro's mouth, in the upper reaches of the Amazon. This setting of a wooden mark in territory presumed to be Spanish would undoubtedly have been anathema to all Spaniards, but the act did not spark outrage from Acuña. It is as if the chronicler sought to diminish the captain (and therefore his deeds) by quite disregarding them.

The descriptions of Teixeira that do exist are so bland as to be suspect. In the Brazilian *Biographical Annual* (published in Rio in 1876) he is venerated 'for his virtues, his indomitable bravery, and famed for the prudence of his counsels . . . [He] was certainly one of the great characters in the history of Brazil in the seventeenth century'. In *Os*

Pedro de Teixeira

Descobrimientos Portugueses (by Jaime Cortesão and also published belatedly) his personality is said to have been *'a maneira de Fernão de Magalhães, enérgico, obstinado e duro ate a crueldade'* ('like Ferdinand Magellan, energetic, stubborn and harsh to the point of cruelty'). The comments are not so much *de mortuis nil nisi bonum* as *de mortuis nil*. Perhaps there were no contemporary accounts. With such a man at such a time it is quite feasible. Without doubt he was brave, patriotic, a good soldier and a wise leader (who could keep an enormous, and disparate, band together for two years); but those are the bones rather than the flesh of his personality.

Or perhaps there was insufficient time for his praises to be sung. After he arrived back at (Nossa Senhora de) Belém on 12 December 1639, he speedily went to São Luís (do Maranhão), where he had fought against the French twenty-five years earlier. There he made a full report of his travels, and was promptly promoted *Capitão-Mòr* and governor of Pará, a post he accepted on 28 February 1640. Unfortunately he was not well, and he yielded the office to another within three months. Eleven days later, on 4 June, he died. There are suggestions that the great journey had over-taxed his strength, and indeed it may have done, but, as with his character, there are no details. It is not necessary to experience a long and demanding journey to be felled by some South American disease. Malaria or yellow fever, for example, are undiscriminating as to whom they kill, and a middle-aged soldier about to rest from his exertions is as good a target as any.

Finally, it is curious that the two men who did most to ensure that Brazil is now Portuguese-speaking – and so vast – should both be so shadowy. Pedro Álvares Cabral stumbled upon the land, thereby giving Portugal a stake in the New World. Pedro de Teixeira sailed up and down the Amazon to bring it under Portugal, even though Spain had a greater claim by right of treaty and discovery. The two men had a heroic influence, for Portugal and Brazil; but it is not even known whether they were short or tall, fat or thin, handsome or the contrary. They played their parts almost unobtrusively and then vanished, one into the obscurity of a country estate and the other into death. Their names live, so too their exploits; but that is almost all.

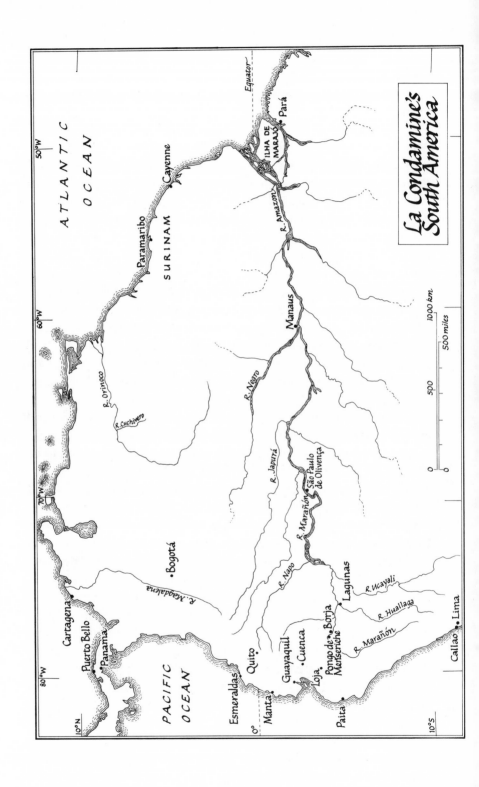

La Condamine's
South America

V

Charles Marie de la Condamine
EQUATORIAL SCIENTIST

The rivalry between Spain and Portugal was as nothing compared with the antagonism between those two nations and the rest of the world. The Americas had been discovered from the Iberian peninsula. They therefore belonged to Spain and, in lesser part, to Portugal. The Pope had partitioned the new lands between these two countries and there had been no question of, for example, England, Holland, France or Ireland being granted any portion. The Spanish and Portuguese were most active in areas encountered during the final decade of the fifteenth century. The invaders and colonizers went west and slightly north of the West Indies. They then took over Central America, and finally went south, exploring and occupying almost all of South America. In time the only exceptions to this wholesale Iberian occupation were the relatively small footholds along the Guianas gained by Holland, France and England, a few pickings in the West Indies, and the far greater invasion of North America by the same three countries.

Northern Europe's powerful seafaring nations did exert most influence on the slice of the New World nearest to them, but they were slow off the mark in consolidating their discoveries. John Cabot, the Venetian-Englishman, explored North America in the fifteenth century but Jamestown in Virginia, for example, was not founded until 1607. Every event described in Chapters 2 and 3 of this book, with Spaniards exploring, conquering, settling, making revolution and having South American families, took place long before Captain John Smith, Jamestown's leader, had even been born. The northern Europeans might not have acquired any of North America had not the Spanish and Portuguese been over-involved with the several million square miles of territory to the south. As it is, the Latin-speaking countries of the New World now cover over eight million square miles, or more than half of the new land. The remainder, almost entirely English-speaking, is the lesser portion, despite the northern Europeans gaining land from the Spanish in later centuries.

To some extent the fortunes of the great river reflect those of the New World as a whole. The Amazon was discovered during Spanish voyages of exploration, although Cabral's Portuguese encounter with Brazil is given priority for the eastern area as a whole. First voyages down the river from Peru were wholly Spanish but, when the sixteenth century yielded to the seventeenth, different visitors arrived at the river's mouth. The English, Dutch and French built forts until ousted from them by the Portuguese. When Spanish domination weakened, permitting the Portuguese to make inroads, Teixeira's journey to Quito and back on Portugal's behalf led to Spain losing control of much of Amazonia.

The river's story also reflects the waxing and waning of power in Europe. Maritime influence emanating from Iberia lost its superiority as France, England and Holland grew in strength. These three competed for a share of the new discoveries, partly in the New World but also elsewhere. When the Spanish Armada was defeated in 1588 the victory not only saved England from invasion but encouraged northern Europeans to range widely in search of profit and adventure. The English and Dutch were particularly active during the seventeenth century, settling, trading, and claiming portions of the planet as their own. The eighteenth century witnessed a great flowering in France, and it is therefore apt that the French should then have played a major role in the Amazon's history. The story of La Condamine, Godin and Madame Godin is not only French but scientific. Never before in the river's history had scientists taken note of it, but then never before had science itself been ready for such a task.

Their story exemplifies yet again the oblique manner in which so many of the Amazon's events came to pass. Cabral's discovery of Brazil occurred when on his way to India. Orellana's downstream venture also happened by mistake, having started out as a quest for cinnamon and gold. Aguirre's bloody journey was initially similar, but became transformed by his longing to conquer Peru. Teixeira's double epic would not have happened had the Spanish not goaded the Portuguese into taking action. The French journey now to be described had a more bizarre trigger even than all these others. It would never have occurred had the shape of the Earth not been a matter for diligent debate during the middle years of the eighteenth century. Did the planet swell at the centre, as Isaac Newton asserted, or was its diameter greater from pole to pole, the prevailing view in France? This argument, fiercely contested, led in a most direct fashion to the first scientific examination of the Amazon and also, no less directly, to the first descent of that river by a woman. She was not a mere member of some later expedition. She was the sole survivor of her own enterprise, and her story a consequence of that academic controversy concerning the Earth and its bulges, whether equatorial or polar.

The controversy was only partly scientific. Its initiators, Newton and Giovanni Cassini (an Italian-born French astronomer), were both dead when the French Académie des Sciences decided to settle the matter. Honour was at stake; so too patriotic pride. The issue was further complicated when Voltaire sided with the English and when, somewhat earlier, Jean Richer discovered that a clock's pendulum beat slower if transported to Cayenne in French Guiana. He had been sent, together with the clock, by Jacques Cassini, French Astronomer Royal (and son of Giovanni), to bring back evidence that Newton was wrong. He did the opposite and, instead of being praised for scientific honesty, was rebuked by Cassini for 'hypocrisy'. In the Age of Reason various people became more and more unreasonable as the Cassinians vied with the Newtonians. The furore, so damaging to the scientific community, had therefore to be resolved. Hence the decision in December 1734 that two expeditions should set forth from Paris. One would proceed to Lapland, as far north as possible. The other would head for the equator. Both would make the necessary measurements to determine whether the Earth was an elongated prolate spheroid (Cassini) or more of an oblate spheroid (Newton).

The shape of the Earth was partly an academic question, with more interest in the contest than the answer; but there was also a practical aspect. Navigation on the planet could never be precise until the planet's shape was known. If the Earth was a perfect sphere the angle of a star would always be proportional to the length of an arc. Go due north until a star's angle had changed by 1° and the distance travelled overland would always be the same. When it had originally been realized that the earth was spherical (rather than flat or sitting on the back of a tortoise) it had been assumed that this roundness was perfect; but by the middle of the eighteenth century no one any longer believed in that perfection. The Earth was some distortion of a sphere. This helped to explain why navigation was such an imprecise business. Measurements of star angles, however accurately performed, did not lead to an accurate reading of a ship's position. Navigators had, over the years, grown accustomed to this fact. As was said at the time: 'If the sailors are not at present sensible how advantageous it would be for them to know the true figure of the Earth, it is owing rather to the imperfection than the perfection of their art.' However, the savants wanted to know. The Académie wanted to know. And all those who wished to raise the Newton v. Cassini argument above the level of bickering – they too wanted to know. Solving the navigational dilemma was a better and more honourable cause than determining which of two dead men had been correct.

With the blessing of Louis XV the double expedition left Paris in 1735. The South American venture had further to go, but the Académie expected that both parties would return and report at more or less the same time. The Arctic group had to wait for summer, and travel in the northern latitudes would present problems. As their report eventually proclaimed, they experienced 'a climate where the heavens are so coy to observation', and 'a cold so extreme, that whenever we would taste a little brandy, the only thing that could be kept liquid, our tongues and lips froze to the cup, and came away bloody'. Despite such difficulties they made the necessary measurements, notably around Tornea in latitude 65°50′50″ N, and then returned to Paris, delivering their report on 13 November 1737.

Neither party was a mere surveying team, instructed what to do and where to do it. The Lapland group was culled from the Académie and completed by Olaf Celsius, Swedish savant and professor of astronomy. The South American contingent was larger, consisting of: Charles Marie de la Condamine, leader and geodesist; Pierre Bouguer, astronomer; Louis Godin, mathematician and scientific director of the expedition; Jean Godin des Odonais, cousin of the mathematician; De Morainville, draughtsman and engineer; Jean Senièrgues, doctor; Joseph de Jussieu, botanist; Hugot, watchmaker and instrument technician; Verguin, captain of the Navy; Mabillon, assistant; and Couplet, nephew of the Académie's treasurer.

The Lapland party returned safe and sound, their journey more or less without incident. The equatorial group would experience death (by illness, accident and murder), marriage, madness, a reluctance to return to France, and also a desire to return via the Amazon, expressed in three expeditions, each accomplished independently. The northern measurements formed the major endeavour of the Lapland group. The equatorial measurements were performed with similar devotion but paled beside the other happenings – the deaths, the mental breakdown, the interference by local people, and those three astonishing Amazon journeys. The venture that set forth from Paris towards the equator in 1735 was not finally concluded until 1770. No one at the outset could possibly have guessed any of its outcomes, such as the separation and eventual union of Monsieur and Madame Godin. Few marriage partners have had such a tale to tell.

A final introductory point is that this equatorial project was the first official incursion behind the closed doors of the New World. Ever since the discoveries had been partitioned between Spain and Portugal no other nation had been welcome. Tordesillas had been signed in 1494. Almost two and a half centuries were to pass before permission to enter was given to a non-Iberian party, a very inquisitive party. These French newcomers were known right from the outset to be investigators. They were a new breed of men, the scientists, forever ready to measure, to sketch, to take note, to examine. There were no limits to their curiosity, and they had all manner of instruments to help them – microscopes, telescopes, measuring chains, astrolabes. Quite suddenly the closed New World was to be opened up to a novel brand of human being who would seek, not gold or spices, conquest or honour, but information of every possible kind.

The War of the Spanish Succession lay behind the shift in policy. Philip V of Spain, who ruled from 1700 to 1746, had a French grandfather, Louis XIV. That longest-reigning French monarch (1638–1715) had always wanted to unite Spain and France, thereby giving France a better stake in the New World, but the advisers of

Charles II of Spain, who reigned from 1661 to 1700, wished to keep the Spanish empire intact. Unfortunately, Charles had no children. To fill the gap, Spain and Louis XIV agreed that Louis's grandson Philip, Duke of Anjou (who was also a grandson of Spain's former king), should ascend the Spanish throne. This act of unification, however deliberate, upset the balance of power within Europe and led to lengthy wars, cumulatively labelled as the War of the Spanish Succession (1701–14). At their end Philip still felt some indebtedness towards France, and when the request came from Louis XV for French academicians to visit a portion of Spain's South American empire, he gave permission. Philip's Council of the Indies was indignant. What was this probing by a foreign power? How would Spain benefit from the visitation? Why open doors that had been profitably kept closed for 241 years? If the Council had been able to predict the future and foresee the effects of this single mission it would have been even more steadfast in its refusal; but King Philip had given his blessing and that was that. La Condamine and the others could set sail.

This leader of the party was the kind of individual who could flourish most freely in the eighteenth century. The writer Victor von Hagen describes him as 'an ensemble of all the forces of that strange age in which religion, debauchery, intellect, fashion and brutality seethed and bubbled together in such an extraordinary pot-pourri'. He had been well born, in 1701, but into troublous times. That war of the succession reverberated around his childhood, and by eighteen he too was in uniform fighting further battles. He proved himself valiant but unwilling to confine his activities to mere military matters. In particular he became interested in mathematics, and especially its relevance to the planet Earth. When aged twenty-nine he was elected to the Académie des Sciences, having also embraced natural history, astronomy and cartography.

Along the way La Condamine had been befriended by Voltaire, partly because the great man admired his '*curiosité ardente*', but also because that wish to examine everything had earned Voltaire a lot of money. A state lottery had been organized which, according to La Condamine, was selling insufficient tickets. It would be feasible for one person to purchase all of them and so be sure of winning more than his outlay. Voltaire followed this advice and became wealthier by half a million francs. Small wonder therefore that La Condamine's career was constantly encouraged by France's leading iconoclast, wit and promoter of every form of under-dog. Not that La Condamine was without other resources – his family had speculated well in the 'Mississippi Bubble', involving alleged mines in Louisiana – but to be favoured by Voltaire was an advantage of a different order. At all events Charles Marie de la Condamine, soldier, scholar, aristocrat, academician and adventurer, became the leader of the first scientific expedition to South America, and also the first foreigner given opportunity to see behind the veil Spain had drawn across her empire for two and a half centuries. 'We have been singularly honoured,' said the thirty-four-year-old, addressing his fellow academicians. And so indeed they had.

Just as Portuguese soldiers had accompanied Spaniards on the first upstream Amazon journey and Spaniards had accompanied Portuguese on the subsequent trip downstream, so two young officers of the Spanish Navy were attached to the French party. Jorge Juan y Santacilla, twenty-two, and Antonio de Ulloa, nineteen, were to meet the scientists upon their arrival at Cartagena, the French having sailed from La Rochelle on 16 May 1735. Orders from Spain were straightforward. The two officers were to assist the French to complete their scientific programme, while also ensuring they made no further investigations. Both these men were from the same mould as La Condamine, being mathematicians as well as sailors, and were equally endowed with ardent curiosity. If their watchful presence might have been expected to quell the sense of hospitality, it did nothing of the sort. They were an asset, in every possible way.

The French did not arrive at Cartagena until 16 November, having passed six months in travel. It was to be a further six months before they would reach Quito (now capital of Ecuador but then within the kingdom of Peru). That city lies 78·30° west of Greenwich (although the world in general did not then favour that observatory for its prime meridian) and a mere 0·14° south of the equator. This location would serve for the measurements, although reaching it entailed much travel, first to Puerto Bello (scene of many a pillaging by pirates, as well as riddled with disease), across the isthmus to Panama (attacked less frequently, and also healthier), and then by boat to Manta. There the

Charles Marie de la Condamine, 'singularly honoured' to work within the Spanish domain.

party split, with La Condamine and Bouguer disembarking and the remainder carrying on to Guayaquil. It was while La Condamine and his single companion were resting one evening, the cicadas sounding 'like scissor-grinders on the Pont Neuf', that the governor of the province of Esmeraldas suddenly emerged to greet his visitors. Pedro Maldonado, aged thirty-two, was a most exceptional colonial official, being a mathematician, a cartographer, an explorer, a mountain climber, a speaker of Spanish, French and Quechua, a road-maker, and an individual entirely right for La Condamine. The two men took to each other instantaneously.

From Manta to Quito the journey is shorter than from Guayaquil to Quito, but at that time it was much more difficult. Pierre Bouguer (who was always to disagree with his superior and prefer some other course) elected to take the heavier instruments, join the others at Guayaquil and complete the journey with them. La Condamine and Maldonado, kindred spirits, opted to travel the harder jungle route and could not resist making detours in every direction. They examined the people, the plants, the fruits, the crops, the rivers and mountains, and also *caoutchouc*. Europeans before La Condamine had seen and recorded this strange latex that could be bounced and would keep things dry, but he promptly fashioned a bag from it for his instruments, and was to become the first to bring this product of *Hevea brasiliensis* to Europe. Already the expedition was proving to involve more than a mere measurement of the roundness of the Earth.

Nevertheless, that work had to be achieved. When the scientists assembled at Quito, slightly more than a year after leaving Paris, they started upon their task. However, there were problems. Quito and its environs were healthier than, for instance, the Panama isthmus, but could still kill. One Indian died during the initial survey work at 8,000 feet above sea level, causing all the other Indians to depart. Young Couplet, nephew of the Académie's treasurer, succumbed to '*paludismo*' (presumably malaria). La Condamine had promised to look after him and had plainly failed. It might have been better to have kept Dr Senièrgues at a distance, given the weakening effect of this physician's enthusiasm for blood-letting. (Cures were then customarily more devastating than the diseases. The recommended treatment at the time for one rectal complaint common in Peru was a pessary of lemon, pepper and gunpowder. The donation of blood, even from a system drained of useful corpuscles by malarial parasites, sounds a lesser punishment.)

There was also the problem of suspicion. Quito then had a population of 6,000 Spaniards, 12,000 mestizos, 12,000 Indians, and 5,000 Negroes, but to all groups the activities of the French were incomprehensible unless, of course, their antics with measuring chains, theodolites, maps and octants formed some new method of discovering gold. What the scientists were doing was to map a grid upon the ground. From this they would measure star angles at positions of known distance from each other. However, as the savants presumably knew before embarking for the Andes, the land around Quito is by no means flat. In fact there is nowhere along the Earth's equator quite so mountainous as the area they had chosen for their researches. Thus, even without disease and suspicion, there was sufficient obstacle to depress all but the most diligent. Pierre Bouguer was a great complainer. Hugot worried about his chilblains. Godin, the mathematician, was frequently ill. Couplet was already dead. Only the enthusiasm of La Condamine and Maldonado kept the unhappy group at its task.

To allay the prevailing suspicion, La Condamine and Jorge Juan, senior of the two naval Spaniards, travelled to Lima. They planned to meet the viceroy, to go over the head of the difficult official at Quito who constantly questioned or harassed the scientists and set spies upon them. The Lima mission was eventually successful but it did take time, by foot, by raft, by horse. Eight months after setting forth the two men were back again with the necessary permission. The date then was July 1737, or twenty-six months after the sailing from La Rochelle. It is steadily becoming easier to comprehend why taking a few measurements at the equator occupied such a slice of all the lives involved.

Then, almost two years later, came not just one body blow but several. The triangulations were being completed, despite the sickness, the bureaucracy, the heat and the cold. The moment of glory was therefore about to arrive. Did the planet bulge as Newton had asserted, making it an oblate spheroid, or had Cassini been correct? A letter then arrived from the Académie. It gave the results of the Lapland team, long since returned to France. Its scientists had shown, by comparing the northerly measurements with those made elsewhere (as in France), that Newton's theories were correct. Voltaire was overjoyed. 'They have flattened the Earth and the Cassinis,' he exulted. There was no such enthusiasm around the Andes. The visitors had laboured, but apparently to no avail. The race had already been won, and the equatorial party could have spared itself all the difficulty.

With hindsight one wonders why this possibility had not been foreseen. Plainly a visit to Lapland was less of a journey. Its landscape was less of a problem. The Swedes were less likely to be awkward than the colonial Spanish, and it was highly probable the northern party would report first. On the other hand, using a touch more hindsight, the whole debate had provided a most excellent excuse for western science, and French science in particular, to have a look behind the closed doors of the New World's southern half. The equatorial party was over twice the size of the Arctic group, positive indication that more work was expected of it. Such a *raison d'être* would not necessarily have been explained to La Condamine or his colleagues, who considered their earth measurements to be paramount. Hence their depression when the letter arrived from the Académie des Sciences, a dejection soon to be compounded from quite different directions.

The French group may have received additional support from Lima one thousand miles distant, but local opposition still simmered; partly from xenophobia, one imagines, and partly from customary resentment at alien activity. In June 1739 – now four years since the sailing – the earth-measurers were encamped at Cuenca, location of one of their fixed triangulation points. This town, second city in the Audiencia of Quito, lay 200 miles south of that city and, according to both Spanish naval chroniclers, was peopled differently from Quito. Those at Cuenca were 'indolent' in general, with many being 'rude', 'vindictive', and 'wicked'. The French as a group may have lost some of their diplomacy and tact over the years, but it was the doctor, Jean Senièrgues, who caused the rudeness and vindictiveness to increase in a most violent manner.

It so happened that the doctor was treating local people freely. Among them were some of the Quesada family, and within that family was Manuela, aged twenty, good-looking, and engaged to Diego de León. This young man then changed his mind and married the daughter of the *alcalde*. As a disinterested party Dr Senièrgues was asked by the Quesadas to obtain a settlement from the faithless fiancé. Manuela's chances of marriage were thought to be reduced now that she had been rejected, and the doctor managed to extract a promise of money from Diego. Unfortunately the payment did not surface. Worse still it was rumoured that Manuela's chances had improved, and in the direction of the doctor. It then happened that Senièrgues and Diego met one day in a narrow street and, after insults had been exchanged, a duel was suggested. At this juncture the impatient doctor drew his sword, lunged at Diego, missed, and fell, causing disgrace upon disgrace to fall upon the French. It was bad enough to use his sword, but even worse to miss.

La Condamine and Jorge Juan attempted appeasement, notably via the Jesuits. The doctor should have lain low but decided, on 29 August 1739, to attend a bullfight. Undiplomatically he was accompanied by Manuela and her father. The crowd was incensed. Nicolás de Neyra, who was a friend of Diego and in charge of the bullring, shouted some remarks at the doctor. Not to be outdone the doctor shouted back and

The fatal occasion in the Cuenca bull-ring when the impulsive Dr Senièrgues so enraged the mob that it killed him.

Charles Marie de la Condamine

Neyra retreated, never a popular move and particularly wrong on bullfight day. Taking another tack, Neyra then cancelled the bullfight. The crowd was outraged. Plainly the Frenchman was to blame and the mob surged his way. Unfortunately the doctor proved to be more brave than sensible. He again unsheathed his sword, leapt into the ring and confronted the enemy. La Condamine and the others, also there that day, rushed to their colleague's defence but were too late. Their friend was stabbed, stoned and generally crushed to death.

A second disaster followed. While the French were wisely lying low in a Cuenca monastery the botanist, Joseph de Jussieu, went off his head. For over four years he had collected plants, carefully tending them through all kinds of hazard. A careless servant then managed to destroy the lot (quite how is not detailed) and this was too much for the collector. He never regained his former powers and was no longer an asset to the expedition. Other botanists after his time were to suffer similar losses, but none took it quite so badly. Jussieu not only lost his plants, his reason went as well.

More was to come. La Condamine applied himself to the business of justice, or at least revenge. In time he persuaded a court to name the guilty parties. These were adjudged to be Diego de León (who had so enraged Senièrgues), Nicolás de Neyra (who had further angered him in the bullring) and the *alcalde* of Cuenca (in charge of the town and therefore to blame for its misdeeds). In fact, none of the three had performed any of the stabbing or stoning that had actually killed the doctor. However, it was all academic. The three were never sentenced, and Maldonado repeatedly urged La Condamine to let the matter slide. It was only dropped when another crisis surfaced. A British fleet had arrived in the Pacific. There was a general call to arms at the threat of attack, and the two naval officers were immediately ordered to Lima to assist their country. From there, having received instructions, they hurried to Callao, Lima's port, to help with defences and wait for the British.

This was the War of Jenkins' Ear (1739–41), a name schoolchildren remember even if they cannot recollect who fought whom or when or why. Robert Jenkins, a seaman, had been the trigger. For years the British had been offended by their commercial exclusion from lucrative New World markets. On one attempt to trade this unfortunate sailor had had an ear pulled from him by his Spanish captors. Jenkins, together with his severed ear in a bottle, was introduced to the House of Commons and made to tell his tale. The members were furious, particularly when hearing that his assailants had said they wished to do likewise to his king. Two great fleets were speedily organized to attack Spanish America, one (under Anson) from the west, the other (under Vernon) from the east. Admiral Vernon sailed with fifty men-of-war, many transports and 28,000 men. His main objective was Cartagena, defended by far fewer military personnel and captained by half a man. Don Blas de Leso had only one arm, one leg and one eye, but these proved sufficient to repel the British. After fifty-six days Vernon retreated, leaving 18,000 dead and half his ships. (This story is not recounted in British classrooms as frequently as, for example, the defeat of the Armada, but the scale of loss was comparable. Approximately forty-four of the Armada's total of 128 ships failed to return.)

Admiral Anson, the other portion of the pincer, had first to overcome Cape Horn and also the six Spanish vessels on his tail.

Vice-Admiral Vernon took Porto Bello in 1739, but he fared disastrously when attacking Cartagena.

Charles Marie de la Condamine

Fortunately one destroyed the other – all six followers either foundered or were rendered useless in a South American storm. Anson's fleet was not unscathed itself and put in at the island of Juan Fernández for repairs. With these completed, he then descended out of the blue on the Peruvian port of Paita, some 600 miles north of Callao, where the two earth-measuring naval officers were strengthening fortifications. Anson gained a lot of doubloons, some satisfaction in setting fire to the place, and also news (from a captive) of Vernon's defeat. He did not then attack Panama, as had been the original plan, but successfully encountered Spanish treasure ships at Acapulco. Thus enriched he sailed west and eventually circumnavigated the globe, though this achievement was considerably marred by appalling losses from scurvy. With his return home the War of Jenkins' Ear, of Spain versus Britain, was peacefully concluded.

The earth-measurers were then in their sixth year of work and this war might have seemed irrelevant to their endeavours. Not a bit of it. The Spanish sense of isolation, particularly on that Pacific seaboard, had been severely upset. Foreigners of all kinds were now more suspect, particularly those in their very midst, taking measurements, making maps, calculating heaven knew what. Local suspicions came to a head over the pyramids. These were permanent indicators of the triangulation points which, as they involved bricks, slabs of rock and inscriptions, had cost considerable labour. In that period of intense nationalism, their inscriptions enraged the Spanish. The names of La Condamine, Bouguer and Godin had been carved; so too the fleur-de-lis, emblem of the French throne. There was no mention of Spain, its king or its subjects, many of whom had worked with the measurers. What was happening? Were the French taking possession of the land? Why, in particular, display the coat of arms of French royalty?

La Condamine was summoned to Quito. He protested that as both the French and Spanish royal families were from the house of Bourbon, the lilies could not possibly be an insult; but they caused, as Von Hagen has phrased it, 'intermittent testimonials, appeals, recesses, dissimulations, indecisions, and procrastinations'. The alleged crime kept the Fiscal of Quito occupied for months while it debated the issues involved.

In the meantime the grand geodesic expedition, soon to enter its seventh year, was not so much being concluded as slowly wasting away. Louis Godin had accepted the post of astronomer at Lima's University of San Marcos. His cousin, Jean Godin des Odonais, became enamoured of a certain Isabela. She was thirteen at the time, and therefore seventeen years his junior. The girl was attractive, and fluent in French, Spanish and Quechua, her father being a Creole of French extraction. When the survey work was finished a marriage was announced between the French chain-bearer and Isabela de Grand-maison y Bruno, causing even the legal wrangles in Quito to be suspended. The earth-measurers assembled for this occasion, those that were left of them.

Couplet had died of fever. Senièrgues had been killed. Jussieu had gone off his head, as had Mabillon, no more than an assistant to the expedition (though their lunacy did not stop these two attending the wedding). Hugot, the watchmaker and technician, had already married locally. And then, shortly after what was apparently a happy day at the Godin wedding, the naval draughtsman, De Morainville, was killed. He was assisting in the construction of a church when the scaffolding collapsed, taking him with it. Soon afterwards Pierre Bouguer and Captain Verguin left for home. They travelled north, via Bogotá and the Rio Magdalena, to reach Cartagena just over seven years after they had first seen the place. Bouguer and La Condamine had never managed to patch their many differences, seemingly arguing over every matter, and it must have been a great relief to both when an honourable parting became possible.

With two men departed, two mad, three dead, one gone to Lima, and two married to Peruvians, Charles Marie de la Condamine was suddenly on his own. Or rather he was free to turn his thoughts and attentions to other matters. In particular he came to know the Jesuits, who still had a few years to go before being expelled from Spanish South America. It so happened that one of his triangulation points lay at the very base of a cathedral the Jesuits were constructing in Quito. It also happened that Pedro Maldonado's elder brother was one of the priests. With his assistance La Condamine was able to look at Amazon maps collected and prepared by Jesuits, notably those made by Padre Samuel Fritz during his forty years upon the river. With curiosity whetted rather than diminished by his New World years, La Condamine became fired with the notion of returning home via the Amazon. Fellow spirit Maldonado offered to go with him. The date was 1743, just 203 years since Francisco de Orellana had also realized he could reach home by travelling down-river. However, this was to be the first scientific descent, the first by a non-Iberian, and the first encounter of the Age of Reason with the most extraordinary river system in the world. Once fired, La Condamine could hardly wait for the great journey to begin.

However, there were still some details to be resolved, such as the matter of the pyramids. After innumerable meetings and considerable debate the Fiscal of Quito's Audiencia concluded that the pyramids could stand, provided the fleur-de-lis was removed and the names of the two Spanish measurers were added. These men would therefore have pride of place upon each monument, and both La Condamine and Maldonado were delighted at this diplomatic outcome. Later the Council of the Indies was to overturn the ruling. It did not like the pyramids and, after six years, ordered them to be destroyed. Very much

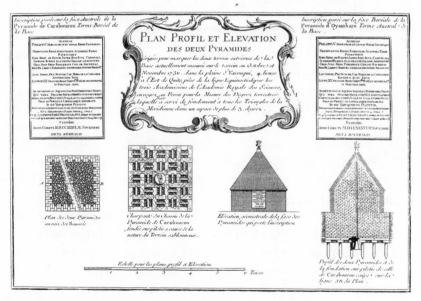

The contentious pyramids were erected by the French earth-measurers when their work was completed, only to be destroyed six years later.

later, in 1836, there was a further change of heart. By then Quito had become the capital of Ecuador and the republic ordered them rebuilt on exactly the original sites, but with new inscriptions, giving credit (and debit) where due: 'The French Academicians . . . erected these pyramids in November 1736 . . . they were destroyed by command of the King of Spain . . . and rebuilt 100 years later . . . by order of his Excellency Vicente Rocafuerte, President of the Republic . . .'

The structures no longer resembled the original pyramids, but did serve as intriguing reminders of an event in Franco-Spanish history. They also explain to the modern visitor how it came about in the middle of the eighteenth century that a Frenchman stood poised to make the first properly investigative study of the river Amazon. Spanish succession, Bourbon expansion, Louis XIV and Philip V, Isaac Newton, the Cassinis, Voltaire, Admirals Vernon and Anson, Master Mariner Robert Jenkins, the beautiful Manuela, Diego de León and many others had played their part, and had helped to set the scene. The play's second act could now begin.

'I found myself in a new world, separated from all human intercourse, on a fresh-water sea, surrounded by a maze of lakes, rivers and canals, and penetrating in every direction the gloom of an immense forest . . .' Charles Marie de la Condamine had spent eight years in the Americas but had lost none of his questing enthusiasm. It was June 1743 when he found himself in that new world, strikingly different from the mountainous terrain of the Andes. The place was Borja, about as far from Cuenca as Cuenca is from Quito. These last two towns are firmly within the mountain chain, while Borja is to the east and low-lying. It lies at the start of the flat, relatively uniform vastness of the Amazon basin. At Borja a man can turn eastwards and know there is nothing before him save trees, water and a gentle descent for a couple of thousand miles. That vast flatness then gives way to the yet greater flatness of the Atlantic. To La Condamine it was almost like looking at home again. It was certainly a change from looking at the Andes.

He must also have felt great relief at finally extricating himself from the vicissitudes of the earth-measuring expedition. No more could the Audiencia restrict, prevent, adjudicate. And no more could the mob at Cuenca threaten. When leaving the country he had had to bypass that town, its citizens still furious that three of them had been accused of complicity in murder (even if no sentence had been passed or would be carried out). There must also have been relief for La Condamine in losing the reins of leadership as his remaining charges dispersed to France, to Lima, or to homes in Quito. He still had his beloved instruments, including a huge telescope, but was otherwise unfettered. Aged forty-two, he could contemplate the forthcoming journey with relish. He was going home via the most astonishing river in the world. At Borja the waters plunge through a narrow gap, the Pongo de Menseriche, before settling down as if in contemplation of the vast distance still to be accomplished. At that spot La Condamine must also have changed his mood, taken a deeper breath or two and put the Andes firmly behind him. Those mountain days were finally over.

While travelling to Borja, and as committed as ever to the needs of collection and observation, La Condamine gathered some *quinquina* seeds. The area was a centre for growing quinine and he thought the plants would be an exciting addition to the king's gardens in France. He had had to evade a band from Cuenca, but even without such murderous intent upon his tail the journey would have been extremely arduous. He had to cross and recross rivers, swaying over the suspension bridges, and was frequently drenched by rain. The perpetual damp made his hide-covered baskets 'stink intolerably'. His paperwork, containing the results of seven years' study, was repeatedly dunked whenever the mules were forced to swim. Once he nearly lost everything when travelling by raft. This became hopelessly caught up in a whirlpool below the pass of Cumbinama. Indians threw lianas to the worried occupants and eventually managed to pull them free. At a different whirlpool, near the Pongo just above Borja, some missionaries had been trapped for two days, spinning round and round and growing weaker from lack of food. La Condamine managed to miss this particular Charybdis, but some nearby rocks almost put paid to his papers. And so did an overnight drop in water-level which left his craft temporarily suspended in mid-air.

No wonder La Condamine was relieved at encountering Borja. The river's sudden peacefulness presaged a more relaxed form of travel in the weeks and months that lay ahead. There was also the astonishing view: 'Accustomed during seven years to mountains lost in clouds, I was wrapped in admiration at the wide circle embraced by the eye, restricted here by no other boundary than the horizon.' La Condamine's enthusiasm must have been infectious. A Jesuit priest at Borja not only arranged canoes for the Frenchman but decided to join him for the next section of his journey, that leading down the Marañón to its union with the Rio Huallaga. The distance is 130 straight-line miles but about twice as far by water. As the boats were paddled ashore at the Lagunas mission station on the Huallaga they were greeted, as La Condamine recorded, by 'Don Pedro Maldonado, Governor of the Province of Esmeraldas – who had been waiting for me six weeks'.

This twin soul had left Quito by an alternative route (there had been three to choose from) and it had proved speedier. Quite what would happen to the province of Esmeraldas in the meantime, or whether it would miss its governor, is not mentioned. Its problems were already some 450 miles to the north-west, and plainly they could wait awhile. 'He, as well as myself . . . felt disposed to proceed down the river of Amazonas . . . after many dangers and great fatigue he had been fortunate enough to arrive at Lagunas six weeks before me . . . He had made requisite observations as he travelled along, with a compass and a portable gnomon . . .' Maldonado was not only intent on seeing the entire Amazon but would complete the journey by continuing to Europe. As he had repeatedly delighted La Condamine with talk of South America, so must his companion have talked of France and its variety of joys.

The journey ahead of them was less hazardous than it might have been a century earlier, or than it would become in the following century when mission stations had been much reduced in number. The French savant and the Spanish governor were to receive every kind of assistance – canoes, canoeists, maps, information, advice, and of course mere hospitality. At every stopping place they asked for similar assistance to be granted to Jean Godin des Odonais and his wife. One gathers from this preparation – it is not positively stated – that Jean Godin wished to follow his leader in due course. He could not do so in mid-1743 because his wife was pregnant. It would be wrong to leave her, and doubly wrong to expect her to travel when either expecting or recently delivered of a child. He, and she, would journey down the river at some more opportune time. At least, that was the plan.

Charles Marie de la Condamine

For their part La Condamine and Maldonado were in their own form of heaven. They measured, observed, recorded, tested, mapped. Then, on 23 July 1743, they left Lagunas in two canoes. These were 44 feet long and 3 feet wide, each fashioned from a single tree-trunk. The passengers were installed at the rear, sitting beneath a palm-frond canopy. The engine-room of paddling Indians was in the front section. Travelling downstream, particularly when propelled by others, may seem a leisurely affair, but La Condamine never relaxed from all his self-appointed tasks, noting the tributaries, the islands, each river's width, the compass bearings, the time of day, the current's speed. His journal does show, from time to time, another less frenetic side to him. He wrote of making the measurements to offset the 'tiresomeness of a weary, though tranquil, voyage through a country in which the continued sameness of objects, however novel in themselves, tended to fatigue rather than please the eye'. The Amazon can undoubtedly cause such lassitude, and all the more so when downstream progress means the banks grow further and further apart.

Of course he and Maldonado were also interested in the Indians. The two men noted the intoxicants (for stunning fish) and the insecticides (containing the alkaloid rotenone) they used, and the poisons with which they tipped their arrows. The scientists learned that there was no danger in eating animals killed with such weapons, 'for the venom . . . is only mortal when absorbed by the blood'. Alleged antidotes were salt or, if that failed, sugar. In experimenting upon a chicken that should have succumbed to curare (from the bark of *Strychnos toxifera*, an otherwise harmless liana), they noted that the fowl did not die after sugar had been applied. It exhibited 'no sign of the least inconvenience'. As for the Indians themselves, La Condamine was less impressed. 'Insensibility is the basis. I cannot decide whether it should be honoured with the name apathy, or debased with that of stupidity. It doubtless arises from the small range of ideas, which do not extend beyond their needs.' An eighteenth-century European scientist, determined on investigation and then on change, was plainly at odds with the simpler life-style of the Amer-Indians whose means of living were long established.

The Omagua, for example, had complex agriculture and saw the forest as a rich warehouse, able to satisfy all their wishes. La Condamine did not appear to distinguish between technically advanced Indians and those who were, by the usual yardsticks, more primitive:

They are all gluttons to the point of voracity, when they have something with which to satisfy it; but sober when obliged by necessity to be so – they can do without anything and appear to want nothing . . . Enemies of work, indifferent to all motives of glory, honour or gratitude. Solely concerned with the immediate object and always influenced by it; without care for the future; incapable of foresight or reflection . . . They spend their lives without thinking, and grow old without emerging from childhood, of which they retain all the defects.

Possibly La Condamine would have thought and written much the same had he investigated the peasants of his own society; or perhaps he was merely reflecting Jesuit opinion. It was not right, he considered, for people to be so relaxed, in tune with the world, in keeping with nature. Seven years later Jean-Jacques Rousseau would publish the famous book in which he advanced his 'noble savage' theory, and maybe La Condamine then changed his attitude. At all events, when upon the Amazon he saw little good in Indians, 'pusillanimous poltroons to excess, unless transported by drunkenness'. Orellana would have disagreed; they had not been faint-hearted or cowardly when he had passed that way. Perhaps the missionaries, in heaping beneficence upon their flock, had transformed them into lesser mortals, at least as judged by one soldier-scientist who happened to be floating by.

It does shock to read of La Condamine's negative attitude towards the indigenous people of the Amazon. In all other spheres he is so forthright in his enthusiasm, seeing the best in everything, whether plant, animal, star, or physical property of the Earth. At first he was reticent about the local people, stating that 'to give an exact idea of the Americans' is impossible; 'one would have almost as many descriptions as there are nations among them'. Having thus discounted generalizations he then proceeds to generalize in noting that he has 'recognized in all of them the same fundamentals of character'. Charles Marie de la Condamine was no Jesuit, nor by any means an unthinking, insensitive colonial. He ought to have been impressed by Indian application of forest materials; but he saw no further than their 'puerile joy', their 'immoderate bursts of laughter without object or design'. It might have been different had he spent time with them, gone on hunting expeditions, learned of their rituals, understood their social laws; but he was more mathematician and natural historian than anthropologist, and he did not take the time.

On factual matters La Condamine's results stand on firmer ground. At the confluence of the Napo with the Amazon, making full use of the instruments he had transported for such a distance, he calculated that the site was 4 hours 45 minutes behind Paris. As one hour equals 15° of longitude, he was assessing the Napo/Amazon confluence as 15 × 4·75, or 71°25' west of Paris. In fact its true location is 72°30' west of Greenwich. With Paris 2°20' east of the prime meridian, he was therefore wrong by some 3°35' of longitude, or about 14 minutes, 20 seconds. He had made his observations 'by a good watch', but it may not have been tremendously good. The general opinion is that, given the difficulties involved and the state of the art at that time, he did extremely well. At least he had given that remote spot a longitude position when no one before him had done anything of the sort.

La Condamine was also most intrigued by the report, culled from Indians and priests, that the Amazon system linked with that of the Orinoco to the north. This alleged union surfaced in the story of Lope de Aguirre, in that his rebellious enthusiasm for returning speedily to Peru may have led him northwards from the Amazon and, by chance rather than intent, directly to the waters of the Orinoco. La Condamine was to stick to the Amazon, but learned all he could about the so-called canal between the two systems. He came to the conclusion that the Orinoco could be reached via both the Rio Negro (leading north-west from Manaus) and the Japurá (the next major river leading north-west). He was wrong about the Japurá and right about the Negro. If a traveller proceeds up it to San Carlos, which lies near the point where modern Colombia, Venezuela and Brazil meet, he can then turn east and find himself voyaging along the Casiquiare Canal. This is a natural waterway that travels within Venezuela's state of Amazonas to join the Orinoco near Esmeralda. La Condamine merely absorbed the story of communication between the waters of the two rivers, leaving it for future explorers to determine where the confluence might be. Not for slightly more than half a century did they finally learn where or why the link occurred.

During his voyage La Condamine noted that Portuguese territory was more prosperous than that under Spanish influence, the change becoming apparent by the time he reached São Paulo (de Olivença). This river town is near Brazil's modern frontier with Peru, showing that the old encroachments – by priests, settlers, explorers – still hold good today. Had Pedro de Teixeira travelled earlier, or had the Portuguese thought sooner of staking claims along the Amazon, Brazil might be an even bigger nation. As it is, some 2,000 miles of the formidable river lie within Brazilian territory, a not inconsiderable portion bearing in mind that the Tordesillas agreement gave all of it to Spain.

La Condamine's many revelations – for instance, the properties of rubber – would later be more fully investigated and exploited. His greatest contribution was to stimulate others. The Spanish had permitted him to enter and investigate their new world. He had taken full advantage of this temporary change in policy and proved beyond all doubt that a feast of great value was available to all who could acquire the necessary permission. For Europeans in particular, relatively starved of species and certainly short on warmth, the tropics held great appeal; but the Amazon became possessed of an extra fascination. It was exotic in every sense, its birds more brightly coloured, its fruits extravagant. The area had been cordoned off politically and was also secretive in itself, with the thick forest concealing almost everything it held in store. Perhaps it did contain serpents forty feet long, as was frequently alleged. If forest and river could produce poison for arrows, latex that bounced, fish with electricity, intoxicants and insecticides, and if they enabled the Indians to lead lives of indolence, the area plainly had more to reveal than could be seen upon the surface. La Condamine, after all, was merely passing by. He had asked, and he had listened, but he had hardly investigated. That task would have to be accomplished by others. He had simply shown the way.

La Condamine and Maldonado left Lagunas (which is still a mission station) on 23 July. They arrived at 'Grão Pará' (Belém) on 19 September. The distance between the two is about 2,600 miles, indicating an average of forty-five miles a day. The river's flow varies, but it would have been possible to have achieved such haste by doing nothing, by being a floating log. However, La Condamine did frequently step ashore, did spend time with his hosts, did set up instruments to measure everything (or so it would seem) within his grasp. He also made detours. For instance, he went many miles up the Rio Negro to discover that this river flowed from the north-west rather than the north as the Jesuit maps portrayed. Therefore, although the canoes frequently travelled at night, the Indian paddlers must have contributed quite substantially for the journey time to have been kept down to fifty-eight days between the Rio Huallaga, almost within sight of the Andes, and Pará, almost in view of the Atlantic. Francisco de Orellana, so impeded by warfare and the ever-present need to look for food, took four times longer in his journey from the mountains to the sea.

When on the river La Condamine enquired about the Amazons. It was over two centuries since Orellana had spread the tale of fighting women, but, even if the story was not generally believed, there was still curiosity. The Scythian name had been grafted on to the river and it was correct for a passing scientist, the first passing scientist, to investigate. No one he encountered had actually seen such people, but their parents had told of them. One man's grandfather had apparently spoken to a group up on the Cuchivero (in modern Venezuela). Although La Condamine constantly asserted that Indians often lied, it did intrigue him that so many different tribes told more or less the same story. The women lived always to the north, always in what is now Venezuelan territory, and they favoured green stones. His conclusion was that a matriarchal society which excluded men may once have lived in that general northern area, but he found no current evidence that this was so.

While staying in Pará the two scientists determined its latitude. Its inhabitants were of the proud opinion that their city stood fair and square upon the equator. La Condamine disillusioned them, perhaps not entirely to their liking, by giving the true figure of $1°28'$ S. He realized rather ruefully that Pará, 'adorned with streets finely laid out, and handsome houses', would have done very well for their hard-won equatorial measurements. It would have been less of a problem than Peru, being nearer, simpler and with fewer obstacles of the Cuenca kind. Had the Académie chosen Pará rather than Quito, and so made life easier for the surveying party, La Condamine would have long since returned home, but he would never have seen Panama or the

Pacific, the height of the Andes or the length of the Amazon. There were undoubted compensations in that choice of the west rather than the east of South America.

When at Pará the two men also investigated Marajó, the colossal island lying immediately to the north-west of the city. On maps of the time it was represented as a confusion of little islands. The scientists discovered it to be a single entity '150 leagues in circumference'. (In fact this one island is much larger, being of greater extent than either Belgium or Holland and about the size of Switzerland.) Although La Condamine wished to head north and home as soon as possible, he was initially delayed by a smallpox epidemic. He learned that a Carmelite missionary had inoculated people fifteen years earlier, not one of those so treated subsequently dying from the disease, and he therefore wondered why this practice was not more in vogue. (The different system of vaccination, which would make use of a cow's immunity to cowpox, was not tried for another half-century.)

La Condamine and Maldonado did eventually leave Pará shortly after Christmas 1743, having spent more time there than in travelling down the great river. They reached Cayenne on 23 February after – needless to say – making observations along the coast. They had again to wait for transport, and utilized the time examining manatees (which they had surely seen along the Amazon) and planting the *quinquina* seeds collected before their embarkation upon the river. They also paid a sort of homage at the spot where Jean Richer had done his work. His experiments, in which he had showed that pendulums beat slower and objects weighed less at Cayenne than in France, ought to have convinced the academicians. The work should have vindicated Newton and confounded the Cassinians, thus forestalling both the northern and the equatorial expeditions, but it seems merely to have antagonized those who favoured an Earth bulging at its poles. So great was this resentment, and so determined were the French (in general) to be proved correct, that a total of fifteen men had been despatched from Paris, to north and south, to bring back the right answer. In 1737 the northern party did so, and in 1745 the leader of the southern group finally returned to Paris.

He and his companion had been forced to wait at Cayenne for five months, and eventually embarked from Paramaribo further west along

Charles Marie de la Condamine

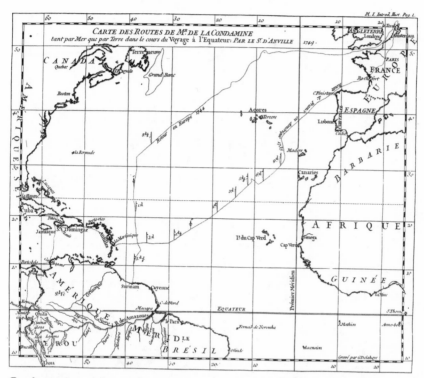

Condamine's travels, as portrayed in his own book, with the prime meridian passing intriguingly by Cape Verde.

the coast. The Dutch governor of Surinam had arranged a passage in a Dutch vessel which sailed on 28 August. It was twice attacked *en route* to Europe, once by a British ship and once, confusingly, by a French vessel. Neither confrontation was severe and Amsterdam was safely reached at the end of November. The acquisition of a *laissez-passer* took time, delaying La Condamine's arrival at Paris until 23 February 1745. The journey down the Amazon had taken a couple of months. Subsequent travel from Pará to Paris, which should have been a lesser problem, took nine times as long. The expedition's results had preceded him (in that Bouguer and Verguin had already arrived), but in any case the Lapland measurements had already settled the issue. Those from Peru were still important, in that they helped to determine the Earth's true shape, but the Newton/Cassini controversy was quite as dead as the two original protagonists.

185

JOURNAL

DU

VOYAGE FAIT PAR ORDRE DU ROI,

A L'EQUATEUR,

SERVANT D'INTRODUCTION HISTORIQUE

A LA

MESURE

DES

TROIS PREMIERS DEGRES

DU MERIDIEN.

Par M. DE LA CONDAMINE.

I, demens, & fœvas curre per Alpes. Juven. Sat. X.

A PARIS,

DE L'IMPRIMERIE ROYALE.

M. DCCLI.

Title page of Condamine's report upon his expedition, prime stimulus for other scientific adventurers, such as Humboldt.

Charles Marie de la Condamine

Far more important was the fact that the scientific history of South America had begun. La Condamine did not waste time before publishing accounts of the expedition, both the scientific side and the problems it had encountered. In 1746, one year after his return (and therefore eleven years after his departure), appeared *Lettre sur l'émeute populaire de Cuenca*. That explosion of riotous behaviour, leading to the death of the French doctor, still rankled. The author vigorously put his side of the affair and demanded that justice should be carried out. He also published a summary of the trip, but his major *Journal du voyage fait par ordre du roi a l'équateur* did not appear until 1751, along with two other publications of a more technical nature. For years he feasted upon his experiences, relating them, stimulating others, and generally being a hero of the time. After all it was a whole new continent he had traversed, and he had returned to a Europe hungry for the sort of news he had to tell.

However, the voyage made by order of the king to the equator was not truly over. There was still Jean Godin des Odonais in Quito. There was still his wife, the youthful Isabela. They too had to return to France and were contemplating the same astonishing scenic route that La Condamine had chosen. And they too, in their turn, or rather in their separate turns, would have more tales to tell.

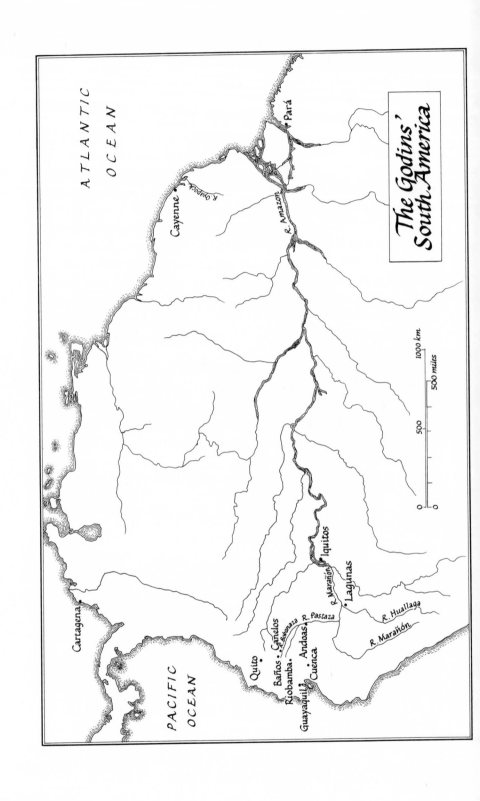

The Godins'
South America

ATLANTIC
OCEAN

Pará

Cayenne

R. Oyapoc

R. Amazon

1000 km.

500 miles

500

Iquitos

Lagunas

R. Marañón

Cartagena

R. Huallaga

R. Pastaza

R. Marañón

Quito

Baños · Canelos
Riobamba · R. Bobonaza

Andoas

Guayaquil · Cuenca

PACIFIC
OCEAN

VI

Monsieur and Madame Godin

AND THEIR SEPARATION

Anyone but you, sir, might be surprised at my undertaking thus lightly a voyage of 1,500 leagues for the mere purpose of preparing accommodations for a second, but you will know that travels in South America are undertaken with much less concern than in Europe; and those I had made during the twelve years for reconnoitring the ground for the meridian of Quito, fixing signals on the loftiest mountains, in going and returning from Cartagena, had made me perfectly a veteran.

The writer of the letter was Jean Godin des Odonais, chain-bearer to the earth-measurement expedition, and married to the Peruvian Isabela de Grandmaison y Bruno. The letter's recipient was his former leader, Charles Marie de la Condamine. It was dated 1749, which explains the 'twelve' years of travel in South America. What he had done, as his letter explained (although in no detail), was to travel down the Amazon solely to discover the rigours of such a journey, and whether they would be excessive for his wife. What he had also done, by the very act of making this trial journey, was to place himself at the wrong end of the Amazon. He was now distanced from Isabela and in no position to help her unless he could return upstream to his starting place. Hence the letter to his former chief, asking for assistance in returning to Peru. Jean Godin had not realized it would be quite so difficult to make the return journey upstream. Indeed he could not have thought greatly about the matter, and had probably set forth governed more by impatience than good sense.

At once one begins to wonder about this man. However lightly he had undertaken journeys to Cartagena (presumably with the intent of booking passage home from there), he should have known that an

Amazon venture was of a different order. Besides it was not one such journey. If all went well, and the conditions were found to be favourable, there would have to be three journeys, including one travelling upstream. It is easy to imagine everyone expressing surprise at his proposed triple expedition. Even La Condamine may have been amazed, despite the letter's disclaimer in its opening words. It would therefore seem, reading between the various lines, that Jean Godin was a man of inaction, a temporizer. He had apparently been encouraged into making the downstream journey because of his father's death (albeit nine years earlier). However, his wife Isabela stayed behind in Peru, and it would seem he had no intention of travelling to France without her, however pressing the demands from home. The voyage down-river was, therefore, no solution to anything. Worse still, it merely created problems.

When La Condamine left the Andes in mid-1743 there was only a vague suggestion that Jean Godin might have wished to accompany him. Perhaps the younger man assumed he would have an easier time going via Cartagena (and sailing from there, as Bouguer and Verguin had done). Or perhaps, when the news reached Peru of La Condamine's fairly effortless journey, Godin changed his mind, preferring the idea of river travel. The wishes and needs of Isabela were undoubtedly critical in all this vacillation. She had been pregnant when Godin (and she) might have accompanied La Condamine to the Atlantic. In the next few years she continued to be either pregnant or very recently delivered of a child. As time passed, however much the confinements were of his making, Godin became increasingly keen to leave. Eventually he did so, promising his wife that he would return for her as soon as possible. (At least his absence would mean, although this is never stated, that she would not be pregnant when he returned, and would therefore be more eligible for travel.)

Jean Godin left Riobamba, their home town, in March 1749 and arrived at Cayenne in French territory during April 1750. The journey cannot have been entirely without incident, but the Jesuits (and La Condamine's instructions on Godin's behalf) made it as easy as could be contrived. Nevertheless a major realization was to assault him at his journey's end. The fact that he, a Frenchman, had been able to wander about Spanish territory for so long, ever since the measurers had arrived at Cartagena in 1735, had blinded him to the political realities of the time. Spain, Portugal and France were three separate nations, occasionally good neighbours but generally suspicious of each other and always rivals. Spain had granted entry to the earth-measurers, but that had been an exception. The freedom granted had made the Council of the Indies most determined that such a passport should never again be issued. Somewhere, probably at Cayenne, it dawned upon Godin how privileged he had been. Quite suddenly his simple plan – of coming down, going back to fetch Isabela, and coming down again – grew hideously complex. As a first resort he therefore wrote to his powerful friend at the Académie asking for assistance.

Jean Godin also wrote to Monsieur Rouillé, the minister of the French Navy, asking him to use his influence upon the authorities in Lisbon. They had to be informed how he wished 'to ascend the Amazon for the purpose of proceeding to my family and bringing it back with me by the same channel'. From the point of view of a former chain-bearer, now residing in Cayenne, the request may have seemed straightforward. From a European viewpoint it was fraught with obstacle. Why on earth should the Portuguese permit a Frenchman to ascend their river for the sole purpose of descending it with some Spaniards? La Condamine was, nevertheless, determined to help his colleague. He visited Monsieur Rouillé personally, explaining that France owed Jean Godin every assistance it could possibly contrive. The man had been in France's employ within the Spanish empire for many difficult years and was now in a quandary. Both Portugal and Spain should permit his passage without delay.

Years passed and nothing was forthcoming. By no means did La Condamine forget his friend, but his requests were disregarded. The matter was primarily a matter for Lisbon, and the Portuguese capital stayed silent. Presumably it could see no gain in granting the permission. Meanwhile Jean Godin continued to live at Cayenne and his wife stayed on in Riobamba. He must have been a loving man not to have abandoned her; but his impotence over the problem of permission led him to think in other directions. Why did France behave in so servile a manner to Portugal? Could she not take some initiative? France had not been doing well in North America in the late 1750s and early 1760s, having been defeated at Quebec by the British in 1759, ceded much of the huge territory of Louisiana to Spain in 1762 (although it was to be ceded back again in 1800), and lost that part of the Louisiana province east of the Mississippi to Britain in 1763. She needed some gains to make good these losses. So why did France not take over the Amazon?

It is easy to imagine how such an idea entered Godin's frustrated and increasingly impatient head. Much of his life was slipping by. The time he had spent in Peru – and that was long enough – had now been equalled by the time spent in Cayenne. France was a powerful nation and needed new possessions. (The Seven Years War, ending in 1763, also lost India for the French.) New lands were essential, and what better than those around the world's largest river flowing through the world's greatest tropical forest? He had seen that river and could give advice. He knew the critical points to be captured and how easily the Amazon might provide a route to the Pacific, for surely anything was better than Cape Horn. He therefore wrote to the French Minister for Foreign Affairs, Étienne Choiseul, a former protégé of Madame de Pompadour.

Godin knew that the writing of such a letter was a risky undertaking. In it he was advocating war against the Portuguese, the very people from whom permission was being sought to retrieve his family. If the letter did fall into enemy hands it would surely put paid to any possible Portuguese assistance. It would deny him Isabela for ever. And it would not help his reputation in France should the facts of the letter be disgorged from Lisbon. Relations between France and Portugal (and with Spain as well) would be terribly damaged by such a revelation, involving as it did the Minister for Foreign Affairs. He therefore entrusted his carefully worded suggestion to a missionary returning from Guiana to France. The man seemed reliable, and would certainly destroy the letter should his ship be captured. However, as the months progressed without any acknowledgement, Godin became intensely worried. Had it been intercepted? Had hopes of a passport been dashed for ever?

This man of inaction, who had been tempted into a positive step, must have been overwhelmed by a fearful feeling of regret. How could he have been so impulsive, so foolish? How could he have put everything at risk? In fact Choiseul did receive the letter but never replied. Even if he thought its proposals interesting he would hardly have despatched an answer across the Atlantic to an *académicien's* former assistant now languishing in Cayenne. It is highly improbable he would risk communication of any kind, and even more so if he warmed to the idea. Godin, desperate with impatience and haunted by self-criticism, became increasingly certain his letter was in Lisbon, which must mean that permission would never be granted. So he ordered the building of a boat – the finances for such an undertaking are not discussed – and actually set sail for France. Self-doubt, uncertainty and straightforward fear then assailed him all the more. Had news of his departure from Cayenne been circulated? Would he be imprisoned and possibly executed in Lisbon? The anxieties proved too much for the former chain-bearer. After only a few leagues of sailing he returned to Cayenne and its security. He might not be gaining anything by staying there, but at least he kept alive.

Suddenly, as a complete turn-about, a small Portuguese vessel arrived at Cayenne on 18 October 1765. It was a galliot and had arrived from Pará. This type of vessel, a form of galley, was equipped with oars. Most suitable for river navigation, it was ideal for implementing the instructions carried on board. These, by order of the king of Portugal, were to collect Jean Godin and transport him up-river for the purpose of collecting his family. There would be an intermediate stop at Pará, and the vessel would travel thereafter as far as possible along the Amazon. It would then wait while the French scientist proceeded to Riobamba and collected the members of his household. He and they would then be transported to Pará.

The miracle had occurred. At long last the requests from Paris had borne fruit. Some thirty years after he had arrived in South America, twenty-three years after his marriage, and sixteen after he had last seen his wife, Jean Godin had been equipped with a suitable boat and, yet more importantly, with permission to reunite his family. It ought to have been the happiest of occasions. In fact it was nothing of the sort. Godin's obsession with his letter, and his assumption that it had fallen into Portuguese hands, led him to suspect everything emanating from Portugal. He was therefore extremely suspicious of the galliot. For years he has been waiting at Cayenne, wanting nothing more than a *laissez-passer* to let him proceed up-river, when suddenly an entire ship, equipped with thirty oars and oarsmen, arrives to do his bidding. It unnerved him wholly. He pretended to be ill. In time he became ill, and still the boat remained. From the galliot captain's point of view, he was under orders from his king and had no alternative but to wait. In Godin's mind the very persistence of the Portuguese ship weakened such resolve to go on board as he did possess. It was plainly a trap. They had intercepted his letter and had come to effect punishment. Revenge would be carried out as soon as he was within their grasp. It was better, by far, to stay in bed.

There was, in short, an impasse. This was settled by Cayenne's governor. He certainly knew of Godin, but in all probability did not know of Godin's letter. He therefore could not understand Godin's reluctance to accompany the Portuguese. For years this unhappy remnant from the equatorial expedition had been bemoaning his lot and begging, beseeching, demanding assistance from Portugal. It then arrived, in a most practical form, and Godin refused to take advantage of it. The governor was also not greatly pleased with a Portuguese vessel endlessly at anchor in a French harbour, and grew increasingly intolerant of its unwilling passenger. He and Godin exchanged unfriendly letters, which became steadily ruder until the governor's patience snapped. He ordered the galliot to leave port.

Jean Godin had lost his courage but not all his reason. In his place was to go 'a person whom I had long known and in whom I had confidence'. To this man, Tristan d'Oreasaval, he gave money and letters. The correspondence was addressed to various people *en route*, and to the principal Jesuit in Quito, and to Isabela. The money was to assist in any way it could, and Tristan agreed to wait at Lagunas for Madame Godin to arrive. He would then accompany her to Cayenne. Jean Godin expected considerable loyalty from his friend, far more than he should have done. Tristan not only used the money on his own account, almost instantly, but was equally disloyal about the letters. Some of them arrived in Quito, where they were read by all sorts of inquisitive parties; but they never reached the Father General and never Isabela. However, as in any land where rumour is the principal communication, she did get wind of them. Apparently some vessel was on some river; this had, it was said, been sent to fetch her; her husband was not on board for he was ill, but he was still alive. Of course Isabela was hungry for all such crumbs of information; but, in truth, was there such a ship? And was it waiting to take her down the Amazon? Her only possible recourse was to despatch a servant to discover the facts. She did so, and in time – in two years' time – Joachim returned. He confirmed the rumours. There was a boat. It was waiting for her. And so was her husband, who was living in Cayenne.

In this story the passage of time slips past almost carelessly. Godin had been waiting in Guiana for sixteen years when the galliot arrived. It stayed at Cayenne until the following year before being ordered to depart. Passage up the Amazon took eight months before the boat's arrival at Lagunas started all the rumours. These had to reach Isabela before her servant could be despatched on his two-year mission. Therefore it was not until 1769 that she could make the most momentous decision of her lifetime. She would somehow reach this boat and sail with it. At long last she would be reunited with her husband. Neither was young any more – she was forty and he fifty-seven – but they were still man and wife. It was plainly up to her, the younger of the two, to effect the reunion. Besides, there was the galliot, there was the permission, and the journey would be downstream. Isabela Godin, born De Grandmaison y Bruno, made preparations to depart. She would travel as her husband had done precisely twenty years beforehand, as La Condamine had done even earlier.

The reason they had not travelled with La Condamine had been her pregnancy. Further pregnancies had then delayed her husband's departure, but all the confinements had been to no avail, as all four of her children had died. Nothing dramatic had killed them. They had all perished from the standard murderers: yellow fever, malaria, dysentery. (These are still the greatest killers in tropical South America.) The last to die was the youngest child, a girl who was nineteen at the time and the only one who had never seen her father. As for the child-bride, now so brutally released from the responsibilities of motherhood, she was about the same age as La Condamine had been when he set forth upon the river, but she might have wished herself a few years younger and stronger. On the other hand her independence from her husband, and her suffering, had tempered her metal in a manner to stand her in good stead. An older woman might have succumbed upon the journey; so too a younger one with less resilience, less steel within her. Moreover her thoughts and cares were no longer divided between husband and children. There was no one left but the Frenchman who had proposed to her back in 1742. Somehow she had to reach him. There was no other way.

Isabela was redoubtable – her decision to descend the Amazon is sufficient proof – and some of her spirit may have emanated from her father. Pedro de Grandmaison neither prevented her from leaving nor, it would seem, discouraged her. Instead, although in his sixties, he tried to smooth the initial part of her undertaking by going ahead of her. Travelling through the Andes, meeting the rapid torrents running down their eastern side, involves greater hazards than floating upon the tranquil Amazon. He therefore left their home town of Riobamba, passed through Baños and reached Canelos, a missionary outpost of the Dominicans. *En route* he made certain his daughter would be comfortable, and each relevant authority was advised of her coming. At Canelos the friars made arrangements for Indians to paddle his daughter and her party down the Bobonaza to Andoas on the river Pastaza. There, at this further mission station, other Indians would paddle her to Lagunas, where the galliot was still waiting to transport the Godin family. (Once again the time-scale and patience can astonish the twentieth century. That boat had arrived at Cayenne in October 1765. It was now October 1769 and there must, one assumes, have been a certain restlessness on board as the months passed, as the years passed.)

Before he left Andoas for Lagunas, where he would make extra provision for Isabela's safety, her father wrote to her. He informed her of the care he had taken on her behalf, of the various arrangements, and recommended as small a party as possible. The canoes were not large; small numbers were preferable. However, by that time she had already amassed a sizeable contingent. It consisted of thirty-one Indians (who could always be dismissed if need be), three female servants, Joachim (the faithful Negro who had already travelled to Lagunas), two of her brothers, and also one nephew, aged twelve. At the last moment a trio of Frenchmen were added to the party. These three, one of whom said he was a doctor, are a bit of a mystery. The men claimed to have arrived from the Pacific, as well they might have done, and they ingratiated themselves into Isabela's party. There is no more information about them. It can only be assumed they were young, experienced travellers, whose potential value to Isabela's expedition outweighed the liability of three more bodies for the small canoes. In any case she accepted them.

Departure from Riobamba took place in late 1769. Isabela had sold all the effects she did not need for her journey. She had said the necessary prayers and had bidden farewell to those of her family still remaining. Now she must reach Canelos, find the canoes her father had arranged, proceed via Andoas to Lagunas, meet up with the galliot, be rowed downstream to Pará, and proceed up the coast to her husband waiting at Cayenne. With luck she would be with him in three months or so. The long years of separation would finally be concluded.

It had always been known that the first leg of the journey would be difficult, the forested, mountainous section leading to Canelos. It proved to be as bad as had been foreseen. The rain poured, the forest was all-enveloping, and the party from Riobamba slid and fell along the path. Fortunately this passage, a straight-line distance of sixty miles, took Isabela and her team no more than seven days. The thought of canoes and a more relaxed form of travel may have encouraged them to make haste through such unpleasantness. What they did not know was that one of Isabela's father's party had been carrying smallpox. This scourge, particularly of Indians, was to destroy Canelos. Don Pedro had left the mission village a flourishing and healthy establishment. His daughter and her contingent, so eager to see the place, found it a disaster. Its inhabitants had first set fire to the place, believing flames would destroy the virulence, and had then fled. The village was therefore totally empty, but still smouldering, when Isabela arrived. She and her mixed group spent their first night within the destruction, save for the thirty-one Indians. They too had vanished into the forest. Anywhere was preferable to a village of death.

On the following morning four local Indians were found a few miles distant. Isabela spoke to them in Quechua, the common tongue along the rivers. From them she learned that everyone from the village had either died or had disappeared in the forest. As for the promised canoes these too had gone; only one canoe and a raft remained. While others in her party lamented their misfortune, or even recommended return to Riobamba, Isabela was beginning to show some of her fortitude. She hired the four men and ordered the loading of both raft and canoe. She would not countenance the notion of return. Twenty years of waiting were not to be lengthened into heaven knew how long because of one set-back. Besides, there were two craft, four Indians, plenty of supplies, and a broad river flowing speedily where they wished to go.

When the next day dawned they no longer had the four Indians. The men had absconded, together with their payment in advance. Small-pox, and the horror of its rampage, could make everything fearful, particularly travelling away from home with a group of strangers, the kind that had brought the disease a few weeks earlier. At first the three Frenchmen argued strongly for return; no longer did the trip in the company of a moderately wealthy lady have much appeal. Working on Isabela's behalf for continuing the journey was the Rio Bobonaza, hurrying along fast enough to render an upstream journey virtually impossible. As she knew from her father's letter the next port of call, Andoas, was but five days distant. The Frenchmen then saw the strength of her argument, and of the current. They agreed to carry on, one of them even offering to be steersman for the canoe. He did the job well enough, negotiating between rocks and trees as the water sped along, until his hat blew off. He grabbed for it, missed, leant too far and fell into the water. A floating log knocked his head and he vanished, never to be seen again. It would seem, in that it is never mentioned again in any account of this voyage, as if the raft was also lost, perhaps on this occasion. At all events the original party of forty-one, including the Indians, had now been reduced to nine. It was the tenth day of travel out of Riobamba.

Later that same day the canoe itself struck a log. All the occupants were thrown into the swirling water but did manage to scramble to the shore. Joachim was a tower of strength, not only assisting Isabela to reach land but then retrieving the canoe. Some of their equipment had gone, more had been damaged, and most of their food had disap-peared. If Don Pedro could have imagined the difficulties that would assail his daughter he would never have carried on to Lagunas. If she had anticipated the problems already encountered she might have been less determined to set forth from Riobamba; but one is beginning to suspect she would have left home whatever the outcome. Her absent husband and four dead children had made her desperate.

The surviving pair of Frenchmen, no longer possessed of illusions about effortless travel with a wealthy entourage, came up with a plan. The doctor in particular was in favour of an advance party hurrying on to Andoas. That place was now four days' travel downstream and would surely provide assistance. Indian canoeists could then return upstream to collect the rest of the party. To Isabela, and also to her brother Eugenio, the scheme had major drawbacks, such as the removal of their transport. She, and he, may even have known of Orellana's story, of how he too had offered to collect supplies but had been unable to return, thereby leaving Pizarro in considerable distress. Nevertheless she did consent to the doctor's departure. With him went Joachim, the tried and tested servant. And with them went their only craft.

Those left behind initially ate handsomely. Sufficient food remained to keep them in good stead for a few days, perhaps a dozen, by which time help would surely reach them. Those dozen days passed and no canoe appeared around the downstream bend in the river. Joaquín, the twelve-year-old nephew, became sick, so Isabela spent the days caring for him. The others sought for food such as tubers, and they occasionally killed a bird, but for the most part their strength dwindled along with their supplies. The Frenchman's appetite altered after seeing the three female servants bathing in the river, and there is mention in the written records of rape along the river-bank; but that passion soon died in the overwhelming misery of the situation. The same individual became hysterical one night after seeing a vampire bat sucking from his foot, and soon afterwards Isabela Godin decided her party should wait no more. It had been four weeks since the canoe had left them. Her nephew was deteriorating fast; all were suffering. It was time to make a move.

She ordered the construction of a raft. This was built speedily, perhaps too speedily. One wonders what equipment they still possessed, and even more about the quality of this piece of work. No sooner had it been launched, with the two brothers using poles at either end, than it hit a tree, disintegrated and caused all seven occupants to fall into the river. Once more they had to scramble to the bank, but on this occasion everything was lost – such foodstuffs as remained, such equipment, such clothes as they possessed, save for those they wore. Don Pedro would, once again, have been appalled had he known one particle of his daughter's suffering. Instead he knew nothing of the kind, no news of any sort having reached Lagunas. However, some apprehension might have begun, some twinge of uncertainty. If all had gone well the canoeing parties from Canelos and Andoas should have brought Isabela to him before that day when everything was lost, but he did not even know – for sure – of her departure date from Riobamba. Travel in South America, certainly in 1769, did not happen to a rigid timetable. Delays and mishaps were integral to every journey, although not necessarily of the scale assaulting Madame Godin. Hers was not a misadventure; it was now a disaster, imperilling the lives of all concerned.

It is difficult to know precisely where this tragedy was happening. Some accounts place it on the Rio Pastaza after that river's union with the Bobonaza, but problems had struck speedily after the water journey had begun. Little distance can have been achieved between the dead village of Canelos and the point where Isabela's party was in grave trouble. It therefore seems probable they were still upon the Bobonaza, and still a few days' travel above Andoas. Not that they now had the means to reach that mission station. Not that they now had the strength or, most of them, the faintest hope of doing so.

Joaquín, the only child in the party, was the first to die. He did not recover after the raft's destruction and succumbed that night. The three female servants were named Rosa, Héloïse and Elvia. The eldest, Rosa, never awoke from a sleep; Héloïse then wandered off, never to return, and Elvia soon perished. None of these bodies was buried; no one had the energy. Both brothers then died, one telling his beads as he did so. By this time the remaining Frenchman was also dead. Surrounded by death, Isabela Godin lay waiting for her own. The stench about her, in that warm tropical air, must have been horrendous. The sense of desolation, with no food, no hope and no friends, must have been equally overwhelming. The others had all been younger, and yet had died. Her time would surely come, probably quite soon.

After two days she did not so much wake from her nightmare as realize she was still alive. It is difficult to imagine the awfulness lying around her. Unknown bodies, rotting and alive with flies, are bad enough. The corpses of loved ones, untended and stinking, must be of a different dimension. Her two younger brothers were there, for whom she felt responsibility as well as love. (It was, after all, her expedition, rather than their own.) Then there was her nephew, far too young for such an undertaking. He had been the first to die; his body was assuredly the most decayed. As for Rosa and Elvia, she had probably known them for years, part of her household even if not related by blood. Then, adding to the stench, there was the single Frenchman, possibly not greatly loved but no less dead than all the rest.

Maybe it was the nausea that pricked her into activity, creating a sudden longing to leave that terrible scene. Before putting it behind her she fashioned some sandals from the shoes of her brothers; then she stumbled off into the forest. She must have been exceptionally weak, having experienced the starvation that had helped to kill the others. She was not a country girl, accustomed to forests, knowing what to do. So she wandered this way and that, scarcely caring where she went. It is proper, when lost in such a place, to walk until finding a stream, to follow that stream downhill so as to meet a larger stream and then the highway of a river. She does not seem to have followed this maxim, but maybe she met no water, or had had her fill of rivers, or – which is most probable – just wandered as Héloïse had surely done, not knowing or minding where she went. She was alone, lost, and too miserable to care. However, unlike the others, she did not die.

For nine days she drifted, staggered, meandered through the forest. She may have found some food; she did not know for sure. She may have proceeded in a particular direction, but she had no plan. She simply wandered, more dead than alive but still not dead. Something in her was succeeding that had failed in all the others. A middle-aged woman, mother of four buried children, was still upon her feet while her companions were rotting, having forfeited their ability to live.

In the meantime Joachim, the loyal slave Joachim, was returning upstream. He should have returned earlier, having left to find assistance over a month before, but he had been under the direction of the French doctor. That man, it would seem, had never had any intention of returning to Isabela. His interests lay only in proceeding further onwards. It took Joachim time to disentangle himself from the uncaring Frenchman, and then to persuade the Fathers at Andoas to render help. They eventually supplied him with a canoe, with paddlers and with some food. Travelling upstream took longer than descending, but they arrived shortly after Isabela Godin had taken to the forest. Later she recollected that she might have heard her name being called, but at the time had not been wholly in charge of her senses. Joachim undoubtedly did call out for her, having landed near the modest shelter he had built. Of course he would have called, in desperation, in misery, for there was nothing else to do.

And then he found the bodies. He did not stop to count them, to assess which corpses belonged to whom. He did not observe that those of Héloïse and Isabela were missing. He simply fled to the canoe. With terrible urgency he and the Indians paddled downriver to tell Andoas the news. Madame Godin and her party were dead. The rescue had arrived too late. Joachim had failed his mistress, had failed her utterly. The bearer of these terrible tidings then continued downriver to inform Isabela's father, still waiting at Lagunas. The old man learned that he had lost not only his daughter, according to the faithful messenger, but two sons and a great-nephew. He surely railed at himself for having failed her, for not having accompanied her. He may even have accused Joachim for arriving with help so late.

He certainly wrote to Jean Godin, still languishing in Cayenne, but the earth-measurer had already heard the news. The bush-telegraph of the river sent facts downstream more quickly than any letter could travel. The same message also crossed the Atlantic, reaching La Condamine. One more tragedy had been added to his equatorial expedition. In France, and much of Europe, the story of Isabela Godin became the talk of every drawing-room. Louis XV's chaotic reign still had four more years to run, but the tale of the Peruvian mother who was married to a Frenchman, had been separated from her husband for twenty years, and had perished in the forest on her way to reach him, became very widely known. It had such pathos, such loyalty, such tragedy, and was the talk of every town. The Amazon backdrop gave it extra potency.

However, Isabela was not dead. After those nine days she encountered two Indians. Some reports suggest she backed away from them, terrified at this extra danger, before realizing she had little to lose. Others say she approached them boldly, striking fear into them, since dishevelled, filthy and partly deranged white women did not customarily appear from the forest. In any case she spoke to them in Quechua, some words of which they knew. Soon they were not only feeding her but transporting her downstream. During the first week of the new year of 1770 they brought her to Andoas, a couple of months after she and forty-one others had departed from Riobamba. The Indians who fled at Canelos were probably still alive, and so were Joachim and the French doctor, but death had otherwise been triumphant, save for this sick, weak and astonishing woman.

Although poorly, she still had spirit. By way of gratitude to the two Indians who had befriended her she took two small 'chains of gold' from her neck. These she presented to them. At once the missionaries removed both necklaces from the Indians, giving them some cotton cloth as substitute. Isabela was incensed, so much so that she immediately ordered canoe and canoeists to take her away. She was too weak to walk, and the good fathers may have felt a touch humble as this redoubtable woman was carried from their presence. They might also have given her some cloth as, until an Indian woman took pity, she was wearing nothing save 'the soles of the shoes of her dead brothers'. Downstream she encountered Loreto, yet another mission station. Its Father, shocked by her condition, offered to send her back to Riobamba, equipped with every need. Once again, although without hatred on this occasion, she rebelled. 'God has preserved me . . . amid the perils in which all my companions perished . . . If I were not to prosecute my first intention, I should esteem myself guilty of counteracting the views of providence . . .' To all the story's ingredients of pathos, courage, terror and love was now added that of divine intervention. No wonder it fared so well.

The priest sent a message downstream to Pedro de Grandmaison. It arrived very shortly after Joachim had appeared bearing his terrible news. The old Peruvian had still lost two sons and a great-nephew, but his cherished daughter was alive. Word was immediately despatched to Jean Godin, and the galliot prepared at long last, at very long last, to move from its moorings. The captain and crew had been unbelievably tenacious in waiting to achieve their mission. Arriving at Cayenne in 1765, despatched from there the following year, reaching Lagunas at the end of 1766, and only hearing good news of their intended passenger early in 1770, they should have received rich reward for their constancy. Even their boat was in good order when the occasion came to move.

Don Pedro did not spend any more time at Lagunas once he had heard of Isabela's survival. On board the galliot, and taking Joachim with him, he travelled the short distance down the Huallaga to its meeting with the Marañón. Then it was upstream to the confluence with the Pastaza, and somewhere along the way he met his daughter being paddled downstream. Nothing is recorded of their encounter. There is no need; the scene is not difficult to imagine. The rest of the journey was simplicity itself, at least when compared with the hardship and misfortune that preceded the meeting of canoe and galliot. The Portuguese ship that had been languishing for four years in Spanish territory took father and daughter downstream for the 2,000 miles to the river's mouth. Then it turned north, as so many others had done on meeting the Atlantic from the Amazon, and it followed the coast to reach Cayenne.

The impossible had happened. The Godins were to be reunited. Jean could not wait on shore after he had heard of Isabela's impending arrival. In a canoe he hurried to meet the ship and was soon climbing on board. Later, and in matter-of-fact manner, he wrote of this meeting, truthfully but hardly effusively:

On board this vessel, after twenty years' absence and a long endurance on either side of alarms and misfortunes, I again met with a cherished wife whom I had almost given over every hope of seeing again. In her embraces I forgot the loss of the fruits of our union; nay, I even congratulated myself on their premature death, as it saved them from the dreadful fate which befell their uncles in the wood of Canelos beneath the eyes of their mother, who certainly would never have survived the sight.

The date was mid-1770. Of Godin's twenty-eight years of married life, less than seven had been spent in his wife's company. For the remainder the width of South America had been between them.

The united family did not hurry on to France. This delay may appear contrary, considering that nothing now prevented them and Cayenne was not their home. On the other hand Don Pedro, Isabela and Joachim were all South Americans, in that they had never lived anywhere else, and even Jean Godin had spent the greater part of his life in the New World. Why bother to go to Europe? They all moved instead into Jean's house on the river Oyapock, some eighty miles south of Cayenne, and there they stayed until 1773. Once again it is easy to wonder about money, and where it was coming from, but this practi-

Monsieur and Madame Godin

Isabela Godin des Odonais, whose epic journey became the talk of every salon when she emerged so dramatically from the forest.

cality is never mentioned. They did attempt to sue Tristan, the friend entrusted with money and letters, and even won the case against him; but the man had nothing, so litigation had been pointless. Don Pedro was not concerned about his prolonged absence from Riobamba, and perhaps his wife was already dead. If not, his efforts to see his daughter reunited with her husband had, in being successfully concluded, caused a different separation. He and Jean Godin had simply changed their roles.

The capricious Louis XV had still one more year on the throne when the most famous South American family eventually left Cayenne. The Boston Tea Party happened that same year, helping to initiate the American War of Independence. France also was moving towards revolution. Europe was in ferment and soon would be in turmoil; but everyone knew, and talked about, the extraordinary story of Madame Godin. Her determination to reach her husband, the loss of her comrades, her own presumed loss, her magical reappearance from the forest, her trip down the Amazon, and the final happy ending – it was all legendary. The principals may therefore have wanted their fame to recede before embarking for France; but they did eventually set sail. Their ship arrived at La Rochelle, the same port as the earth-measurers had used on their departure. Jean Godin had then been twenty-three. Thirty-eight years were to pass by before he saw it again.

A semi-paralysed, extremely deaf old man was standing at the quayside as the ship docked. Recent years had not been kind to Charles Marie de la Condamine. Paralysis and deafness had started when he was in his fifties; neither had improved since then. In 1757, when aged fifty-six, he had married for the first time. She was twenty years younger and also his niece, thus a papal dispensation had been required before the betrothal could take place. At no time did La Condamine's zest for science diminish. At all times he made himself available for consultation on every subject of interest to him – smallpox, the need for a standard measurement, anything and everything to do with South America. In scientific circles he *was* South America. No man knew more about the place, or had experimented more with its products, such as curare, rubber, quinine. A rival might have been the brilliant Pedro Maldonado. He too became an *académicien*, and he was elected to other learned societies. The Royal Society in London made him a Fellow. When he visited that city to be present at his election, he caught measles. As with so many others before and after him, he could not survive being transplanted to a different world. He had survived many South American perils, but succumbed to rubeola.

La Condamine was to die the year after he stood at La Rochelle waiting for his friend. A few months earlier, calling himself only 'half a man' as he did so, he had listed the members of the equatorial expedition and recounted their fates. Even before he had left South America there were three dead (Couplet, Senièrgues, Morainville) and two insane (Jussieu, Mabillon). Since then Louis Godin, Jean's cousin who had accepted a post at Lima, had died while living in Cadiz, in Spain. Pierre Bouguer, who had carried on his form of personal warfare with La Condamine long after returning to France, had also died. Hugot, the man in charge of the instruments, was still in Quito. Antonio de Ulloa, younger of the two Spanish naval scientists, had spent time as Governor of Louisiana (that huge area awarded to Spain in 1762) and was also still alive. The expedition was therefore a fragment of its former self, but at last Jean Godin had returned safely. It must have given the former chain-bearer inordinate pleasure to see his old leader waiting at the docks. It must have given that leader equal pleasure to see one last accomplice safely home, together with his bride. For a quite extraordinary length of time it had seemed as if such an event would never come to pass.

After such an astonishing reunion, prevented for so long and achieved with such courage and fortitude, the Godin family cannot be left on the dock at La Rochelle, however completely they had at last detached themselves from the river Amazon. It is true they did not go back, but their lives had a few more years to run.

Jean Godin's father had died in 1740, well before the expedition had completed its work within Peru. His mother had died in 1751 shortly after Jean had started his long sojourn in Cayenne. His only brother had died in France even before the expedition had begun, and there were two widowed sisters. Pressure therefore existed for Jean, as the surviving male, to take charge of the family's concerns, notably the land bought by Jean's father near the family home at Saint-Amand

Montrond on the river Cher. In Cayenne he had resisted this, even after his mother had died. So far as Jean Godin was concerned his greater duty lay in waiting for his wife to come downstream.

That duty done, it was to Saint-Amand in Berry that Jean, Isabela and her father proceeded, once the business of arrival had been completed. La Condamine had managed to acquire a royal pension for his colleague, merited by 'zeal and labour during the operations on the equator of Peru'. From Saint-Amand the pensioned Jean Godin was able to write to his dying leader: 'My wife is now with her father in the bosom of my family where she has been received with tenderness.' It was surely a joy to La Condamine that this final episode of his expedition was ending so happily. Presumably the family members most welcoming to Isabela were the two widows. They must have been relieved and delighted by Jean's return, together with his wife, after such a span of time.

Isabela's father never returned to Peru. According to one account he was 'locked up in his reverie', an old man frittering time away until time was ready to kill him. He believed himself back in the splendour of life among the Andes. In essence he never truly recovered from the loss of two sons and a daughter, followed by the extra shock of that daughter emerging from the forest. A happy event was the arrival in France of Jean-Antoine de Grandmaison y Bruno, the old man's grandson. After the tragedy he had been living with his uncle, his father having been one of Isabela's two brothers who had died in the forest. At Saint-Amand he first lived with his grandfather and aunt and then married a local girl, Magdeleine Picot. There was then another death. The old Pedro, who had taken every precaution for his daughter's journey, who had preceded her down-river, and who had then heard that his precautions had been as good as valueless, died in 1780. They buried him in the larger of the two cemeteries within the parish of Saint-Amand.

The two sisterly widows had died even before the old Peruvian. The Godins were without posterity, since their children had perished before the journey and no more had been born to them. Jean and Isabela were therefore now alone in the family home on the Rue Hôtel-Dieu in Saint-Amand. Jean occupied himself primarily with the lands that were his inheritance, but his thoughts, apparently, were forever

Monsieur and Madame Godin

On 14 May 1988 a bust of St Amand's most famous citizen was formally unveiled near her final home.

turning towards South America. He gave advice to the 'interested minister' concerning the transport of cattle to Guiana, and how business should be conducted with the Portuguese. He also worked diligently, and presumably with the considerable co-operation of his wife, on a Quechua-French dictionary and a Quechua grammar. Isabela was fluent in this Inca lingua franca from the Andes and the upper reaches of the Peruvian Amazon, but it is easy to wonder about the potential sales of such a volume. Admittedly French was a global lingua franca at the time, but Spanish was dominant among the Spanish possessions. In any case, neither the Quechua grammar nor the dictionary was ever published.

Isabela was physically in France but remained emotionally in South America. Only once did she recount the details of her terrible drama, but, when alone, she would frequently open a little ebony box. In it were the soles of the shoes she had prized from her brother's corpse as well as the cloth she had been given by the Andoas Indians who, more than the missionaries, had helped her to cover her nakedness. Her original beauty had been marred by insect bites and she had developed a nervous tic. This increased when reference was made to her adventures and would only diminish when the subject had been changed. It was, wrote a chronicler, a souvenir of those terrible times.

Jean Godin des Odonais died at his home on 1 March 1792. He was then seventy-nine and still, despite the revolution three years earlier, receiving his state pension. It would probably have been terminated before long, being a privilege from earlier and regal times. His wife, Isabela, seventeen years his junior and married to him half a century earlier, survived him by only six months, dying on 28 September in that same year. Despite their tremendous and famous separation they had, by the end, spent the greater part of their married life in each other's company. As they were without issue their property passed mainly to Isabela's nephew, Jean-Antoine. His marriage to Magdeleine Picot had led to three children, but only one survived, Félix de Grandmaison y Bruno.

The town of Saint-Amand Montrond lies 150 direct miles south of Paris, just where the flat terrain of France begins lifting itself up to meet the Alps. Those who know about the history of this town, and certainly those who administer its library, are adamant that its two most

Monsieur and Madame Godin

renowned citizens have been Jean Godin des Odonais and his lady, the beautiful Isabela whom he married in Peru and who, after considerable adventures, was brought safely to his family home in France. There they lived, most peacefully, for their final nineteen years.

London Pari[s]
Bordeaux
Corunna
Lisbon

Azores

Madeira
Canary Is.
Tenerife

ATLANTIC

Washington •Philadelphia

Tropic of Can[cer]

Cape Verde
Is.

Havana

OCEAN

Acapulco

Cartagena   Cumaná
        Caracas
    Bogotá   R. Orinoco

PACIFIC   Equato[r]

Quito   Casiquiare Canal
Riobamba •Cotopaxi   R. Napo   R. Amazon
        ▲Chimborazo
Cuenca

Callao •Lima

Tropic of Cap[ricorn]

OCEAN

        R. Paraguay

Humboldt Current

                URUGUAY
        Buenos Aires

0   1000 miles
0   2000 km

The New World of
Humboldt and Bonpland

VII

Baron von Humboldt
INSPIRATION TO THE WORLD

The 'last great universal man' was born a few weeks before Isabela Godin left Riobamba in Peru. Often given that flattering description, or called the 'greatest man who ever lived', Baron Friedrich Wilhelm Karl Heinrich Alexander von Humboldt started his life in Berlin, capital of Prussia, on 14 September 1769. He was therefore four years old when the Godins left South America, five when La Condamine died and twenty-three when Jean and Isabela so finally concluded the great expedition to measure the planet's shape. Nevertheless his journeys within South America were next in line to those of the earth-measurers. As soon as he was able he picked up the baton they had carried. He had been inspired by their achievements, their tales from the fantastic continent, and their science; but he quickly realized they had scarcely scratched the surface. The more he read of South America, virtually all of it penned by La Condamine, the more attracted he was, and the more determined to go there. Those closed Iberian kingdoms, kept from foreign eyes (as far as possible) for two and a half centuries, and only temporarily opened to a small team from France, were to be investigated by the most critical gaze of all. In the last year of the eighteenth century Alexander von Humboldt arrived in South America.

The fact that he was wealthy, well-connected, fluent in several languages, burning with ambition, and a renaissance man able to take full advantage of South America, did not mean he could get there immediately. La Condamine's expedition had taken place after a remarkable chain of circumstance starting with the War of the Spanish Succession and ending with Anglo-French rivalry concerning the

213

planet's shape. No individual, however talented, could expect immediate permission to follow in his footsteps, receiving similar Spanish co-operation. The door had been prized open to let in the French contingent. It was then closed – if anything, yet more firmly. More providential circumstance was necessary before the door would open once again.

Besides, Humboldt was consumed with such fire that anything and anywhere seemed to attract him. La Condamine's writings had been a stimulant to explore tropical South America, but the universities were also attractive in their way; so too Goethe and Schiller, or places like India and the Nile, or the new worlds of electricity and magnetism. If South America should prove difficult there were other places, other people, other things galore. Somewhere or something would inevitably be investigated with all that energy, but it did so happen, when a number of years had passed by, that the longing for tropical America was finally fulfilled. However, there were those intervening years, and the story makes most sense if started at its outset.

The year 1769 also produced Napoleon, Wellington, Cuvier; the following one created Beethoven. It was an exciting time to be born, but not necessarily at Schloss Tegel, near Berlin. His mother was cool to both Alexander and his brother Wilhelm, and their father died when the boys were young. Education was placed in the hands of private tutors, notably Gottlob Kunth, who was to stay with the Humboldts for fifty years. In the early days there were higher hopes for Wilhelm because he learned speedily, was healthier, and seemed well equipped for high office. Alexander was more difficult, and had initial thoughts of a military career. No one taught him science in those childhood years but he became a skilful artist and, along the way, acquired Russian, French, English, Spanish and Italian as well as German. As a developing youngster he was not so much sensitive as susceptible. Just as he had read La Condamine and wanted South America, so did he read James Cook and long for the Pacific. He met the Jewish physician Marcus Herz, and determined upon philosophy and experimentation. He met Frau Herz and loved her company, writing to her in English or Hebrew if secrecy was demanded. He was clay, happy and willing to be moulded in any direction, particularly if it involved learning, travel and yet more learning.

Baron von Humboldt

When aged eighteen Alexander was sent, together with his brother Wilhelm, to the university at Frankfurt an der Oder. This was an unsatisfactory establishment, and no place for learning any science. In any case the unwilling Alexander had been instructed by his mother to study economics. Within six months Wilhelm had been despatched to Göttingen to study law, while his older brother was brought home. There, as susceptible as ever, he encountered botany, or rather he met the young Karl Willdenow who had already published a *flora* of local plants. From that moment Alexander knew he would be a botanist, along with everything else. After joining his brother at Göttingen, an institution incomparably superior to Frankfurt, he discovered philology, archaeology, and natural history in general. He shared rooms with Klemens Metternich (later to be an Austrian statesman and Chancellor) and went on his first field trip, examining basalts on the river Rhine. Most important of all, he encountered Georg Forster, fifteen years his senior.

Everything that Forster had to say was wholly welcomed by the younger man. Forster was traveller, natural historian, enthusiast, author, and had sailed around the world with Captain Cook. Even now, when the world is fully mapped, Cook's exploits can make irresistible reading. To a young man intent upon exploration, who had not only studied Cook's three voyages but had then met an actual participant of his second expedition, the excitement must scarcely have been bearable. That particular voyage had visited the Cape of Good Hope, then the Antarctic circle and New Zealand, then Tahiti, the Society Isles and the Friendly Isles. It had searched for the alleged southern continent, inspected Easter Island, and visited Tonga, the New Hebrides and New Caledonia before reaching Cape Horn and South Georgia to travel further south again, eventually to England via southern Africa. It was one of the most stupendous journeys of all time, and surely seemed a hundred times more so when recently completed.

Georg Forster's sailing had been fortuitous. The chief scientist from the first voyage, Joseph Banks, had wished to sail again. The old *Endeavour* had proved a most suitable vessel, and two newer ships were purchased from the same Whitby builder for the second voyage. (The *Endeavour* was sold by the Admiralty, became a French privateer, was then bought by a Rhode Island company and finally allowed to rot in Newport harbour.) The newer ships, re-named *Resolution* and *Adventure*, were both modified for the voyage. The larger vessel, severely altered at Banks's request, became extremely top-heavy. Her first lieutenant informed the rich and powerful scientist: 'I think her by far the most unsafe ship I ever saw or heard of.' Her upper works were then altered again, so much so that Banks refused to sail in her. The post of chief scientist therefore fell vacant and was awarded to a recent immigrant from Germany. Cook's journal relates: 'It being thought of public utility, that some person skilled in natural history should be engaged to accompany me on this voyage, the Parliament granted an ample sum for that purpose, and Mr John Reinhold Forster, with his son, were pitched upon for this employment.' The son was then eighteen and had been living in England for six years.

To take a couple of Germans, recent arrivals in England, may seem odd for an Admiralty expedition, but the Forsters were of Scottish lawyer stock. Their forebears had emigrated to Prussia in the seventeenth century. There they had continued to practise law, doing well until Reinhold, Georg's father, made the continuance of their comfortable existence impossible. After switching from law to divinity he outraged his new masters by spending little time on his clerical duties, preferring to study botany. The young Georg used to accompany him on these floral ventures, and then emigrated with him to England when Prussia would no longer provide employment. A job at Warrington as science and language teacher in an academy proved to be equally unfortunate for Reinhold, his temper and conceit having travelled with him. He would appear entirely ineligible as a shipmate who would have to share modest quarters for years on end, but Lord Sandwich proposed him, the Admiralty accepted him, and Cook had to suffer him.

Reinhold Forster wrote a journal of the voyage, but was not allowed to publish it. He had so aroused Cook's antagonism that this refusal was almost inevitable. In the journal he frequently criticized the expedition, even the crew's habit of speaking in traditional below-decks manner. Forster was also deeply shocked by the *Adventure*'s unfortunate separation from *Resolution*, when the ships lost touch off New Zealand before returning individually to England. And he hated 'the dreadful energy of the language' used when the event occurred.

Baron von Humboldt

While south of the Antarctic circle and meeting ice, gale and fog, Forster described the scene on board. It 'looked like the wrecks of a shattered world, or as the poets describe some regions of hell; an idea which struck us all the more forcibly as execrations, oaths, and curses re-echoed about us on all sides'. One gunner's mate, by way of comparison, wrote that 'under all these hardships the men were cheerful over their grog'. It would be comprehensible if Cook preferred the gunner's mate to the critical, short-tempered and conceited ex-divine who was his naturalist.

Cook certainly preferred the son to the father. Georg was permitted to write *Voyage around the World on H.M. Sloop 'Resolution'*. This was published in England in 1777, two years after the voyage's completion and while Cook was on his third and final expedition. The translation *Reise um die Welt*, printed in Germany in 1778, created much more fame for its author than the English version had achieved. The book was eagerly devoured by Humboldt, and the author himself was consumed as avidly once the two of them had met. Indeed, Humboldt offered to accompany him to England. Georg wanted a publisher for his planned book on Pacific geography, and Humboldt relished the opportunity for further stimulating talk with this global traveller. He would also see England and, for the first time, a stretch of sea.

This proved to be an astonishing journey, a pot-pourri of science and history. Humboldt visited the British Parliament and heard Richard Brinsley Sheridan, the younger William Pitt and Edmund Burke address the Commons on the very same day. He briefly attended the (seven-year) trial of Warren Hastings, former Governor-General of India, and met the scientists Henry Cavendish, William Herschel and Sir Joseph Banks. Whether Forster also met Banks is not specifically recorded, but Banks's enthusiasm for the Pacific and any Cook voyager probably outweighed all complications stemming from Cook's antagonism towards Georg's father. Humboldt certainly saw the Banks herbarium, the largest in the world. He also went caving in the Peak District and visited Bristol. Assiduously he made notes on (seemingly) everything – beer, crops, wool, economy, rocks – and then, to crown the journey, returned via Paris. His arrival there coincided with the earliest anniversary of the Bastille's storming, the first *Quatorze Juillet*. Humboldt was as excited as the Parisians. The revolution had not yet begun either to eat its own or to lose sight of its high ideals, and for Humboldt the experience was unforgettable.

So was his companion. In later years Humboldt wrote that Georg Forster had been his guiding star, his major influence:

With him began a new era of scientific travels, that of comparative anthropology and geography . . . Endowed with a fine aesthetic sensibility [he] was the first to describe with charm the varying stages of vegetation, the climatic conditions, the nutrients in relation to the customs of people in different localities. Not only in his excellent description of the journey of Captain Cook, even more so in his smaller publications is to be found the germ of something greater, brought to fruition in a more recent period.

In fact there were to be very few publications by Forster, and his great work on the Pacific's geography never materialized. That visit to Paris had been far too unsettling. Georg did not simply approve of the revolutionaries, he joined their ranks. When Mainz fell to the French he was firmly on their side. When it was reoccupied by the Germans, and the revolution itself had taken a turn for the worse, Georg Forster had many enemies on both sides of the Rhine. Humboldt's 'most distinguished teacher and friend', whose name could never be mentioned 'without a feeling of the most heartfelt gratitude', died miserably in Paris at the start of 1794. The individual who had described 'with charm' the stages of vegetation, and through whose influence 'a new spirit in exploration' had been born, perished partly from starvation at the age of forty.

Humboldt did not see his powerful mentor after they had both returned to Germany. Nevertheless seeds had been planted, or rather given hot-house treatment. Only time and opportunity were necessary before the young Prussian would also be savouring, investigating, analysing some distant portion of the planet just as Georg had done. Neither the hour nor the occasion had yet arisen, but both would surely do so. In the meantime, and most perversely (or so it seems), Humboldt took a job in the Prussian Ministry of Industry and Mines.

This was an inefficient organization, bureaucratically replete. Its mining officials knew nothing about rocks or even the elements of geology. Humboldt's job – Assistant Inspector of Mines – did not pay a living wage. As a polymathic would-be explorer, richly equipped in talent and scientifically well grounded by Göttingen, it is small wonder that the Ministry welcomed him enthusiastically. The greater wonder is that, without pressure from anyone, this should have been Alexander von Humboldt's first choice of employment. Initially he may have regretted his move, having been given an unhappy office task in Berlin, but he made the most of it, wrote the report they demanded of him, damned and praised where need be, and received prompt promotion to Chief Inspector. This was still a far cry from the Pacific or South America, but, in his curious fashion, he was on his way.

Next, which Humboldt may have foreseen and regarded as sensible inducement for joining the mining industry, they sent the inspector on an inspection. This was no casual trip. It would take him from the Alps to Poland, from Austria and Berchtesgaden via Bohemia and Moravia to Silesia and Wieliczka, some 3,000 miles in all. As extra attraction the mines were extremely varied, involving all manner of rock and all kinds of desirables, whether gold or tin, copper or salt, antimony, cobalt, iron or coal. Gases were also involved, and Humboldt invented breathing apparatus. He also concerned himself with the health and welfare of the miners, noting how they suffered differently in the different kinds of mine but never received assistance when struck down by sickness or accident. As for Humboldt, his adolescent frailty was turned inside-out by his labours underground: 'I consider that the improvement in my health is entirely due to my work in the mines.'

The authorities continued to promote Humboldt, but the mining service was only a stepping-stone. He had no need of their money but did require to see the world, somehow. He knew he had to be a traveller – and further afield than anywhere encompassed by the mining ministry. However, he still bided his time, spending much of it performing experiments, on plants, on magnetism and electricity, on muscles and nerves, on whatsoever took his fancy: 'The fact is I can't exist without experiments.' He performed thousands, and very nearly produced the first battery. Both he and Luigi Galvani had been so preoccupied with the relationship between electricity and twitching muscles that they assumed an animal's physiology somehow played a crucial role. Alessandro Volta tested electricity in 1795 without the involvement of animal material, and Humboldt never forgave himself. This tremendous stride forward had been within his reach, and he had failed. He could so easily have omitted the animal tissues – and we would now have the humboldt rather than the volt.

It is easy to believe the young Alexander was more than one man. His mining chiefs were astonished that he could achieve all he did for them. He was also writing *Experiments on the Excited Muscle and Nerve Fibre with Conjectures on the Chemical Process of Life in the Animal and Vegetable World*, the results of his several thousand experiments. He had already produced *Florae fribergensis*, about the plant life of Freiberg, which had earned considerable renown (and even a gold medal from one enthusiastic reader). His drawing was extremely competent, as can be seen from excellent self-portraits. He spent time with Schiller and Goethe, being criticized by the former and warmly welcomed by the latter. To be with Goethe, he said, is to be equipped with new organs. Goethe, twenty years senior to the mining inspector, said he could not learn as much from books in a week as from Humboldt in one hour. To receive this kind of testimony from Germany's most eminent intellectual, the genius of his time, was undoubtedly heart-warming. Humboldt replied that Goethe's descriptions of nature were as good as Georg Forster's, the highest praise in his vocabulary.

Although Humboldt behaved as if he were several men, there was a major lack. He had no wish for home, family, or even women. 'Alexander will never be inspired by anything,' wrote his sister, 'that does not come through men'. 'I can't believe that he will ever form a real relationship,' observed his brother. Echoing this belief, Alexander himself wrote to a former teacher that 'a man should get used to standing alone early on in his life'.

The best-loved friend in those early years was Reinhard von Haeften, an army officer four years Humboldt's junior. Little is known of this man. There is no sketch, and Humboldt's letters to him were not discovered until this current century. They are, as is quite plain, letters of passion: 'My love for you is not just friendship, or brotherly love – it is veneration, childlike gratefulness, and devotion to your will as my most exalted law.' He wrote those words after Reinhard's marriage. The adoring Alexander had put on a brave face for that occasion. He had generously given a great ball in Bayreuth Castle and had then suggested a threesome arrangement. To the lady he wrote: 'I can well imagine the feeling of bliss you must have felt when you saw him . . . I have felt the same myself . . . Tell Reinhard how much I loved the lakes of Lucerne and Sarnen . . . If we can't go to America, that's where we should go, removed from all so-called educated people, to live a happy life in harmony together.' No reply from either bride or groom has been preserved, but really none is needed. The proposed *ménage* did not take place.

After the wedding other events augmented the sense of loneliness – or of freedom. His mother died, aged fifty-five, of cancer of the breast. From her he inherited tremendous wealth, far greater than his earlier stipend. The date was February 1797, and Alexander von Humboldt was twenty-seven years old. The world lay at his feet, and what part of it he chose to walk did not trouble him. He could go wheresoever he pleased, more or less.

Having planned his life so meticulously so far, he could not possibly have foreseen that the next stage would prove so difficult. The freedom he thought he had acquired grew more elusive, seemingly every way he turned. Initially he went to Jena in eastern Germany to join his brother, Wilhelm. They planned a joint investigation of Italy's volcanoes. Unfortunately Napoleon Bonaparte, also twenty-seven, was busy in Italy at the time, winning the battles that would establish his reputation. As a further blow Wilhelm's wife became sick. Schiller and Goethe wrote mocking letters, laughing at Alexander's ill-luck and helplessness, until the brotherly expedition disintegrated. Wilhelm moved his family to Paris and Alexander chose to visit scientists in Vienna. He did indeed meet many, but then encountered an old friend, the very rich, terribly shy (some say he only looked at skirting boards) and eccentric geologist named Leopold von Buch. The proposed family get-together that winter in Switzerland fell apart at once. Humboldt opted to spend the time with Von Buch, to learn from him however possible and tramp the Alps together. On their journeys Humboldt measured the atmosphere, taking note of temperature at fixed times, of pressure, humidity, gas content and electrical charge. He became the first weather station, setting the pattern of observation so commonplace today. However, he was still neither in South America nor the Pacific, nor anywhere truly far afield.

Lord Bristol, Bishop of Derry, was ludicrously rich and slightly weird. He was planning an expedition up the Nile, fully equipped with artists, musicians, savants and a cook. This traveller, who allegedly caused the proliferation of Bristol hotels around Europe, invited Humboldt to join his entourage. A couple of sociable ladies had already accepted, notably Countess Lichtenau, former mistress of Friedrich Wilhelm II. Humboldt agreed to join them. 'I may be blamed for associating with the noble lord; but he is the eccentric of eccentrics . . . If it goes against the grain, I can leave. Besides he is a man of genius, and I cannot let such a wonderful opportunity pass. I may be able to do something for meteorology.' One wonders what the Countess might have thought of a young man who, in her company beneath Cleopatra's skies, worked at meteorology; but she had, in the end, to decline the invitation. Humboldt immersed himself in Egyptian history as the expedition prepared to depart. The year was 1798.

Unfortunately his irritating contemporary also had plans for Egypt. Humboldt was in Paris buying instruments when rumour became reality. Napoleon had slipped past Horatio Nelson's fleet and had landed near Alexandria. Later Nelson would annihilate the French ships, but the Bristol expedition had already foundered. Its leader, the noble lord, had been arrested in Milan. He was accused of acting as agent for the British government – which may have been the case – and the Italians imprisoned him. There he stayed for eighteen months, but Humboldt did not grieve for more than a modest portion of that time. Paris was the most magnificent city in the world, particularly for a scientist. Joseph Lagrange was there, and the Marquis de Laplace, Baron Cuvier and Geoffroy Saint-Hilaire. The terror of the revolution had passed; its virtues had arrived. There was an astonishing spirit abroad, of change, of fresh discovery. They were just completing the great triangulation of France as Humboldt arrived. The last measurements were being made to form the basis of the new metre, intended as one ten-millionth of the distance between pole and equator. (And how La Condamine would have relished such measuring!) There was a suggestion that Humboldt should join the additional savants requested by Napoleon to examine Egyptian history, and Humboldt most willingly prepared himself to go. This planned expedition then crumbled into dust. News came of Nelson's victory at Aboukir Bay and Humboldt's second Egyptian venture was no more.

One way and another, despite putting great energy into every

Alexander von Humboldt, botanist, geologist, linguist, traveller, and inspiration to all nineteenth-century naturalists.

initiative, the young Prussian had failed to study Italian volcanoes, had failed to examine the Nile with an English lord, and had failed to visit Egypt with the French. His frustration must have been extreme, but, at that moment of despair, further opportunity suddenly arose; he met Louis Antoine de Bougainville. As with encountering Georg Forster, the effect was dynamic. Bougainville had sailed the world in the year Humboldt had been born, and of course his *Voyage autour du Monde* had been eagerly devoured. Meeting a shipmate of James Cook had been overwhelming. Meeting the nearest French equivalent to Cook, who had travelled even before the Yorkshireman, was equally devastating. Worse still, in terms of calming Humboldt's agitation, the septuagenarian admiral was planning another voyage. With the full co-operation of the French government this expedition would initially concentrate upon central and southern America. Then it would move to the Pacific and, hopefully, reach further south than Cook had ever done. Finally it would move to Africa. The old sailor asked Humboldt to join his corps of scientists. Humboldt, of course, instantly agreed.

The first blow fell when Bougainville was replaced. Parisian officials decided that a younger man, Thomas Baudin, should be in charge. Humboldt regretted the change, but continued energetically to make preparations. He met and liked the other scientists. He offered to take Bougainville's son, aged fifteen, under his care. The frigate *La Hardie* was to be the principal vessel and was waiting at Toulon. There existed the problem of the British blockade, but this was not all-seeing, all-powerful. Those taking part in the French expedition moved south and were ready to sail when a message arrived from the Directory in Paris. New wars were imminent, notably with Austria. These would be expensive. The global expedition would cost money that could be put to other purposes. It was consequently cancelled without additional delay.

Italy, the Nile, Egypt in general and the world at large had all been dangled before Humboldt. He had been excited at every prospect. He had then despaired as they were all annulled, each and every one. Other people's expeditions were plainly not the answer. He would have to make his own. As companion he would take Aimé Bonpland, a botanist four years his junior. Both men had been stranded by the Directory's cancellation, Bonpland having been recruited even before

Humboldt. Their sense of frustration was equal. So too their determination to travel, somehow, somewhere. They decided to join the savants busy labouring by the pyramids (even though the French fleet had been sunk). To do this it was first necessary to get across to Africa. And where better to find a boat than in Marseilles?

There they made arrangements to travel in a Swedish frigate destined for Algiers. This ship's arrival at Marseilles was imminent, so people said. Quite how the two scientists would proceed east from Algiers, whether with pilgrims travelling to Mecca or in some other form of caravan, did not concern them for the moment. The thought of Africa was sufficiently tantalizing. Its promise danced before them as days passed, as weeks passed, as months passed. Finally news arrived that the frigate had put into Cadiz for repairs. In their despair the two men promptly booked passage for Tunis on a cattle-boat. They then cancelled these reservations on hearing that all passengers from France were imprisoned on arrival. Their sense of frustration had now reached breaking point and, as others have done in similar circumstances, they turned upon their heels and walked from the scene. Enough of other people's expeditions, ships and promises – the two of them would walk, initially to Madrid, and see what happened there. They were young with sound limbs. Walking seemed the only way.

The delays in Marseilles had permitted the two men to learn about each other, their similarities and differences. Humboldt had money, Bonpland had none. Humboldt had been born in Prussia and Bonpland in France. (His birthplace had been La Rochelle and he had first seen daylight during the same month of the same year that the Godins arrived at that port after their departure from South America. The famous story, repeated to him over the years, helped with its coincidence to arouse his interest in the New World.) Bonpland had started life as a doctor, qualifying at twenty and voyaging with the French navy as a surgeon. However, botany had been more compelling. When at the Sorbonne in Paris he met old Joseph de Jussieu, muddle-headed remnant of the earth-measuring expedition. This man, who had lost his reason along with his collection, had returned from Quito to France in 1779. The very sight of him, if not the wisdom of his words, had been inspiration for the young medico-botanist, eager for news about tropical luxuriance. There were other differences between Bonpland and Humboldt, such as the former's love of ladies, but the similarities – such as their joint longing to explore, to discover, to collect – were striking. These had been reinforced by their shared experience, their selection for the circumnavigation, their disappointment, and their inability to reach anywhere – except by their own four feet.

It took the men six weeks to reach Madrid. Humboldt measured and observed as they progressed, finding errors in the alleged locations of towns through which they passed. Having fixed their geographical position more accurately he would hurry on, through the snow on occasion, past people bewildered by his activities. The two friends traversed the high plateau of central Spain – Humboldt being the first to reveal it *was* a plateau rather than lower-lying land. Spain was not then the happiest of countries, with her ships always in danger from the powerful British fleets, her colonies simmering with republicanism, and neighbouring Napoleon trampling Europe wheresoever he chose. However, it was to be the most wonderful of places for the two travelling scientists. Their fortunes would be altered from the low of repeated frustration to an astonishing, unparalleled high.

The Spanish had now been in the New World for 307 years. Throughout that time, save for their uneasy alliance with Portugal, they had resisted foreign involvement. It is true that La Condamine and his party had received permission to visit sixty-four years earlier, but they were only allowed into a limited area, were under constant supervision, and suffered interference by suspicious authorities. Even so, the French scientists had been astonished at the French good fortune. Humboldt was to be yet more astounded at his own good luck. This arose not so much from what he was as from whom he knew. The Saxon (not Prussian) chargé d'affaires in the Spanish capital was Philippe von Forell. Humboldt had met Forell's brother in Dresden and this acquaintance formed an excellent introduction. Better still, the Saxon ambassador liked science. Best of all, he knew personally Spain's principal minister, Mariano Luis de Urquijo. This statesman was said to be a lover of the Spanish queen, which would give him access to the king. If the queen approved of their plans, then the king would agree, and indeed the matter was soon settled. Humboldt and Bonpland would receive assistance from every Spanish official they encountered wherever they wished to go. It was an amazing *laissez-passer*. The Nile, Italy, and even the Pacific were all instantly forgotten in the breadth of this amazing liberty. From not even being able to reach northern Africa it was a remarkable shift in circumstance. Quite suddenly all of Spanish America was opened up to a pair of men entirely suited to take advantage of this brand new world. No wonder they made haste to leave in case their fortunes changed.

'Never before has a traveller been granted such unlimited permission,' wrote Humboldt, 'and never before has a foreigner been honoured by such marks of confidence from the Spanish Government.' He had done even better than La Condamine. He and Bonpland could travel wherever they chose in the Spanish dominions. These lands reached from the 38th northern parallel to the 42nd latitude in the south. It is surprising the two of them did not lose their wits as poor old Jussieu had done.

Alexander von Humboldt and Aimé Bonpland arrived in the New World on 16 July 1799. There was no longer a Spanish requirement to travel via Cartagena, and their first American port of call was Cumaná, 850 miles to the east and very near the spot where Lope de Aguirre had landed from the Island of Margarita when he and his diminishing band had had plans to conquer Peru. Whereas Aguirre encountered resistance on all sides, reasonably enough if the rumours of him were one-tenth true, the two scientists were taken straight into the presence of Don Vicente Emparán, governor of northern South America. He offered every assistance, spoke excitedly of their plans, and helped them find a house. They were truly free at last.

The journey to South America had not been entirely straightforward. The travellers had started off from Madrid as they had reached Madrid – on foot. At the port of Corunna the two men had boarded the corvette *Pizarro*. Its captain thought little of their chances of escaping the British. Three enemy vessels had recently been observed off the Tagus, further to the south. No one was optimistic about the corvette's fate, save for Humboldt, who apparently did not entertain the thought of capture. 'In a few hours we shall sail,' he wrote to a friend. 'I shall make collections of fossils and plants. I intend to institute chemical analysis of the atmosphere and I shall make astronomical observations. My attention will be ever directed to observing harmony among the forces of nature, to remarking the influence exerted by inanimate creation upon the vegetable and animal kingdoms'. Not much concern there about looming men-of-war. No thought other than the meticulous excitement lying over the horizon, particularly to the west and south.

In the afternoon of 5 June, with a north-easterly wind blowing, the *Pizarro* weighed anchor. Initially the wind proved a problem, threatening to run the corvette on to the rocks (at which further frustration the two scientists would surely have gone mad), but Captain Cagigal knew his business and all went well. He had luck and skill, for he escaped both the rocks and the waiting ships. After three days they did spot a British convoy, and Humboldt single-mindedly regretted the dousing of lights that this caused because it meant he could see less well for taking measurements and observing marine specimens hauled on board. One wonders if Cagigal welcomed such a passenger, so aloof from normal cares, so enwrapped in concerns that others did not share. Humboldt, too enchanted to waste himself with worry, wrote: 'The nights were magnificent; in this clear, tranquil atmosphere it was quite possible to read the sextant in the brilliant moonlight.'

Before leaving the Old World the *Pizarro* called in at Tenerife, one of the Canary Islands. Fog and poor maps made the approach difficult, but both hazards helped to save them. When conditions improved they saw four British ships which could well have captured them had the *Pizarro* been visible, or had it sailed a more conventional course. Of course Bonpland and his mentor hurried ashore the moment their ship docked, and of course they saw Tenerife's volcano. The Pico de Teide rises 12,200 feet above the sea, and loomed above them irresistibly. 'What a fantastic place,' he wrote to his brother; 'what a time we had. We climbed down into the crater, perhaps further than any previous scientist.' Suffering heat (from the sulphurous vapour) and cold (from the altitude), the two men were ecstatic. 'I could almost weep at the prospect of leaving this place. I should be quite happy to settle here, but am scarcely out of Europe.' They did leave, after six days.

In theory the *Pizarro*'s next port of call was Havana. In practice this intention had to be changed when fever became rampant. Humboldt and Bonpland were not the only passengers on board; there was also an assortment of Negroes, mulattos and Spaniards. All suffered from the heat, and the insanitary conditions of an eighteenth-century vessel assisted in the spread of disease, either typhoid or typhus (or both) being on board. A young Spaniard was the first to die and plainly others were going to follow his example. The ship's surgeon had no recourse but to bleeding, a practice still disastrously in vogue. What should have been pure excitement, as the Americas hove into Humboldt's view, was quite the reverse: 'We were assembled on the deck, lost in melancholic thought . . . Our eyes were fixed on a hilly coast on which the moon shone occasionally through the clouds.' This was not an exultant Humboldt, delirious at novelty. It was someone only too aware of pestilence on every side.

The nearest port was Cumaná. It was decided the corvette should dock there with minimum delay. However, as at Tenerife, the charts and pilot's notes were a problem. Each was different from the other and none was accurate. The *Pizarro* approached the shore in a cautious and circumspect manner. Two canoes, both manned by Indians, came to inspect the new arrival. After satisfying themselves that the ship was Spanish, and not an unwelcome intruder from northern Europe, the Guayquerias climbed on board, laden with local produce. They offered to act as pilots, but not until the following day. Thus it was that during the morning of 16 July Humboldt and Bonpland landed at Cumaná, were hurried to the governor, received his support, and were pronounced free to go where they wished, whether up into much of what is now the United States, or over to Mexico and the band of land between the two Americas, or anywhere along the Andes stretching south to Tierra del Fuego. The piece of territory at their command was therefore about twice the size of Europe. It had deserts, mountains higher than Mont Blanc, and vegetation of a kind never seen back home. 'What a fabulous country we're in,' he wrote to Wilhelm. And so they were.

To begin with there was no method in their exultation. They collected. They measured. They drew and took note. The original notion of proceeding to Havana had only been postponed, but neither man wished for the moment to re-embark on any form of vessel. There was ample to be investigated in the northern lands of South America, so why risk further travel elsewhere, particularly by sea? Not all of

Humboldt's letters reached Europe (mailbags being generally jet-tisoned when enemy vessels hove in sight), but those that did so struck a uniformly happy note. 'What an extravagant country we are in. Amazing plants, electric eels, armadillos, monkeys, parrots . . . We have been running like fools; for the first three days we could not settle on anything. We were always leaving one object, to throw it away for another. Aimé Bonpland declares that he should go mad if this state of wonder were to continue . . .'

With their microscopes they, and the respective ladies, examined lice of many varieties found in the ladies' hair. They measured plant growth, which exceeded by far anything in Europe. They heard of and then found a man suckling a child with his own milk. On their first foray inland they encountered the oil-bird, or *guacharo*. This cave-dwelling species, slaughtered for its fat, was quite new to science. They also took advantage of a solar eclipse in late 1799. This was immediately followed by climatic change, with red mist hanging thickly in the sultry air. Locals blamed the sun, but the lack of wind, the black clouds and the thunder were presage to an earthquake. Caught at the time in his hammock, Humboldt instantly recorded everything recordable, such as an abrupt shift in the magnetic needle's dip. No sooner had that spectacle been concluded than the sky was rich with fireballs, a shower of meteorites whose timing was precisely detailed (and which helped to form a basis for understanding their periodic return).

For a man who had revelled in Paris on 14 July 1790, the first anniversary of Bastille Day, it was a shock to encounter a land where liberty, equality and fraternity were frequently in short supply. There was still, for instance, slavery. A peasant class had not been imported from Europe; instead Negroes had been shipped from Africa to work the land, Indians having proved not wholly suitable for this task. The slave market was a short distance from Humboldt's house, and about as far a cry from the *Quatorze Juillet* as one could get on the planet. Humboldt watched the slaves' teeth being examined. He saw oil being rubbed into black skins to give them an attractive sheen. And of course he questioned the priests, who, in the main, considered that both sides benefited from the arrangement. 'Religion,' he concluded, 'is able to comfort people for wrongs performed in its name.' Nothing had changed since the earliest days of conquest, when, so it was reported, the 'soldiers first fell upon their knees and then fell upon the Indians'.

For 300 years there had been little social change within the Spanish empire. That stability did not have long to last when the eighteenth century gave way to the next. Britain would cease its involvement in the slave trade in 1808. The French would follow suit in 1815, and Spain and Portugal five years later. Such legislation did not cancel slavery, but at least the transportation of slaves would be made illegal. A general desire for freedom, a longing to be rid of European shackles, also swelled as the nineteenth century began. America's War of Independence had not been unnoticed further south, and the first uprising in Caracas occurred in 1797. It was suppressed, but Venezuela became independent of Spain in 1811. Humboldt and Bonpland were therefore seeing the eclipse of the old ways. No link existed between their arrival and the new order, but the ferment of those times invaded the scientists as much as anyone. For Humboldt the revolution in France had shown the path. It was up to other countries to follow that leadership as fast as possible.

After half a year in the New World, and with thoughts of Havana now shelved, Humboldt and Bonpland made plans for their first thorough examination of the interior. It was the start of a new century and they were ready for a new adventure. They had not experienced much hardship, having spent most time in Cumaná and Caracas, and were eager for greater trials. Humboldt was thirty, Bonpland twenty-six, and they could consider themselves experienced in South American travel. They therefore decided to answer, if it were possible, the one major question posed by La Condamine about the Amazon. Precisely where did the Amazon basin connect with the Orinoco system? La Condamine had been informed, and had believed, there was such a union. Who better to solve this intriguing riddle than the first pair of scientists with the money, time, permission and energy? They were quite a distance from the possible connection, but nearer than any of their kind had ever been. Besides, they welcomed a definite goal to replace their vague wish to see more of the land in which they had arrived. La Condamine's alleged canal would serve their purpose most appropriately.

This inland expedition began on 7 February 1800. After initial river travel it encountered the *llanos*, a formidable flatness knowing only two seasons. Either the land was baked pitilessly hard during the time of drought or it was drowned in flood-waters following the rains. 'Neither hill nor cliff rises, like an island in an ocean, to break the sameness of the unending plain,' wrote Humboldt, as much attracted by awfulness as by the clarity of the sky, the plumage of the birds. The men filled their hats with leaves to make better insulators and longed for trees beneath which to escape the searing sun. From a distance, the land appeared like a 'vast ocean covered with seaweed . . . Here no oasis recalls the memory of previous inhabitants; no carvings, no ruins, no fruit tree, once cultivated but now wild, speaks of the work of former generations.' Indeed it had not been much settled by Indians, but did prove suitable for imported cattle, and there were some two million in the area – of 250,000 square miles – when Humboldt and Bonpland made their crossing.

A major diversion was their arrival at Calabozo, a lonely cattle station. In its vicinity were many gymnotids, the electric fish that La Condamine had tantalizingly mentioned. They were not eels, but swam in eel-like manner and possessed an eel-like smoothness to their skins that had earned them their scientific name, *gymnos* being Greek for 'naked'. Be that as it may, they undoubtedly created electricity, 600 volts or so. This was sufficient to stun, or even kill, any animal to come their way. Humboldt was already obsessed with electrical phenomena, the work being in its exciting infancy, and he was enraptured with natural history. The union of the two was therefore doubly enthralling, or ten times so. But how to catch such a devastating fish?

The locals had a technique, which Humboldt was to call picturesque. A large number of mules and horses were driven at speed into a marsh where the fish were known to be resting in the mud. This violent act brought them out into the water, and their electricity caused the mules and horses to leave it speedily. With bamboo sticks the Indians sent the frightened animals back again. There they lunged about, terror in their eyes. A few succumbed, falling into the water and even drowning. The others continued to thrash until the gymnotids exhausted their battery-like supply. With dry lengths of wood acting as insulators the fish were then coaxed from the water. Some picturesque catching had done its work and the creatures were ready for science.

It was inevitable that a man who had already raised blisters on his

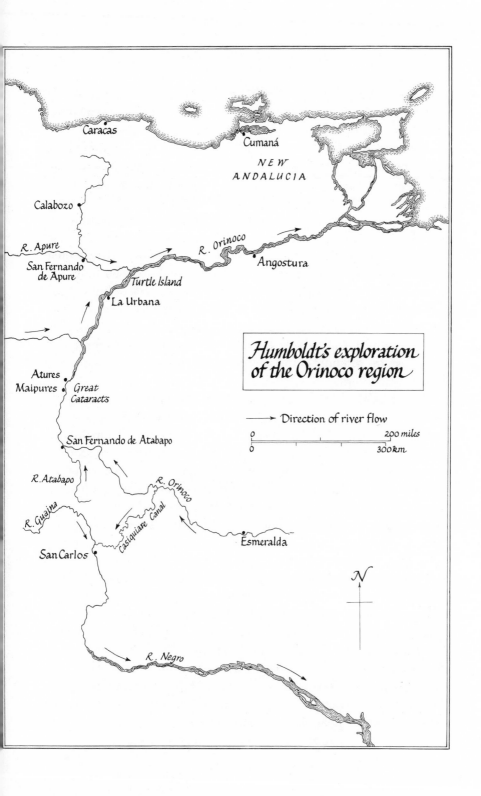

Caracas

Cumaná

NEW
ANDALUCIA

Calabozo

R. Apure

San Fernando
de Apure

R. Orinoco

Angostura

Turtle Island

La Urbana

Atures
Maipures • Great
Cataracts

*Humboldt's exploration
of the Orinoco region*

Direction of river flow

0   200 miles
0   300km

San Fernando de Atabapo

R. Atabapo

R. Orinoco

R. Guainía

Casiquiare Canal

Esmeralda

San Carlos

N

R. Negro

back when experimenting with primitive electrodes in Germany would learn personally (and painfully) about electric fish. 'I cannot remember ever having received a more terrible shock,' wrote Humboldt, having inadvertently trodden on one recently taken from the water. Had the horses not already been used he would have been killed by such an error, but as it was he had 'violent pain' in his knees, and almost every joint was affected for the remainder of the day. He and Bonpland were amazed that the fish, now known as *Electrophorus electricus*, did not convulse themselves with their own electrical impulses. Or, come to that, each others'. Humboldt dissected them, discovered that their fibres of electrical generation were equal in weight to their muscular tissue, and was first to detail the Hunter organs and Sachs bundles, as they came to be known. He also described how in relaxed circumstances the fish transmit small impulses, these being greatly increased when the animal is stimulated. If many fish are roused (and they do live in groups), the offender is speedily punished for its transgression, as if by batteries in series.

The New World was living up to its fame as a repository of unending astonishment. There was, for example, the milk tree. This *palo de vaca* grew in the *llanos* and, so locals said, had drinkable sap. Humboldt and his companion, now vividly aware of electric fish, were less scornful than they might have been, particularly after seeing a specimen of the tree with many scars across its trunk. One more wound was added, the whiteness poured forth into the waiting vessel, and Humboldt was ready for the tasting. He thought it a touch acid, and thick, but otherwise potable. 'Cow's milk,' he wrote in his journal, 'and from a tree!' The continent was living up to all those childhood dreams.

After seven weeks of inland travel across the flat wastes of the *llanos* they arrived at a tributary of the Orinoco. Apart from the question of the river's alleged linkage with the Amazon system, there was also doubt concerning the Orinoco itself. Did it flow from the Andes, as some asserted vigorously (from their vantage point in Europe), or was there some other source? If so, where was it, and might the mysterious canal lead to a solution of both unknowns? At San Fernando de Apure, the Capuchin mission station that gave them hospitality after their *llanos* crossing, Humboldt and Bonpland received bland instructions concerning the canal. 'Go down the Apure. Meet the Orinoco and travel upstream until the current is too strong for further progress. Take your boat from the water and take it through the forest until you can descend to the Rio Negro. Journey down that until the canal appears on the left-hand side.' In short, nothing could be more straightforward, save that the distances were considerable, the biting insects voracious, and the rapids they would meet were known as the Great Cataracts. It was not to be an easy journey. In fact, and more than once, it threatened to be the death of them.

The mouth of the Orinoco had been discovered by Columbus three centuries earlier. The river had been a major lure for Sir Walter Raleigh two centuries beforehand, and yet at the start of the nineteenth century no one knew (at least in the outside world) whether its course bent like a fish-hook to its source or proceeded to the mighty Andes. The reason for such ignorance was twofold: a Spanish ban on exploration, particularly foreign exploration, and the strict control on river traffic exerted by the monks. Whether they were Capuchin, Franciscan or other did not matter. The Orinoco was a missionary waterway kept under tight supervision.

Columbus, aware that it was a major effluent, argued correctly that such a flow could come only from a continent. A hundred years later Raleigh travelled far upstream, and even further in his enthusiasm: 'Men shall find here more wealth and beauty than in either Mexico or Peru . . .' Even the land, of *llanos* and forest, of biting flies and brown water, he found supreme: 'I never saw a more beautiful country, nor more lively prospects; hills raised here and there, over the valleys, the river winding into different branches, plains without bush or stubble, all fair green grass, deer crossing our path, the birds toward evening singing on every side a thousand different tunes, herons of white, crimson, and carnation perching on the riverside, the air fresh with a gentle wind . . .' With the assurance of Columbus that this was no island, and the heady exultation of Raleigh, who praised every aspect, there should have been scores of successors; but then came the missionaries to seal off the waterway. And then, years later and with his extraordinary *laissez-passer*, came Humboldt. The enigma of the Orinoco would finally be solved. How could it possibly meet the Amazon?

The Capuchins at San Fernando de Apure ordered a special boat to be prepared for the scientific party. Basically it was a *lancha*, a large form of canoe, but a roofed compartment had been constructed in the rear. In theory this would protect Humboldt and Bonpland from the elements. In practice, due mainly to all their precious instruments, the cabin was quite inadequate, though slightly better than nothing at all. The monks gave the travellers stores of food, four paddlers and quantities of the local currency – guns, brandy, fishing gear and tobacco. A willing companion for this forthcoming journey was Nicolás Sotto, brother-in-law of the local province's governor. There was also a mulatto servant, hired at Cumaná, and a pilot in charge of the four paddlers. Therefore nine people were on board the modified *lancha* when, shortly before dawn on 30 March 1800, this first major Humboldt expedition sallied forth. Europe was still in turmoil. Nelson would soon be destroying the Danish fleet. Napoleon was gaining in strength with every year that passed. But all of that was far away. On the Orinoco one small boat was about to make its form of history.

The nine travellers took six days to journey down the Apure, the largest tributary of the Orinoco, before reaching the main stream. There they turned south, up-river, and travel became a greater labour. Among the joys were flamingos, spoonbills, herons – more birds than Bonpland had ever seen. Among the less pleasurable aspects were the biting flies such as *pium* that were scarcely visible, and the mosquitoes, all too easy to see and hear – these and similar insects being collectively known in that locality as '*la plaga*'. 'How beautiful the moon looks,' said an Indian; 'surely no mosquitoes are there.' There were dolphins cavorting near the boat, and capybaras forever leaping from the shore to the water. Peccaries ran along the river banks, and an occasional tapir would swim ahead of them. 'It is paradise,' said another Indian when in a swarm of flies, having learned the word but possibly not its fullest meaning. Humboldt was thinking more of the inferno. 'All hope abandon, ye who enter here,' he quoted in his journal, a strange sentiment for a man who could enthuse where so many others could not. Plainly, paddling upstream along the Orinoco through all its insect life was not one permanent enchantment. 'How can anyone believe,' said a suspicious inhabitant, 'that you have come to be bitten by mosquitoes and measure lands that are not your own?' He also informed them that worse was to come, further up the river.

Baron von Humboldt

A curious source of pleasure, quite unlike anything the Europeans had ever seen, then hove into view. It was Turtle Island, a chain of three and most correctly named. Human families considered it worthwhile to paddle even from the Orinoco's mouth, some 400 miles downstream, to collect turtle oil. Hundreds of thousands of turtles laid their eggs in early March, shortly before the spring equinox. The conditions of sand and warmth were then entirely right – and therefore no less right for the egg-collectors. Having been informed that 5,000 jars of turtle oil were produced annually, and having observed the egg-to-oil procedure, Humboldt decided that half a million female turtles were involved. These each laid about 100 eggs, of which some hatched prematurely, some were broken, and some were eaten by the egg-collectors. The missionaries originally controlled the quantities gathered, thus ensuring sufficient turtles in future years, but this system lapsed. Today, as has become a refrain with so many species in so many areas, the animals are almost extinct. The islands are still there, and their name, but not the multitudes (of turtles *and* humans) that used to visit them.

At La Urbana, near to Turtle Island, the Humboldt party had to change boats. The Apure Indians knew nothing of the Orinoco further upstream and were ready to return. A new boat had therefore to be bought. This was slimmer than its predecessor, being no more than two feet wide, and so more suitable for the rapids that lay ahead. It was also less stable and contained even less space for the scientists, their instruments and their expanding collection. On board there was still the Cumaná servant, but a new pilot and four new paddlers had been recruited. Nicolás Sotto was still on board, and there was one new-comer, Father Bernando Zea. This up-river missionary found the venture as irresistible as Sotto had done, and he offered to act as guide at the cataracts and beyond. In addition there was a menagerie of animals, a little zoo that had grown as the journey had progressed.

The expedition embarked with its new craft on 10 April, arriving five days later at the foot of the Great Cataracts. This forty-mile stretch of rocks and turbulence acted as a natural barrier, deterring those down below from proceeding upstream and those up above from descending to the lower Orinoco. Humboldt and his team had known all along of this obstacle, realizing that the empty canoe would have to be dragged up-river, either through the water or, if need be, overland. That problem was conveniently left to the Indians. Bonpland therefore had opportunity for collecting, and Humboldt for taking measurements, while both of them tried to escape the flies. Father Zea built a small tree-house for anyone who wished to use it, the insects being most numerous at ground level. There was also the Indian form of retreat: small dwellings of clay filled with smoke to discourage the blood-suckers. Within them normal respiration was also discouraged, but any price to pay was small if the rapaciousness of the attacks was lessened.

A particular trouble, as anyone knows who has been in such parts, is that the attackers come in waves. No sooner has one species relented, perhaps completely gorged, than another takes its place. There are insects that prefer sunlight and others that like the shade. There are the day-time kinds, the night-time varieties, and those choosing dusk and dawn, such as most mosquitoes. Sometimes self-slapping does good. On other occasions it merely stimulates, drawing attention to oneself. There are miserable creatures that relish walking up one's nose, or immersing themselves in the exciting moisture of an eyeball; but worst of all for sanity are those that choose to walk into ears. They do not take blood. They do not even bite. They merely flutter their wings upon one's tympanum. There is no other noise like it. Mosquitoes, *pium*, nose-strollers and eyeball suicides are forgotten when the flapping dominates.

The Orinoco's Great Cataracts consist of the rapids of Atures and Maipures. The latter are wilder, greater, and even noisier. From suitable vantage points the scientists looked down upon this cascading majesty, trying to forget the insect hordes and understanding full well how the turbulence had formed such a barrier to human progress. A little was known in the outside world of the Orinoco up to the rapids. Virtually nothing of it was known beyond those formidable falls. It was even rumoured (and believed and told by many friars) that people lived up there whose bodies ended at their shoulders and whose mouths opened below their navels. There were men with dog's heads, it was said. Anything was possible beyond the cataracts.

Most amazing of all was the realization, once the scientific party had launched its craft again, that the insects were lessening. By the time Humboldt's boatload reached the mission station at San Fernando de

Atabapo the miracle had occurred. There was not a biting insect to be seen, or felt, or loathed. The reason was the constitution of the water on which the expedition was now travelling. The Orinoco is a white-water river, which means it is a muddy silty grey. The Atabapo looked and felt, smelt and tasted quite different, being a black-water stream. The travellers could now see the fish, often deep down, over which they passed. They could drink the clear liquid and had no need to strain it. (Water colour relates both to the type of soil involved and the degree of erosion. A dark colour is caused by dissolved organic substances derived from leaf litter, making the water acidic. White water is due to an increased load of suspended solids and is more alkaline. The composition of rivers can change according to season or it may remain constant.)

Humboldt was suitably impressed when they entered the darker, clearer, tastier and altogether more attractive waters of this portion of the upper Orinoco. 'Nothing can be compared with the beauty of the Atabapo,' he wrote, in sharp contrast to many earlier diary entries. The fact that his body had ceased to be a feasting slab for insects surely helped him to this conclusion. The date was 26 April, eleven weeks since their inland expedition had begun. It had been almost eleven months since the *Pizarro* had weighed anchor, leaving Europe in its wake, and the two scientists were now thoroughly settled in South America. Indeed, on the far side of the Orinoco cataracts they were seeing more of South America's hidden lands than they had even dreamed about when, beset by frustrations, they had seemed incapable of leaving Europe. Now they were as embroiled as could be within the New World, and all set to solve one of its greatest riddles. How could the Orinoco and the Amazon possibly be joined?

Travelling with Father Zea meant transporting a man who could open all known doors. So far as anything was understood about the Orinoco's rivers, it was known by his missionaries. The Atabapo, the beautiful fly-less Atabapo, was a tributary of the Orinoco and not its main stream. The expedition had made this diversion in order to reach the Casiquiare canal from its Amazonian end. San Carlos was a mission station conveniently near this point, and Father Zea had recommended a route well known to him. However, this did mean leaving the Orinoco's drainage area and moving up and over into the

Amazon's. Almost all the world's rivers are separated by such a watershed, with rainfall arriving either on one side or the other without a middle course. The Casiquiare is an exception to this rule, and Father Zea's suggested route would lead the scientists straight to it. They could then traverse the so-called canal, meet up with the main stream of the Orinoco, and paddle down it to prove the linkage between the two systems. It would be a formidable journey but would achieve its end, provided all went well.

Having departed from the main stream *en route* to San Carlos, the cramped canoe was made to travel up smaller and smaller rivers to reach the watershed. The Atabapo had been first, but then, after four days of sheer delight, they reached the Temi. This lesser river was in flood, and a straighter course could be achieved by paddling through the forests it had flooded rather than meandering along its proper course. Next came the Tuamini and that brought the boatload to Javita, another lonely mission station. From this outpost the canoe had to be dragged over the divide. The monks arranged the necessary Indian labour, there being seven miles between this portion of the Orinoco's system and that of the Amazon. Sometimes rivers are separated by a mountain range or merely a line of hills. Here was no more than slightly higher ground. Nevertheless it was still a watershed, and rain falling in the area seeped towards either the Amazon or the Orinoco. There was no other way.

On 5 May, having been trundled carefully on tree-trunk rollers, the canoe was launched into Amazon water. The spot lay some 300 miles north of the Amazon itself, but was emphatically part of its enormous basin, being on the river Pimichin that flows into the river Negro that flows into the Amazon. For the first time on their grand inland expedition the scientists were now travelling downstream, no doubt a most welcome change for the front and paddling section of the boat. Within just a few hours, and with unaccustomed speed, they reached the Negro (called Guaina in its upper reaches), the black river named by Orellana over two and a half centuries earlier. The river had brought no particular delight to that Spanish explorer, so beset with the perils of survival, but it did to the Franco-Prussian expedition. The famous canal now lay within its grasp.

Two days later the boat and its mixed contingent of men and animals arrived at San Carlos. Just as the various creatures had found passage on the canoe, so should they invade any description of this voyage. They included one dog, seven parrots, two manakins and one motmot (other forms of bird), two guans (hen-like), and a total of eight primates, ranging from small squirrel monkeys up to a large woolly monkey (now known as Humboldt's). Even at San Carlos, as if that troupe was insufficient, a hyacinth macaw and one young toucan were welcomed on board. Father Zea was not so welcoming, being concerned about 'the daily augmentation of this ambulatory collection', but he gave the squirrel monkeys shelter within his habit's sleeves during any rain.

From San Carlos the canoes had to return upstream for eight miles before turning right, and eastwards, into the famous canal. (On the journey downstream when *en route* to San Carlos this union of waterways had been temporarily neglected.) The Casiquiare is no more canal-like than any river, but the scientists knew immediately that it was also unlike the Rio Negro. Once again the insects were all about them, the canal being white water flowing to meet the Negro's black, and once again they were heading upstream; but the important fact, which no doubt helped them to forget both current and insects, lay in their certainty that this was the canal, the union between Orinoco and Amazon, the disputed waterway. Plainly, as the friars had asserted all along, it was Orinoco water. Some of it flowed along the canal to meet the Negro and the Amazon; the rest pursued a more northerly course to continue as the Orinoco. Only two years beforehand a prominent French geographer (the man who first used contours) had called the postulation of such a connection 'a monstrous error in geography'. Instead it was an amazing truth, and the Humboldt party was travelling on it.

Humboldt may now have thought himself as far from the vicissitudes of politics as he could possibly get. Unfortunately this was frontier country, dividing not only two great river systems but also the territories of Spain and Portugal. The route that Humboldt's party took when travelling south from Turtle Island to the San Carlos mission coincides almost exactly with the border between modern Colombia and Venezuela. Had he proceeded another hundred miles or so down the Negro, he would have encountered what is now Brazilian territory. During his expedition there was much less certainty about the actual frontier, but the rivalry between Spain and Portugal persisted. While on the canal, which is now entirely within Venezuela, he encountered a Brazilian garrison. Plainly the Europeans were spies, they said. Equally plainly they should be transported down-river to Pará, for the officials at that city would know what to do. Father Zea wisely interrupted. Why not send a soldier to receive instructions? This suggestion was happily accepted, but no reply came back. In any case Humboldt was on his way again, measuring, mapping, recording. (Decades later Humboldt was asked to intervene in a border dispute between Venezuela and Brazil. He favoured Brazil's claim and received a major medal as his reward. Venezuela had apparently offered no such inducement.)

The Casiquiare canal proved to be 200 miles long. It seemed to be interminable. Humboldt's journal lost its jauntiness and Bonpland had not been himself since they had left the Atabapo. All hands and faces were swollen from insect bites. Father Zea, who had lived long in the general area, said the Casiquiare insects were the most painful he had felt. Humboldt's unhappiness was compounded on the expedition's final night on the canal. The dog, which had joined the party of its own volition, was carried off in the dark by a jaguar. One was known to be in the vicinity, and the dog had barked its warning, but in the morning both jaguar and dog had gone.

Having emerged from the canal, and after all possible measurements had been taken to prove the existence of this link, the canoe was paddled upstream along the Orinoco to Esmeralda, another mission settlement. The canoeists had departed from the Orinoco at San Fernando de Atabapo and had covered two legs of a triangle before meeting it again. Although the Amazon deserves all the superlatives, being by far the world's largest river system, the Orinoco is no mean stream. At the dividing point where it gives some of its substance to form the Casiquiare it is 500 yards wide and 1,000 miles from the open sea. However, for the Spanish explorers in previous years that point had been far enough inland. The mission station at Esmeralda possessed the reputation of being at the end of the world. It is a lovely site with a background of mountains, but insects make it practically untenable and certainly undesirable. Today's Venezuela does reach a hundred miles further in the southerly direction, but only because there is a convenient chain of hills down there to make a formal frontier. Today's Esmeralda does not look greatly different, say travellers who have reached this outpost, from the way it appeared in Humboldt's day. Lacking much appeal, it seems now, as then, a good place to turn around.

Bonpland's listlessness had turned into illness, another reason for heading downstream. The expedition left on 23 May, giving up all thoughts of tracing the Orinoco to its source. Nevertheless it had ascertained that the Orinoco's origin lay more or less south of its mouth and assuredly had no relation with the Andes over in the west. Progress down-river was speedy, partly because of the current but also because of the travellers' sense of urgency. The immediate destination was Angostura (today's Ciudad Bolívar), some 200 miles from the river's union with the sea. By the time they reached it Aimé Bonpland's life was in danger. At the house of a doctor he was given great quantities of quinine and also Angostura *corteza*, the famous bitters made from a bark that can reduce fever. Humboldt was in misery: 'I could never hope to meet a friend again so loyal, courageous and energetic. Throughout the journey he had shown many astounding proofs of courage and resolution . . .' The rich explorer had previously awarded Bonpland a large slice of money in his will, but there seemed every chance this would never be collected. However, at the end of a terrible month, the powerful botanist suddenly recovered.

From an ague of the body to one of the heart. No longer was his life threatened, but now his equilibrium, his general sanity. She was part-white, mainly Indian, and apparently enchanting. Poor Humboldt, having watched his friend succumb to fever, now had to wait in Cumaná while this new form of fire raged. The facts are skimpy – Humboldt does not dwell on them – but the girl allegedly agreed to marry the European botanist, and then disappeared. Bonpland went in pursuit, consumed several weeks in searching but failed to locate her, found himself in an excellent collecting area, spent much time in an ecstasy of botany, and eventually met again a most relieved Humboldt in late November 1800. The Orinoco journey was then formally concluded. It had lasted, one way and another, for nine months. The two men had collected 12,000 specimens of plants. They had journeyed for 1,500 miles and had absolutely verified, with latitude and longitude, the existence of the Casiquiare canal. La Condamine's outstanding question had been answered most emphatically, fifty-seven years after it had first been posed.

Although he had solved the most perplexing Amazonian riddle remaining when the eighteenth century became the nineteenth, it is arguable that Baron Alexander von Humboldt was not a true explorer of the great river. He could not claim the kind of acquaintance with it that had been experienced by Orellana, Aguirre, Teixeira, La Condamine and the Godins. He never saw the main stream, mainly because his *laissez-passer* had been issued by Spaniards rather than Portuguese. It is extremely possible he would have been arrested and sent to Lisbon had he trespassed into Brazil. He did subsequently meet the Amazon's headwaters in various other Spanish lands, and he even corrected the map La Condamine had made, but he did not see the river where it is most enormous, at its mouth or even a couple of thousand miles upstream.

Nevertheless, no account of South American exploration would be complete without considerable mention of Humboldt. He made the most complete investigation of the continent that any man had ever made. He produced what is now known as a data base of the area. His relentless measuring provided a foundation on which others could build. He was far more accurate than La Condamine could ever have been, science having advanced in the intervening years. His expedition was more wide-ranging, untrammelled as it was by imposed objectives like La Condamine's earth-measuring commission. Humboldt could go wheresoever he chose, and in his own time. He did not have the complications of a retinue, either to assist or to make trouble (such as Dr Senièrgues, who had aroused a mob to revenge).

Humboldt's investigation of the Casiquiare canal was the high spot in his South American journey. Once he was reunited with the recovered Bonpland the two of them travelled to Cuba, their original destination. There they learned that Captain Baudin had finally sailed on the long-planned circumnavigation that had brought Humboldt and Bonpland together in the first place. They left Havana for Cartagena, hoping to meet the French squadron at Lima. Then, instead of heading for the Peruvian port by sea via Panama, they chose to travel overland via Bogotá. The next major stop was Quito where they saw evidence of

Humboldt and Bonpland collected 12,000 plant specimens and travelled 1,500 miles on their journey to discover a link between the Amazon and Orinoco systems.

the terrible earthquake of 1797 that had killed 40,000 in Riobamba, the home town of Doña Isabela's family. By then it was 1802, a couple of years after the Orinoco expedition.

When at Quito they received word that Baudin had changed plans and would not be calling in at Lima. Humboldt and Bonpland were therefore left, once again, to their own resources – always more reliable. After Quito and then Riobamba they called in at Cuenca, where Senièrgues had met his death. A positive indication of happier times was that several bullfights were arranged in their honour. Eventually, with enviable lack of haste, the two men did arrive in Lima. From Callao, Lima's port (where La Condamine's Spanish companions had strengthened the defences against Admiral Anson), they took ship for Mexico. Cotapaxi erupted as a formal farewell when the scientists were taking their leave of its continent. In March 1803 they arrived at Acapulco (where Anson had so enriched himself), and in March 1804 the two men left Mexico for Cuba once again. There was much to do concerning the specimens left there three years earlier. Finally, having investigated more of the Spanish New World than any others had ever done in so spirited and scientific a manner, the Prussian and the Frenchman took ship north for the United States. First stop was Philadelphia, largest city of the new country, where Thomas Jefferson was their principal host. Then came the city of Washington, made the capital only three years earlier and still a modest place with some 5,000 inhabitants. Back afterwards to Philadelphia and a French frigate to Bordeaux. The momentous journey came finally to an end.

It had lasted five years and had covered 6,000 miles on land. Some 60,000 plants had been gathered, as well as hundreds of artefacts, rocks, skins. Dozens of notebooks were packed with information. Thereafter, if something from the area was 'new to science', as the phrase goes, it was probably something new to Humboldt. A good many of his pioneering efforts have already been mentioned, such as his establishment of basic meteorological data, but he certainly did not relax after the Orinoco voyage. For example, in what he said at his life's end had been his greatest achievement, he climbed Chimborazo, the huge volcano in today's Ecuador. He did not reach the summit, climbing 19,286 of its 20,562 feet, but this was higher than any man had ever been. (The record was not beaten until the development of Himalayan climbing. Before the Asian mountains were properly measured later in the nineteenth century Humboldt believed Chimborazo to be higher than anywhere else on earth. As for altitude reached by any means, the French scientist Joseph Gay-Lussac, a friend of Humboldt, went to 23,000 feet by balloon in 1804.)

Humboldt observed the transit of Mercury when he was in Lima. He encountered the cold current running northwards up the coast of South America that is now named 'the Humboldt Current', and was the first to record its changing flow and temperature, thus to some degree earning his honour, even if the phenomenon was already well known to everyone who had ever sailed those seas. He informed the United States president about the frontier territory between Mexico and the USA, and was liberal with maps that he had made. In all he had ranged from latitude 12°S to 40°N. The facts he had collected were to be of major use in astronomy, geology, biology, meteorology, oceanography and geography. Until his time no one had even correlated rise in altitude with drop in temperature, or had realized that volcanoes are frequently aligned. He saw more of a relationship between natural happenings than anyone had ever supposed to exist. He was the founding father of many sciences and the hero of many later scientists. There has never been another – or so it is frequently said – like Alexander von Humboldt, the 'greatest man'.

His life after South America continued to be one momentous endeavour after another, but he never travelled again on such a large scale. A trip to Siberia in 1829 was his greatest subsequent journey. The British refused to grant him access where they held dominion, assuming the foreigner to be an agent. Napoleon snubbed him at their single meeting, saying no more than that his wife was also interested in botany. It took Humboldt until he was sixty-five to publish his final volume on the South American travels. There were thirty in all and, coupled with the expense of the voyage, they absorbed his inherited fortune. However, many of Humboldt's works were to give great inspiration to others. Charles Darwin took *Personal Narrative* with him on HMS *Beagle* and wrote: 'I formerly admired Humboldt, now I almost adore him.' Lots of ladies were also to adore him, but all to no avail. There is nothing but the barest hint of possible marriage before

Humboldt published 30 volumes on his South American travels, a labour that absorbed his inherited wealth and lasted 30 years.

the subject is finally forgotten. He was eventually to die during his ninetieth year in May 1859, revered, venerated, the friend of kings and emperors, and with his intellect untarnished to the end.

So what of Bonpland, of Aimé Bonpland, Humboldt's friend and most loyal companion? He may have been an excellent travelling colleague but he was a less satisfactory editor. In the publication of their joint endeavour he proved to be slow, inaccurate and uncooperative. Perhaps he was far more interested in his new job than in writing about an earlier labour. He had certainly acquired a most enviable post: superintendent of the royal gardens at Malmaison, near Paris. The Empress Josephine was his employer, and all went well until she fell from grace for having borne no heir to Napoleon. Bonpland was loyal to her until she died in 1814, but then had to look elsewhere. In 1816 he accepted the position of museum director at Buenos Aires. South America then was not the relatively stable society it had been during his earlier visit. When on a collecting expedition near the Paraguay river four years after his arrival, some cavalry swooped upon his party. The servants were all killed at once. Bonpland was wounded by a sabre gash to the head and then made captive. He was not imprisoned but had to act as physician to a nearby garrison. For nine years his freedom was withheld, even though Humboldt was pulling every possible string (as La Condamine had done half a century earlier for Godin and his wife).

In 1830 Bonpland was finally set at liberty, the various entreaties – some by the British prime minister – having been successful. For a time he was renowned, receiving medals and awards from Europe, but these came less often as he stayed on in South America. He chose a small town in Uruguay and there he lived for the remainder of his days. The wife he had acquired when in Paris had left him at the start of his restraint. On achieving freedom he lived with an Indian girl who produced a large number of children for him. (Details of this liaison are imprecise.) He occasionally thought of returning to France, but decided not to leave his plants or, one assumes, his many offspring. In May 1858 he died aged eighty-five, slightly resenting the fame that had fallen upon Humboldt, but always grateful for the annual pension granted to him by the French government fifty-three years earlier when the two of them had returned to France. In the end he preceded his old companion to the grave by but a single year.

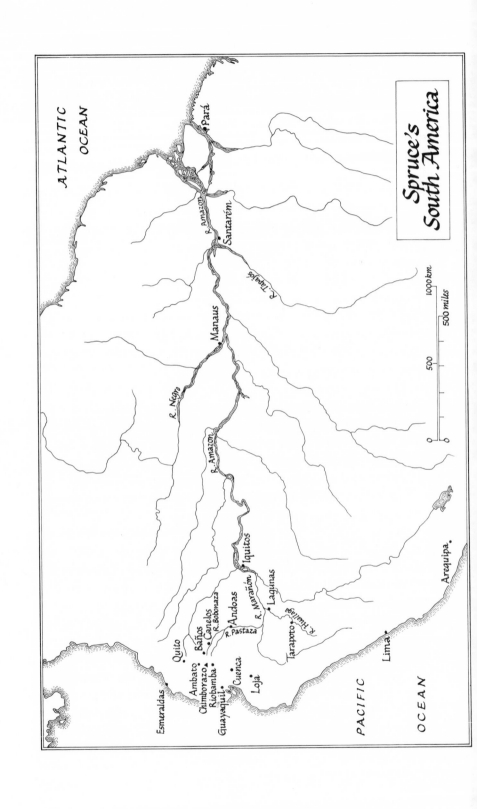

ATLANTIC OCEAN

Pará

R. Amazon

Santarém

R. Tapajós

Manaus

R. Negro

R. Amazon

Iquitos

Lagunas

R. Marañón

Andoas

R. Huallaga

Canelos

R. Bobonaza

Taraporo

Baños

R. Pastaza

Quito

Ambato

Chimborazo

Riobamba

Cuenca

Guayaquil

Loja

Esmeraldas

Lima

Arequipa

PACIFIC

OCEAN

Spruce's
South America

1000 km

500 miles

500

500

VIII

Spruce and Wickham
COLLECTORS EXTRAORDINARY

Humboldt's visit to South America had been accompanied by revolutionary rumblings. The American War of Independence and the creation of the French republic had helped to pave the way for thoughts of independence in these other lands. When that freedom arrived, and the colonial shackles from Spain and Portugal were undone, one result was easier access to South American countries. Humboldt and Bonpland had been amazed by their *laissez-passer*. Later travellers accepted such tolerance more as a matter of course, considering it right that people should come and go on the planet as they chose.

They also thought it right to take. They took specimens of every kind, collecting them in their thousands. Such acts were considered to be neither irresponsible nor in any way detrimental to the countries concerned. Science needed these examples of the world's riches, and science existed back home. Most items were of interest solely to the taxonomist. However, a few involved different motives, such as profit. Why should South America be the sole possessor of certain plants merely because it was their place of origin? Why should the blessing of cinchona be restricted to the high Andean regions in which it flourished? And why should rubber only grow in the forests that had given birth to this most desirable commodity?

With hindsight – such a useful attribute – it is easy to realize that this form of looting was bound to occur. What is impossible to visualize is how such thievery actually took place. Who were the miscreants and why were they chosen? What odd sets of circumstances caused them to be (more or less) in the right places at the right times? Why, in particular, was Richard Spruce selected to take cinchona, bearing in mind his predominant interest in mosses? Why was he overshadowed by such an imperialist as Clements Markham? As for rubber, the name of Henry Wickham is for ever associated with the taking of seedlings from the Amazon, for this unlikely man succeeded where many had failed. He was not a botanist nor even a collector, but he managed to gather one of the most lucrative species the New World had to offer. The stories do make sense once the facts have been established, but, as with all tales, it is necessary to begin at the beginning. Or rather at a point when not even the principals knew they would embark upon the particular exploits for which they are now renowned. The events that led to the taking of cinchona by Spruce (and others), and of rubber by Wickham, can be said to have begun in 1849. Admittedly Wickham was then only three years old and Spruce thirty-two, but their stories, and the deeds for which they are most famous, started with Spruce's arrival on the Amazon.

Many individuals might give their soul for a time machine. Personally I would more than welcome a chance to have attended a certain dinner at Santarém in 1849. The host was Captain Hislop. This Scotsman did not own the town of 2,000 people on one bank of the river Tapajós, but he was its most ebullient citizen – and probably its richest. On the evening in question he had invited Alfred Wallace, Henry Bates, Richard Spruce, Robert King (assistant to Spruce) and two English residents of Santarém, Messrs Golding and Jeffries. The natural history of the Amazon was, as it were, gathered in that one room, Wallace, Bates and Spruce being (or about to be) the dominant collectors of the region.

In essence it was Alexander von Humboldt who had arranged the meeting, even though he had left the continent forty-six years earlier. His books had acted as a crucial stimulus throughout Europe for a variety of youngsters who subsequently saw South America as the most desirable goal on earth. Charles Darwin's *The Origin of Species* was not to be published until 1859, by chance the very year of Humboldt's death, but his earlier books arising from the voyage of the *Beagle* were also vital reading matter for anyone interested in South America. Darwin had not actually seen any portion of the Amazon but he had certainly enthused about its continent: 'The day has passed delightfully; delight is, however, a weak term for such transports of pleasure: I have been wandering by myself in a Brazilian forest.' One day later he continued: 'I can only add raptures to the former raptures . . . I collected a great number of brilliantly coloured flowers, enough to make a florist go wild . . . The air is deliciously cool and soft; full of enjoyment, one fervently desires to live in retirement in this new and grander world . . .' The *Beagle*'s circumnavigation was completed a dozen years before Wallace and Bates set sail from Liverpool. Ample time had therefore passed for this further infusion of zest concerning South America to invade ardent natural historians such as those gathered round the dinner table in Santarém.

On that evening Wallace and Bates had already been in the area for over a year. Spruce and King had arrived more recently. All four men were young, the eldest being the thirty-two-year-old Spruce. Unlike every scientist before them, such as La Condamine and Humboldt (who had had their own wealth to support them) or Charles Darwin (who had had no need of salary and did have transport), this new breed was without resources. The new naturalists were to earn their slender needs by selling their collections, perhaps for threepence a specimen, perhaps for less. They certainly suffered, primarily from disease.

Henry Bates spent 11 years around the Amazon and achieved fame with his vividly illustrated memoirs.

Wallace, in particular, experienced terrible bouts of malaria and decided to leave South America after only four years. Spruce stayed for fourteen years before returning home to Yorkshire, but there he was an invalid for the remainder of his life. Bates experienced innumerable hazards during his eleven years by the great river, all splendidly chronicled in his *The Naturalist on the River Amazons*. (The title's plural echoes a former assertion that the huge river was in fact two rivers, becoming the Solimões above its junction with the Negro.)

Wallace, Spruce and Bates might have gone anywhere in South America, in that it was largely uncollected (the Spanish and Portuguese having been so lax scientifically during their lengthy occupation), but they concentrated upon the Amazon. Count François de Castelnau had already been to Peru, Robert Schomburgk to British Guiana, and Codazzi, Pissis, Karsten and Wagner had linked their names respectively with Colombia, Chile, Venezuela and Ecuador. The botanists Von Martius and Von Spix had also worked in Brazil, De Castelnau had travelled down the Amazon when his Peruvian days were over, and Pöppig had visited the region after considerable time west of the Andes. Despite all this endeavour, European involvement of a scientific nature within Amazonia was still modest during the first half of the nineteenth century. The Spanish had been the first to travel down the great river, the Portuguese the first to ascend it, the French (with La Condamine and Godin) the first scientists on its water, and Humboldt the first in many of its upper and northern reaches, yet it was the British who, scientifically, embraced the Amazon most wholeheartedly in the excited wave of interest that followed Humboldt.

Great Britain was busily embracing much of the planet during those Victorian years, via trade, the gospel, straightforward annexation, or a mixture of all three. The world's largest river was having its name linked with that of Britain quite differently, via some impoverished collectors. It is easy to suspect that the British naturalists yearned for a yet greater involvement by their country, and Spruce, for example, wrote in his diary:

How often have I regretted that England did not possess the magnificent Amazon Valley instead of India! If that booby James, instead of putting Raleigh in prison and finally cutting off his head, had persevered in supplying him with ships, money and men until he had formed a permanent establishment on one of the great American rivers, I have no doubt but that the whole American continent would have been at this moment in the hands of the English race!

As it happened, and as the gathering at Santarém could not possibly have conceived, the British were to collect the greatest prize the Amazon then had to offer. They did so without resort to normal imperialist practice. They just took it, without Bible, rifle or colonist in sight. That they were able to do so was a direct consequence of that happy, youthful, exuberant and infectiously exciting evening on the southern bank of the Tapajós. Without those naturalists' endeavours it is highly improbable that Britain would ever have acquired *Hevea brasiliensis* in sufficient quantity to be planted elsewhere. The story of rubber would in that case have been entirely different, and Britain's name would not be so frequently vilified, notably in South America, when this subject is raised. However, one event had to happen before this most notable deed, perfidious or otherwise, could take place. Richard Spruce had to create the precedent.

Ten years after the dinner party he was its only guest still in that continent. King had departed fairly speedily. Wallace, so beset with illness, had left the area less than three years after the evening in Santarém, but did not leave travelling; the Far East became his new obsession. Bates had only recently left the Amazon, having amassed 14,712 animal species of one sort or another, over half of which were new to science. Richard Spruce was still collecting and, in that year of 1859, had reached the western headwaters of the Amazon, having been treading in various famous footprints. He had been busy on the Huallaga river, where Don Pedro had waited for his daughter Isabela Godin while she was all but perishing on her journey from Peru. Spruce had left there to proceed up the Rio Pastaza, as he wished to travel further west. He therefore passed Lagunas, where La Condamine had discovered Pedro Maldonado waiting for him before they travelled together so successfully down-river. Spruce also reached Andoas, the settlement to which Madame Godin had been brought by the two Indians after they had found her wandering, distraught, desperate and lost. These events of a century earlier must have been vivid in Spruce's mind, until the bells tolled in Ecuador upon Humboldt's death to remind him of a mere half-century beforehand, when the Prussian explorer and Bonpland had examined that area.

The reason he was travelling so far westward, and entering a country busy with revolution, had been outlined in a letter from London: 'Her Majesty's Secretary of State for India has entrusted the Hon. Richard Spruce, Esq. with the commission to procure seeds and plants of the Red Bark Tree which contains the chemical ingredient known as quinine.' To be so entrusted was to be ordered, and the letter had further 'suggested' he should 'proceed' to Ecuador, collect money at Guayaquil, make arrangements for shipment with Her Majesty's consul there, and gather the necessary seeds.

From the point of view of the letter's author the commission was undemanding. Spruce had already spent ten years in some of the wilder parts of South America. He was known to be in the upper reaches of the Amazon – but a stone's throw, in South American terms, from the general location of *Cascarilla roja*, the red bark tree. Moreover, the effort was so blatantly worthy. Malaria was a terrible scourge in many portions of the British empire. The supply of quinine from South America's western seaboard had become unreliable. It was plainly preferable, or so this simple argument concluded, to gather some of the *Cascarilla*'s seeds, propagate them elsewhere and success-fully produce as much as was necessary of the 'chemical ingredient known as quinine'. Richard Spruce was undoubtedly the most suitable candidate for this work. He was therefore 'entrusted' with the commission.

The straightforwardness of such imperial reasoning was not matched by the actual task. The revolution in Ecuador was one undoubted problem. If Spruce had not stood at the door of his temporary dwelling one day, with shotgun and revolver ready for use against a belligerent bunch of revolutionaries, he would have lost his possessions, and perhaps his life as well. After leaving Andoas he had journeyed to Canelos, where Isabela had encountered the ravages of smallpox, causing all thirty-one of her Indians to prefer the known forest to an unknown infection. Spruce was able to recruit some 'shirted' Indians at that same place. Definitely without shirts were the Jivaros whom he next encountered. These head-hunting and head-shrinking Indians had guns as well as poisoned spears, but they befriended the Yorkshire botanist and his party, offering them shelter.

The indefatigable collector Richard Spruce, whose commission to collect cinchona proved so valuable to others.

The recruits from Canelos were miserable at this hospitality, cowering 'like a bunch of frightened guinea pigs', while a freshly shrunken head gazed down at them, adding to their qualms.

The Jivaros not only housed Spruce but led him and his quivering entourage to the Puyu, a Pastaza tributary that had to be crossed if they were to continue along their chosen route. The stream proved to be in flood. A delay was inevitable, with Spruce writing of his 'chagrin' at this enforced halt. However, like so many of his fellow-countrymen whose curious interests have surprised onlookers in countless portions of the globe, he found much to enjoy. It was raining, it was cold, the local Indians might change their mood, the river might not subside for days, or weeks, but Spruce's unhappiness 'was somewhat lessened by the circumstance of finding myself in the most mossy place I had yet seen anywhere . . . I found reason to thank heaven which had enabled me to forget the moment of my troubles in the contemplation of a simple moss'. There was more than a simple or single moss, this being an area encased in mosses in the most moss-laden portion of the planet. Spruce always found his greatest joy in cryptogamic company (and is best remembered for a significant publication upon this kind of plant).

He proceeded reluctantly when the Puyu waned in strength, particularly as conditions in general then deteriorated. No one, from Orellana onwards, has taken much pleasure in their passage through this portion of the Andes. The rivers are always torrents. The rain is remorseless. The contours are considerable, making progress difficult along tracks unworthy of the name. It was all very well for some servant of the queen to suggest that Richard Spruce Esq. should proceed towards the growing area of the red bark tree, but the indefatigable botanist was all but vanquished by the Andes. An attack of catarrh was so virulent that blood appeared from his nose and mouth. On an earlier occasion, when sickness had laid him equally low, he had heard an old lady 'with a scowl almost demoniacal' request his death: 'Die, you English dog, that we may have a merry watch-night with your money.' As those earlier days passed, with the hag repeating her miserable message, Spruce had switched from fever to chill, but he did not die. In the heights above the Rio Pastaza, at an unattractive place called Baños, his teeth chattered in the cold and again he thought that death was imminent. He could not (apparently) take advantage of the area's hot and sulphurous springs, fed with warmth from the nearby volcano, but he forced himself onwards. He passed the crosses of those who had perished on this same journey, and heard tell of a man observed grinning on an icy rock. 'Why is he laughing?' a child had asked. The boy was admonished with instructions to keep quiet or say a prayer; the man and his grin were dead.

Ecuador had become politically independent twenty-eight years earlier, both from Spain and from the enormous Gran Colombia that Simón Bolívar had attempted to create; but the nation was still unstable. Further on from the springs of Baños lay Ambato, starting point of Spruce's search for the cinchona seeds, but revolution was on every hand. So too was counter-revolution, with warring bands making life problematical for a solitary botanist who merely wished to rob the country of a major asset. The landowners were adamant he should not remove any of the valuable bark. Spruce affirmed his interest only in the seeds, and slowly made advances. A most awkward local man was Francisco Neyra, none other than the grandson of Nicolás de Neyra. Everyone who knew La Condamine's story, and how Dr Senièrgues had been killed by the mob, would have remembered the part played by the bullring's manager, Nicolás de Neyra. Spruce certainly knew the century-old epic and therefore knew the name. It seemed absolutely appropriate for the new Neyra to be as difficult and unhelpful as his grandfather.

Spruce steadily realized that there was more to receiving a commission from the Secretary of State for India than just proceeding to the correct area. There was certainly more to seed collection than simply gathering them. There were, for instance, people like Neyra. Spruce could fend off malaria, frustrate crones longing for his purse, and keep together shirted Indians while he gathered moss, but he was not immediately adept at dealing with intransigent landowners. Nevertheless, once he had met Her Majesty's consul in Guayaquil, he did have money. The British, he knew, would pay whatever he spent in acquiring the source of quinine. It was up to him, Neyra or no Neyra, to collect his seeds and send them on their way to India.

He therefore packed his equipment at Ambato and set forth for Riobamba, some forty miles to the south. In that area, so he had learned, the trees were growing more thickly and were most suitable for his purposes. Humboldt had also been along that road, and the straight line of cause and effect was very clear. The Prussian had opened up so much of this hidden world. Its gold had been plundered long before even he arrived, but the British were about to take something yet more valuable. And, having taken that, there was rubber next in line.

No one knows when it was discovered that the bark of cinchona trees contained curative properties. It is also uncertain when these healing characteristics were first learned by European man. The Indians of Peru were undoubtedly the earliest to associate the bark with its medicinal powers, realizing that it could dispel fever. It could also, as an early form of chemotherapy, attack malarial parasites in the human bloodstream. (It may even have been the first drug to attack the cause of *any* disease.) Cinchona trees, native to South America, belong to the Rubiaceae, of which the gardenia is a favoured example. There are about sixty-five species of evergreen shrubs and trees within the *Cinchona* genus, and most live naturally in the mountainous and forested regions of Colombia, Peru, Ecuador and Bolivia, generally between 3,000 and 6,000 feet above sea level. The plants need high humidity and considerable rainfall.

The word quinine comes from the Quechua language, where *kina* (or *quina*) means 'bark'. The active therapeutic substance found in cinchona is an alkaloid, but only four or so of the species in this genus contain the substance in significant quantity, either within the root bark or, more importantly, in equivalent regions of the stem. The Andean Indians were presumably unenthusiastic about passing on helpful, life-saving suggestions to the all-looting, all-demanding invaders. There is certainly no reference to any Spaniard using the bark until the year 1600, and that event was not recorded at the time. There is stronger evidence of a cure for fever being effected in 1630, and again in 1638. The first involved the *corregidor* (or magistrate) of Loja, and the second – a better-known story – concerned the Countess of Chinchón. As she was the Peruvian Viceroy's wife, the cure had therefore moved to the top of the social scale. Her name was subsequently used for the tree itself, a potion of cinchona bark having allegedly saved her life. It may well have done. The bark's active ingredient, quinine, is considered to have saved millions of lives in the centuries since its incorporation within the western pharmacopoeia. (Unfortunately the tale of the countess may not be true. A.W. Haggis, in his excellent *Fundamental Errors in the Early History of Cinchona*, published in 1941, doubts the authenticity of the original account written by Sebastian Bado, a seventeenth-century Spanish doctor.)

By 1649 *los polvos de la condesa* (or 'the Countess's Powders') had reached Europe, vigorously marketed by the Jesuits. (Other names given to the drug were Jesuit's Bark, Cardinal's Bark and Peruvian Bark.) The Church kept its precise origin secret and monopolized supply, thus antagonizing doctors. In Protestant areas it was considered to be popish (and, so another story goes, Oliver Cromwell had to die for lack of it). Charles II, when in similar straits, was given a secret elixir (of wine plus quinine) and recovered. The quack concerned was instantly knighted and made a royal physician, adding to the fury of the established medical profession. *Sir* Robert Talbor next saved the French Dauphin's life. For this he received a lump sum, a pension and a promise that the secret would be concealed for his lifetime. In fact he died one year later, aged forty-two, but such secrecy would have been difficult to maintain. Too much was at stake, and the fame of the fever bark tree would have been difficult to suppress. In any case it was officially recorded by the great taxonomist Linnaeus in 1742. He called its genus *Cinchona*, thus, despite the mis-spelling, compounding the countess story. La Condamine had brought back specimens from his earth-measuring expedition and had published a description of *Quinquina condamine* in 1738. However, Linnaeus then had his say, and his word ruled.

By this time cinchona bark was a valued medicine, used in the form of a powder, extract or infusion. In 1820 quinine and cinchonine were successfully isolated, and these two bitter alkaloids became even more favoured than the crude extract of bark had been. To disguise their bitterness it became the custom to add some sweetener. From this habit arose the notion that bitterness should be added to improve the carbonated soft drinks that suddenly became popular in the nineteenth century. Quinine Tonic Water originated in 1858 when Erasmus Bond achieved a patent for an 'aerated tonic liquid'. To improve a drink's flavour was one advance. To improve its flavour and add a therapeutic agent was doubly agreeable.

No wonder that the demand for quinine steadily increased. It could not be created artificially (and still cannot be manufactured economically). Its use as an anti-malarial agent and general febrifuge assured a market for all the bark that could be collected in South America. Demand from the drinks industry added to that requirement. South Americans in the tropical belt, mainly between 10°N and 22°S, were doing their best to satisfy the world, but the trees had suffered too much from these depredations. As the species did not grow elsewhere, and fear was arising that the supply would diminish or even cease altogether, it was inevitable that someone would think of a better solution: namely to take the seeds, grow them in controlled conditions, ensure that demand could be satisfied, and bring eternal reliance upon South America and South Americans to an end. At that period in history the wealthier countries were still annexing and colonizing other countries. What was the problem, therefore, in removing a few seeds? The act would even be humanitarian; it would save lives by ensuring the supply of a vital prophylactic. It was the proper thing to do.

It was such a good plan that, once initiated, there was increasing impatience. Where was Spruce? Were others, such as the Dutch, ahead in the commercial race to be humanitarian? And should not further collectors be despatched west of the Andes? In 1859, the famous year of Humboldt's death and Darwin's *Origin*, another individual steps on to the scene with considerable pomp: '. . . the urgent importance of introducing chinchona cultivation into India was brought to my notice . . . I resolved to undertake its execution . . . being convinced that this measure would confer an inestimable benefit on British India, and on the world generally.' He was also adamant concerning his personal merits: 'My qualifications for the task which I thus set myself to accomplish, consisted in a knowledge of several parts of the chinchona region and of the plants, an acquaintance with the country, with the people, and with their languages, both Spanish and Quichua.' The person was Clements R. Markham, then aged thirty, but later to become Sir Clements Markham, president of the Royal Geographical Society, a leading protagonist of British polar exploration after the turn of the century, and principal promoter of Robert Falcon Scott, who died in 1912 while returning from the South Pole.

The young Clements Markham, 'irritatingly destined for high office'.

(Sir Peter Scott, the British artist and naturalist, and the only child of
the explorer, was Peter Markham Scott.)

Clements Markham had served in the Royal Navy for seven years,
but left – as one book phrased it – 'in hazy circumstances'. In *Scott and
Amundsen* Roland Huntford wrote of him: 'He liked good looks, fresh
complexions, nice manners. He was suffused by an ill-disguised
feeling of romantic attachment. Though married, with a daughter,

Markham was a homosexual. He sometimes went south to indulge his proclivities safe from criminal prosecution. He liked earthy Sicilian boys.' Perhaps he also liked earthy Peruvian boys. He was certainly a most vigorous Englishman, with all the fervour of a Victorian missionary. To him it was absolutely right for Britain to take the cinchona seeds and produce quinine elsewhere. It would be laudable, it would produce profit, and it would serve the empire. (Markham always spelt the quinine genus as 'chinchona' because the famous countess had been of Chinchón. Linnaeus had undoubtedly erred when he named the trees *Cinchona*, but his error had to stick because that was the given name.)

Whereas Richard Spruce had received his cinchona commission at the instigation of Kew Gardens, principally via George Bentham and Sir William Hooker, who had been receiving his collections, Clements Markham operated on a higher plane. His initial approach was to Lord Stanley, First Secretary of State for India. By then, April 1859, Spruce was already battling his way across the Andes. In July, when Spruce had reached Riobamba, Markham was submitting his proposal, 'a plan in the execution of which I persevered until success had been secured in every particular'. Here was a man irritatingly destined for high office. 'I, of course, foresaw the probability of failure in one or more points, but I was fully resolved that no failure should be accepted as final, and that, whether through Government or private agency, every detail of the undertaking, as I then submitted it, should be eventually carried out.' He left England in December 1859 and set forth into the South American hinterland on 6 March 1860. His wife stayed behind at Arequipa 'to conduct all the business on the coast', leaving him free to go to work within the interior.

By now Spruce had set to work around Limón and was sending reports to Sir William Hooker:

I have succeeded in hiring the forests producing the *Cascarilla roja* after about ten times as much correspondence as would have been necessary in any civilized country . . . I am also in treaty with the owners of the woods . . . which produce the *Cinchona condaminea*, but as this species seems to flower and fruit at the same time as the *Cascarilla roja*, and the localities of the two species are 15 miles apart . . . it is plainly impossible that I can see with my own eyes the seeds of both species gathered which is the only way of having the right sort . . .

Spruce and Wickham

Having to be in two locations simultaneously was one problem; another was the zealous enthusiasm of the local work-force, who started gathering seeds before these had ripened. There was also the continuing revolution. Limón lay between Quito and Guayaquil, two warring cities, and a constant movement of troops passed by, taking horses and food, and caring nothing for the needs of a visiting seed-collector.

Clements Markham now begins to take over: 'I considered it necessary that a practical gardener should assist Dr Spruce in the forest. For this work I selected a very able and painstaking Scotch gardener named Robert Cross, who was recommended to me by Sir William Hooker.' In the middle of 1860, when Spruce was waiting for that year's batch of seeds to ripen, he met Mr Cross, who had with him a large number of Wardian cases (named after Nathaniel Ward and specifically designed for moisture-loving plants). Throughout that July and August the two men struggled to box cinchona cuttings, while ants and caterpillars simultaneously struggled to consume them. When the seeds ripened in August and fell from the trees, the men put out sheets to catch them. All in all they gathered 100,000 seeds, and were then faced with the problem of transporting seeds and cuttings to Guayaquil. Fortunately the civil war temporarily ceased, enabling everything to go down-river on a huge balsa raft. Markham was then far to the south (in modern Peru, as opposed to Ecuador), but took a little credit, if not (and most humbly) all of it: 'I shall ever look upon my good fortune in securing Dr Spruce's able co-operation as the most fortunate event connected with my conduct of the enterprise.' In his book *Peruvian Bark* (published in 1880), in the chapter entitled 'My Fellow Labourers', Markham is gracious about Spruce, Cross and three other assistants, much as some general thanks his soldiers for having won the fight.

This particular general did also encounter problems on his own account. On 6 May 1860 a certain *alcalde municipal* sent word that *un estranjero inglés* should be both arrested and prevented from taking a single plant. Rather than risk arrest, Markham 'saw that in an immediate retreat was the only hope of saving the plants'. He considered himself 'the last person to injure the Peruvians or their interests' and would defend his property with force, if need be. Whereupon, and with some difficulty, he and his party took a longer, and less obtrusive, route to the coast. At one awkward moment he brandished his revolver, damp powder rendering the weapon 'harmless but efficacious'. The Peruvians were blatantly not in favour of their valuable trees being replanted elsewhere, but the Englishman managed to extract an export permit from Lima's minister of finance. His four bundles of seedlings were then immediately despatched.

Markham's book, written twenty years after these exploits, includes a preface that is brief, clear and not overwhelmingly coy:

The enterprise undertaken by me . . . is an assured success . . . There are now 847 acres under chinchona cultivation on the Nilgiri Hills, besides 4,000 acres of private plantations . . . The annual bark crop from Government Plantations of British India alone is already 490,000 lbs. . . . In 1879–80 the quantity of bark sold in the London market, from British India and Ceylon, was 1,172,060 lbs. . . . The work itself has conferred an inestimable blessing on the people of India, while it has, at the same time, become a remunerative public undertaking.

As for South America, and its valuable trade in Peruvian bark, Markham has neither lamentation nor even doubt:

It would have been a source of deep regret to me if [exporting chinchona] had been attended by an injury to the people or the commerce of Peru, Ecuador, or Colombia. . . The demand for quinine will always be in excess of the supply from South America; and the cultivation of chinchona plants in India and Java will have the effect of lowering the price, and bringing this inestimable febrifuge within the reach of a vast number of people. . . Hitherto [the South Americans] have destroyed the chinchona trees in a spirit of reckless short-sightedness, and thus done more injury to their own interests than could possibly have arisen from any commercial competition . . . they themselves may undertake the cultivation of a plant which is indigenous to their forests. . . It will then be a pleasure to supply them with the information which will have been gained by the experience of the cultivators in India.

He affirms that there was no law forbidding export of these plants, 'although a decree to that effect was issued by the Ecuadorian Government on May 1st, several months *after* the collection of plants had been embarked'. In short, the British got them, just in time, and the South Americans did receive a lower price for their bark once the foreign trees had grown sufficiently to provide commercial competition.

Spruce and Wickham

The arrival of Clements Markham on the scene, and the casual manner with which he incorporated others into his plans, can make one forget Richard Spruce. This individual was a pioneer to begin with, and then became no more than an employee. He had been on the track of cinchona while Markham was still gathering support, but the moss-lover was a different kind of man, unambitious and certainly uninterested in self-promotion. This greatest collector of South American plants and cinchona seeds stayed in South America for three more years. After watching Cross depart with the all-important cargo he placed his accumulated wealth (some £700 – the quoted figures differ) in a Guayaquil bank. The precise amount swiftly became irrelevant because the bank then failed. Spruce was forced to collect again, just when he thought he might soon be travelling home, but ill-health dictated his return before too long.

Back in Yorkshire Spruce existed on an annual pension of less than £100 – again the figures differ, but the sum is never grandiose – and walking and sitting were both difficult. Nevertheless he did manage to finish *Hepaticae Amazonicae et Andinae*, a 600-page volume that had its origins in the moss-laden world he had encountered when waiting for that stream to abate in a sodden portion of the Andes. He was to gain eponymous posterity via a moss, Sprucea, and a liverwort, Sprucella. (Spruce trees have nothing to do with his name. That word is thought to derive from 'Prussia' where, as in many parts of the northern hemisphere, those trees of the genus *Picea* are abundant.) Despite his afflictions, his poverty, and living precariously within a couple of rooms, Richard Spruce did not die until 1893, when he was seventy-six. Although Humboldt, Bonpland, Wallace, Bates, Spruce and Darwin all experienced considerable illness either during or after their expeditions, the six men died at an average age of eighty. Wallace, most fever-ridden of them all, was also the most tenacious, dying at ninety.

The work of Darwin, Wallace, Bates and Spruce reverberated around the world in the same fashion as Humboldt's labours had resounded half a century earlier. The collections they sent back constituted one form of stimulus. Another was their thinking and writing, inspired by travelling through such novel regions. As for the removal of species likely to benefit other parts of the world, this was not a new practice, although a more positive deliberation now lay behind the deed. Since 1492 considerable two-way traffic had existed between both portions of the globe. The Old World had received tobacco, the potato, pineapple, groundnuts, cashew nuts, cocaine, tomatoes, paw paw, cocoa, cassava, arrowroot, maize, custard apple and such moderate blessings as cascara sagrada, ipecacuanha and vanilla. In stating the case for removing cinchona Clements Markham argued that South Americans owed to India 'the staple food of millions of their people'. Apart from rice they had been given 'most of their valuable products – wheat, barley, apples, peaches, sugar-cane, the vine, the olive, sheep, cattle and horses'.

In the early days potatoes and so forth were taken without a hint of regard for the consequences. The nineteenth-century takers realized that benefits were likely to accrue and therefore convinced themselves of the virtue of their case. With ministers of finance having to be persuaded, or maybe bribed, the procedure of extraction was no longer as simple as it had been. Nevertheless a removal of even greater economic consequence than that of cinchona would soon take place. Markham, Spruce and co. had shown how it could be done, and quinine production in the East had fulfilled the promise of the deed. Rubber could now follow in the self-same path.

To some degree it was logical that Spruce should gather the cinchona. He was a botanist, a collector and near the relevant area when the commission was despatched to him. It is also comprehensible that Markham should wish to absorb the enterprise. There is a similar logic with the rubber story, but here chance was more involved. No one could possibly have predicted that a somewhat aimless traveller, intent upon nothing in particular, should be the man to remove a species offering even greater rewards than did the cinchona tree. However, as with the story of quinine, it is necessary to begin before even those to be involved could possibly have known what was in store for them.

Many a traveller has encountered the phenomenon whereby some modest settlement, perhaps a town with fitful electricity, seems transformed when that same individual returns to it after a spell in more natural surroundings. Its originally laughable plumbing becomes positive indication of an advanced form of civilization. The shacks and other humble dwellings prevent rain – or most of it – from falling on the traveller's head. Richard Spruce returned to Manaus after a long spell up-country and might have thought he was merely encountering the world of developed blessings once again; but, as he approached the town and as the Rio Negro steadily widened, the area seemed to be suffused in an abundance he had not remembered. There was more river traffic in its vicinity, much more. The various vessels sped by in great haste. They were weighed down with cargo. At Manaus itself, instead of an idle mid-nineteenth-century Latin American scene, there were smoking steamships from countries an ocean distant. The place had possessed some 3,000 souls. Now it was a boom town, with people and imports flooding in where nothing but local produce used to arrive – and that most lazily.

'What has happened?' Spruce shouted to a friend.

'Don't you know?' the man shouted back. 'Rubber has happened, that's what!' With one gigantic leap, Manaus had boomed into the nineteenth century.

Christopher Columbus was allegedly the first European to take note of rubber. He observed white milk oozing from certain trees as they were felled. Later voyagers mentioned how Indians played with the stuff, bouncing it (without there 'being need for any inflation') and even pouring it over their feet as a form of waterproofing. Some called it *cao o'chu*, or 'weeping tree'. The French, naming rubber *caoutchouc*, are therefore loyal to its source. The English word recalls Joseph Priestley's discovery that it erased pencil marks, a most trivial use of this exciting material. The Spanish and Portuguese, with their lack of zeal for commodities that did not smack of instant wealth, were initially uninterested in the bouncing juice. Charles Marie de la Condamine, first in so much, was also first to import it into Europe and coined the word 'latex' (after the Spanish for milk). He even, as mentioned in his chapter, used it to protect certain of his instruments. For several decades afterwards the import of rubber was restricted to Indian-made artefacts fashioned from this curious substance.

Then in 1791 an Englishman, Samuel Peal, patented a procedure for infusing rubber into materials such as cloth, leather and wool. His technique made them 'perfectly waterproof'. It also made them brittle in cold weather. Charles Macintosh did better but his 'mackintoshes' also tended to go hard as boards in winter and melt in summertime.

(Perhaps such unfortunate garments could only gain fame and popularity in Britain, where waterproofing is so desirable, and heat and cold generally of lesser consequence.) Brazil was the principal supplier of raw rubber to the world, and exports reached eight tons a year by 1827. This gentle situation was to change dramatically, largely owing to the inventive Charles Goodyear, a Connecticut American born in the first year of the nineteenth century. When aged thirty-four, and with an impressive list of disastrous enterprises to his name, he applied himself to rubber, a substance that had also not been tremendously successful. Goodyear guessed that pre-heating rubber to a certain temperature was a critical prerequisite for processing it into a usable form, but ten years were to pass before he hit upon vulcanization, whereby rubber is heated with sulphur. This prevented the brittleness and suddenly permitted a wide range of possibilities for Brazilian latex, such as mackintoshes that did not crack apart in wintertime. The date of this new patent was five years before Wallace, Bates, Spruce and Hislop enjoyed their joint evening in Santarém. The first step had therefore already been taken towards the transformation of both Manaus, further up the Amazon from Santarém, and Belém, the river's principal port at its mouth.

That convivial evening had been in 1849. Another ten years were to pass before Spruce was instructed to proceed to Ecuador, and four more before that exhausted man left South America. In the decade of Spruce's departure a very different individual was wandering about in the central and southern portions of the New World. His travelling was casual and the publication describing his adventures was equally relaxed. *Rough Notes of a Journey Through the Wilderness from Trinidad to Pará, Brazil, by way of the Great Cataracts of the Orinoco, Atabapo, and Rio Negro* appeared in 1872. It possessed 'illustrations drawn on the spot by the author', one of which would single out this man for immortality. The author and artist in question was Henry Alexander Wickham. The rough notes were indeed rough, being packed with errors and inconsistencies. They were not even seen through the press by the writer, as a 'Notice' explains before the contents list. The book's first half describes the journey of the title, while the second recounts an entirely different trip to Central America some three years earlier. Bates and Wallace were abrupt in their opening sentences but Wickham's start is

Spruce and Wickham

even more perfunctory: 'New Year's Eve, 1869, we lay at St Thomas's and witnessed a curious effect in the sky: a rainbow at night, caused by the moon-rays falling on a rain-cloud.' There is no location given for St Thomas's, no explanation for the journey, and no description of his travelling companion, Rogers, who never achieves a Christian name. Wickham is equally uninformative about himself – how old he is, why he travelled to the New World, where his money came from or what he wished to do.

The book's second portion mimics Wallace and Bates precisely: 'The Bremen schooner "Johann", 350 tons, in which I was a passenger, sailed from London on the 3rd of August, 1866, and after a tedious voyage we sighted the island of St Lucia on the 4th of October.' As before there is no elucidation of anything, and no first name for another companion, Temple. This offhand and irritating book concluded with an equally unexplained *Report on the Industrial Classes in the Provinces of Pará and Amazonas, Brazil*. Its author is not Wickham but James de Vismes Drummond Hay, C.B., H.B. Majesty's Consul at Pará. The report is thorough, including such facts as that beef cost tenpence a pound in England as against sixpence in Brazil. Its inclusion in Wickham's volume is bizarre, but a dedication thanks Drummond Hay for 'many kindnesses', and perhaps the *Report*'s publication was a fair exchange.

In the two portions written by Wickham he seemingly describes everything to come his way, pleasurable or not:

Nothing was to be had from the slothful people of this miserable pueblo but a little poorly-made cassave. Drunken carousals continued without intermission (*El Governador* being chief instigator): the noise and annoyance was most disgusting to a person who was obliged to be an involuntary spectator. Castro at length reduced himself to such a pitch of phrenzy, that I thought it advisable to give him an opiate, which had the desired effect.

Everything is written in like manner, the good, the bad, the handsome, the ugly, and Wickham displays none of the enthusiasm so blatant in Wallace, Bates and Spruce. A reader feels no immediate longing to be either Temple or Rogers. Other companions are acquired *en route*, such as Ramón and the pleasingly named Level and Angel María Oviedos, but these men also remain mysterious. In one of Wickham's drawings there is a well-dressed woman apparently reading a book, but with her back to the artist. This picture's caption is powerful in its lack of explanation: 'Our first (temporary) home near Santarém, 1871.'

During his second expedition, the first to be described in his assortment of rough notes, Henry Wickham encounters rubber. As with everything else there is no additional explanation; the 'india-rubber' trees appear abruptly as he goes in search of them. Quite suddenly the author is planning a spot of rubber-tapping with a varied crew. Together with Rogers and Ramón, there was a 'queer weazened-looking old fellow' – Mateo, a stolid old man called Benacio 'with no particular attribute to mark him . . . except that he ate more than his comrades', and two boys. Of these Narciso was 'decidedly stupid' while Manuel was 'very bright . . . somewhat approximating in character to a London street boy'. Manuel later becomes 'roguish' and 'given to pilfering', neither characteristic rendering the first description invalid in that age between Fagin and the Baker Street Irregulars.

On 13 December 1869 Wickham hoped 'to have 1,000 trees ready for tapping in the ensuing month'. By 8 January 'I had tapped the first hundred trees, but the yield was very small which disappointment I attributed to their being loaded with green fruit'. In February he recruited three more tappers when he fell ill. By the end of the month, 'I was unable to tap the india-rubber trees, and Ramón is laid up with what is called "a game leg", and most of the other people were suffering more or less from calentura; consequently, I took very little ciringa'. With fever taking its toll, the poor showing in rubber was perhaps inevitable.

Through the remaining pages there is frequent but equally casual mention of rubber. Some flood-waters make the trees difficult to tap. Ramón is on his feet again, and then he succumbs once more. The two boats become 'heavily-laden', one assumes with rubber. There is no mention of selling the stuff, or of a worthwhile enterprise. Tapping rubber, it would seem, was part of life, like sleeping or eating, or encountering biting flies and avaricious humans, friendly natives or a spiteful forest. On one page, in the same throwaway fashion, is a simple botanical drawing: 'Leaf and Fruit of the Ciringa Tree (Indian Rubber), Size of Nature'. There are no suggestions concerning this famous plant, and no complaints about tapping an income from a tree growing wild in a difficult environment. Instead the rough notes

Wickham encountered rubber-tapping on his wanderings in South America as casually as he met everything else that came his way.

continue, in diary form, with their day-to-day events. As a final statement about the wilderness through which he had been progressing, he reaffirms what so many, starting with Francisco de Orellana, had said before him:

I have come to the conclusion, that the valley of the Amazon is the great and best field for any of my countrymen who have energy and a spirit of enterprise as well as a desire for independence, and a home where there is at least breathing room, and every man is not compelled to tread on his neighbour's toes.

Wickham's miscellaneous volume, published in 1872, was publicly available when yet another consignment of rubber seeds arrived at Kew Gardens, London. A certain Mr Farris had despatched them, but plainly with insufficient care as only twelve germinated. Following the success with cinchona it was inevitable that plans should be afoot for the same sort of deal with rubber, and Mr Farris's efforts were a part of them. There was no humanitarian aspect as with cinchona – no one's physical health would benefit from the translocation of *Hevea brasiliensis* – but the commercial possibilities became more desirable every year. Three decades had passed since Goodyear had patented his vulcanization, and industry was steadily discovering more and more applications for this elastic, non-conducting, water-proofing material. Manufacture as a whole was booming, with various wars to help its progress, such as the Crimean, and that between North and South in the United States. The Franco-Prussian conflict of the early 1870s was another boost, and the Brazilian product was everywhere in demand. On the day when Spruce, Bates and Wallace had sat down to that dinner in Santarém the value of rubber had been about three US cents a pound. When Spruce came down the Negro it had reached $3 a pound, and in every succeeding year it bounced even higher. The men in Manaus knew that. So did industrialists. And so did the botanists at Kew.

Suddenly there appeared *Rough Notes of a Journey Through the Wilderness*. Its author had plainly learned a thing or two about rubber. He had worked with it and, presumably, had sold it. Most important of all he had made a drawing of it, or rather of one leaf, one pod, and one fruit. It is easy to imagine the men at Kew falling upon this heaven-sent book and wanting to meet the heaven-sent individual who had penned it. In one of their tropical houses a miserable twelve seedlings were

Spruce and Wickham

FRUIT(S) IN POD

FRUIT

H.A. Wickham

*Henry Wickham's simple drawings of the 'leaf and fruit' of the rubber tree,
so enthusiastically noted by the men at Kew.*

struggling and failing to survive. It was very clear that this man
Wickham should be contacted without delay. He knew about rubber.
He seemed to be some sort of botanist, in that he often gave the Latin
names of plants in his *Rough Notes*. And he had even expressed an
interest in returning 'to the triangle betwixt the Tapajós and the
Amazon'. As Spruce had performed with cinchona, so should Wickham bring rubber from the forests for the good of all, and for Britain in
particular.

The principal enthusiast at Kew for such a scheme was Joseph
Hooker, director of the Gardens. It was his father, William Hooker,
who had been the main instigator for the cinchona snatch, when he too
was director. Together, father and son, William and Joseph, reigned
over the increasingly important gardens for a span of forty-four years.
(A book about them, *The Hookers of Kew*, by Mea Allan, is said to have
had its sales affected, notably in the United States, by its exciting title.)
Joseph was the greater collector of the two, first travelling to the
Antarctic with Captain James Ross and then favouring the more
abundant vegetation of the Indian subcontinent. He also enjoyed the
Mediterranean and, although never travelling to the botanical luxuri-

ance of South America, was fervent for the plan that would bring a piece of it to grow at Kew – an important piece, and possibly the most important piece of all. As the world knows, and Brazil certainly knows, the plan did succeed. The author of *Rough Notes* did return to the *Hevea* forests around the Amazon. He did collect seeds and did export them, but not until the twentieth century had begun did he put pen to paper detailing the plantation story in general and his part in particular.

On the Plantation, Cultivation, and Curing of Pará Indian Rubber is a slimmer but more scholarly work than Wickham's *Rough Notes*. It was published in 1908, by which time the author could style himself 'Sometime Commissioner for the Introduction of the Pará (*Hevea*) Indian Rubber Tree for the Government of India and Inspector of Forests B.H.'. Instead of starting off in relaxed fashion, apparently with the first thought to enter his head (as in *Rough Notes*), he begins the new book with a trenchant flourish:

The plantation of rubber-yielding trees having evidently come to play an important part, and in growing magnitude, in the planting interests of the day, it has been suggested that, as having exceptional working knowledge of the subject – extending back to the sixties – I should give it, and in such a way, as to be accessible to my fellow planter and forester, the 'man on the spot'.

He mentions that his original report, written shortly after doing the deed for which he became famous, 'would appear to have become buried in India Office and Forestry Reports'. Hence the need for a further statement from the individual 'personally responsible for the getting out and the bringing away from their native forest in the valley of the Amazon of the original stocks from which the "Plantation Pará" of today are derived'. In this further statement he explains that Sir Joseph Hooker, 'then directing at Kew, was attracted by drawings of mine of the leaf and seed of the tree in a volume of the time on the forest of the Orinoco-Amazon, and he did not rest until he succeeded in inducing the Government of India to grant a commission for its introduction'.

The commission seems to have been both totally generous and totally the opposite. There was 'a straight offer to do it; pay to follow result'; but there was also, apparently, no limit to the funds that might be spent, providing success was assured. Wickham's recollections of himself as written in 1908 do not entirely tally with those recorded in his *Rough Notes* (published thirty-six years earlier). Perhaps failure of personal correlation over the years is not a unique event, but those *Rough Notes* contained no argument for the transplantation of *Hevea*. By the twentieth century Wickham was asserting that he had been 'as one crying in the wilderness'. His proposals for relocating rubber had, so he said, been received unfavourably: 'Dead weight of inertia, not to say opposition, prevailed. The idea of cultivating a "jungle forest tree" was looked upon as not less than visionary.' Perhaps he did come back from that Orinoco journey in 1871 proclaiming that rubber should be transplanted forthwith. Perhaps he had withheld all such argument from a mere travelogue, considering it an improper place for such personal vociferation. Or it could be that he only found out how desperately the world cried out for rubber after he had returned from the forests where it was abundant. Only then, perhaps, and following the publication of his *Notes*, would he have realized that the solution was at hand – at *his* hands – should he find some willing sponsor.

At all events he encountered Joseph Hooker. Wickham is most gracious about him, saying that he 'looked upon the matter in another light'. Indeed he did. Those seeds from Mr Farris had failed, and were not the first such failures. The instructions to these other seed transporters were assuredly given before Wickham began crying in the wilderness (if indeed he did), but perhaps (the most generous conclusion) Wickham had been proclaiming in the wrong kind of place. Only when he had caught Mr Hooker's ear, or after Mr Hooker's eye had sighted those *Notes*, did like minds come together. From that moment the various longings coalesced. Clements Markham, now a principal of the India Office, was eager for a further piece of brigandage. India was enthusiastic for additional plantations. Kew was happy and able to act as midwife yet again. And Henry Alexander Wickham, aged twenty-eight in 1873, was wanting to act as intermediary. A commission to collect rubber seeds was set in force without further ado.

The exploit undertaken by Wickham is indeed famous. It is touched upon in many books, but no uniformity exists in the telling of the tale. Sometimes Wickham is worse than a scoundrel, a thief who absconded with Brazil's crown jewels. At others he is an itinerant naturalist, earning modest keep by sending botanical specimens to academic establishments. On yet other occasions it is as if a gunboat (not unknown in those days) had sailed up the Amazon. And sometimes the deed seems quite guiltless, as if Wickham was only behaving like the thousands of tourists who have pocketed seeds in the hope that they will grow back home. At the end of this charge and counter-charge it is easy to wonder instead if the act was not unavoidable. Rubber, like so many natural creations, had become one of the world's basic commodities. Minerals can be retained, and exclusively sold, by those nations in whose earth they lie, but crops are in a different category. They can be grown elsewhere. Even if their original habitat is located within a single country there can be conditions elsewhere entirely to their liking. Or possibly even more to their liking than their original abode.

Thus it has happened that pineapples, first from South America, are now doing nicely in Hawaii. Coffee, which started in Arabia, is a mainstay in much of South America. Potatoes from Peru became so crucial in Europe that a failure of this one crop caused terrible famine in Ireland during the 1840s. Where would Virginia or Zimbabwe (or a hundred other producing countries) be without tobacco? What would Ghana do without cocoa, or all of Africa without the Indian corn that was native to South America? What was HMS *Bounty* doing when the mutiny occurred, save transporting breadfruit trees from Tahiti to provide cheap food for West Indian slaves? In a present-day food store one may wonder where everything originated – not where it was encased in plastic or a can, but where it grew before modern times began. We certainly make things harder for ourselves by wrong nomenclature, as with that 'Indian' corn, 'turkeys' from North America or 'Muscovy' ducks that still look best around the Amazon where men first saw them fly.

Wickham's description of the rubber-taking venture, recorded in the middle of his slim, scholarly volume on the planting and cultivating of 'Indian rubber', may not be entirely accurate, but is probably more reliable than anyone else's account. Although written over thirty years after the events it describes – and memory does play false – Wickham's account has to be foremost because he travelled alone on this particular foray. He is quite explicit, and kind, concerning remuneration for his enterprise, the 'pay to follow result': 'Fortunately, I was left quite unhampered by instructions as to ways or means.' He is also clear about his anxieties, and the 'question came to me, how on earth to bring it

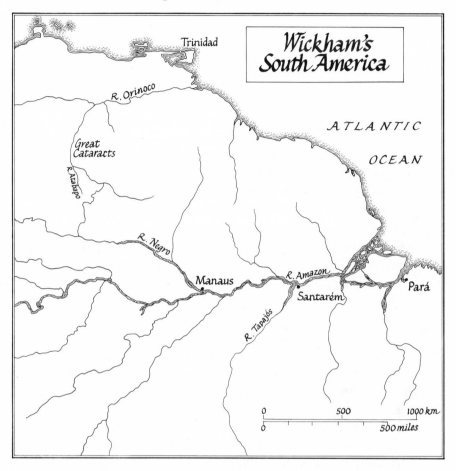

off . . . I had by that time given up the over-sea project, and had turned to planting near Santarém, on my own account, on the Tapajós plateaux.' There is no explanation of the 'over-sea project', unless it was the plan for bringing rubber-seeds to England. Therefore it can only be assumed that the commission reached him after his return to Brazil.

'About this juncture, and whilst I was still boxing about for, or to find, some practicable way, the few European planters in that remote locality were surprised and startled by news of the arrival on the great river of a fully-equipped ocean liner.' Wickham and others were invited to dine on board the SS *Amazonas* by Captain Murray. 'The thing was well done. The ship's boats took us off at Santarém, and we found the ship dressed out in blue lights.' The *Amazonas* was the first of the Inman Line, inaugurating 'Liverpool to the Alto-Amazon direct'. On board were 'two gentlemen' in charge of the event, and everyone enjoyed the evening with its 'well-appointed supper in the saloon'. The guests from Santarém were then decanted on shore, and the following day the vessel proceeded upstream.

Wickham thought no more about the ship, or that evening, for the time being. His rubber seeds were ripening, and anxiety was expanding in similar fashion. How on earth to bring it off? How could he despatch thousands of seeds and seedlings back to Kew without being forestalled by the Brazilians and without them arriving in such a condition that, once again, Kew could not do its work? A bizarre and fortuitous answer to his prayers came down-river with the news that the *Amazonas* had been abandoned. Those two hospitable gentlemen, the ship's supercargoes, had 'stripped' the vessel. They had absconded with the outgoing merchandise and Captain Murray had nothing to transport to Liverpool, there being no money to pay for the rubber he should have loaded. At once Wickham was intensely interested: 'I determined to plunge for it. It seemed to present an occasion either "to make my spoon or to spoil the horn".' (The expression is unknown these days, but the meaning is clear.) Wickham had no cash, and could not raise any in that locality, but he wrote to Murray 'chartering the ship on behalf of the Government of India'. He suggested a meeting where the Tapajós flows into the Amazon, a few miles downstream from Santarém. Captain Murray, one gathers, was pleased at any chance to fill his empty holds, however remote the possible payment.

With transport having become feasible, if not yet certain, Wickham worked with greater zest to provide the cargo. He hired as many Tapuyo Indians as possible. He loaded their pannier baskets with as much seed as these, and the Indians, could carry. The women were instructed to make open-weave crates from split *calamus* canes. These were carefully dried, as were the seeds themselves, along with their packaging of banana leaves. The loaded crates were slung high in suitable shelters, an aid to ventilation and, hopefully, to germination later on. 'There was no time to lose,' writes Wickham, using the phrase three times in his account of those days. He surely said it to himself yet more frequently as the suggested date of rendezvous drew near.

Spruce and Wickham

When that day came Murray was still 'crabbed and sore', as well he might have been. The two supercargoes had been entirely successful in their infamy, having sold all the outgoing shipment and then vanished – no one could or would say where – within Manaus. Murray had waited at the *boca* of the Rio Negro, as the men had advised, and had only lifted the anchor on realizing how well he had been duped. It must have been difficult for Wickham to commiserate when so blatantly gleeful that an entire ship, a British ship, had arrived quite empty for him to fill. He and his Indians did so without delay. Murray's 'grumpiness' was brushed aside as the 'prospective *Hevea*' were slung, fore and aft, in their little crates. However, all problems were not yet at an end. There was still Pará ahead of them, the port from which clearance was required before SS *Amazonas* could lawfully put to sea.

Any notion that Wickham was innocently unaware of the gravity of his act is dispelled by his own writings: 'It was perfectly certain in my mind that if the authorities guessed the purpose of what I had on board we should be detained under pleas for instructions from the Central Government at Rio, if not interdicted altogether.' He knew that Clements Markham had had a difficult time extracting cinchona from Peru. He realized that any delay in his own project would be disastrous, with the seeds deteriorating into uselessness in all their splendid, roomy holds. And he also knew, as the most cogent fact of all, that Pará was an obstacle of appalling magnitude.

But again fortune favoured. I had 'a friend at court' in the person of Consul Green. He, quite entering into the spirit of the thing, went himself with me on a special call on the Barão do S—, chief of 'Alfandiga', and backed me up as I represented to his Excellency my difficulty and anxiety, being in charge of, and having on board a ship anchored out in the stream, exceedingly delicate botanical specimens specially designated for delivery to Her Britannic Majesty's own Royal Gardens of Kew.

Wickham confirmed that the ship's captain was keeping up steam, partly to reduce any delay and partly in the hope that his Excellency would see his way to granting an 'immediate dispatch'. This all-important interview was 'most polite', and full 'of mutual compliments in best Portuguese manner'. Consul Green must have done a superlative job, quite in the spirit of the thing, for the 'dispatch' was granted without a qualm. The *Amazonas*, needless to say, got under way as soon as Murray had the 'dingey hauled aboard'. Wickham's chuckles must almost have been audible to men working on the distant Pará waterfront. Some of them were probably heaving bales of rubber while others, marking up their value yet again, were rejoicing at taking part in another bumper year. This rubber was unlike any other form of produce they had ever known.

Wickham's troubles were not over, but the ensuing problems were in a different class from the nail-biting interview. He had to keep the crates clear of the ship's rats. He had to ensure ventilation. He had also to deal with a varying climate as they crossed the equator and headed north, but at least they were travelling during the northern summer. At Le Havre Wickham hurried ashore and 'there posted over to Kew', so as to hasten preparations. A night goods train was despatched by the authorities to meet the *Amazonas* when she docked at Liverpool, and the Kew hot-houses were made ready for the sudden invasion of *Hevea.* Joseph Hooker must have been ecstatic at the prospect of an entire ship-load of rubber seeds to come his way.

At Pará, while the S.S. Amazonas *kept up steam, Wickham hurried ashore to receive permission for exporting his precious cargo.*

Spruce and Wickham

'The *Hevea* did not fail to respond to the care I had bestowed on them,' Wickham writes, and they provided a joyful sight for everyone concerned. Instead of twelve sickly seedlings, as had been acquired from Mr Farris, 7,000 young plants were alive and well a fortnight after their train journey south from Liverpool. At Kew they were arrayed, tier upon tier, row upon row. Rubber had finally left the Amazon.

The eventual destination planned for the rubber was Burma, but the rupee fell in value and that scheme fell with it. Ceylon was the next choice, and proved more enduring. Wardian cases, so successful with cinchona, were used for the rubber seedlings. These were sent down the Thames in barges and then loaded aboard British India liners. The year was 1876. There would be much error and considerable experimentation before those 7,000 developed into the overwhelmingly successful rubber plantations of the East, but that is what did occur, in time.

Meanwhile Manaus boomed, like some reveller unaware that the party had already ended. The world's demand for this extraordinary latex rose day by day, and so did the product's price. In 1885 Karl Benz created the world's first petrol-driven motor car, and it ran on rubber wheels. Two years later John Dunlop helped his son to win a cycle race by binding a rubber hose to each wheel and then inflating them. The motor industry took time to prosper, but it and the rubber plantations were to flourish in tandem. Wickham's 'snatch', 'vile deed' or 'sensible development of a global requirement' (think of it as you please) had happened at a most appropriate moment. The awful labour of rubber-tapping *seringueiros* could never have supplied the twentieth-century lust for the substance they collected. Rubber trees had to be in plantations if their yield was to have any hope of satisfying demand, and Amazonian plantations proved to be unworkable. (*Dothidella ulei*, the leaf blight, saw to that.)

Of the various protagonists in this story of cinchona and rubber, both Clements Markham and Joseph Hooker were knighted long before the rubber industry had shown how successful it would become. Henry Wickham, the principal, did not receive his knighthood until 1920, eight years before his death. As for Richard Spruce, in many ways the most likeable and admirable, he only received that pittance of a pension, some say £50 a year, some say not much more. He had really done it the hard way, and he then died the hard way too, after years and years of debilitating illness. The cinchona plantations and the rubber trees were growing well when he, so much the pioneer in all this enterprise, gave up the struggle in 1893.

Henry Wickham, who did not receive his knighthood until 1920. By this time the eastern rubber plantations were a resounding success.

IX

Julio Arana
KING OF THE PUTUMAYO

'Ridley, whose active life was cut short in 1956 at the age of 101, played an important part in the establishment of rubber in Malaysia.' With this happy phrase Wilfrid Blunt (in his book on Kew Gardens) lays gentle emphasis upon a man crucial to the rubber story. Without doubt Hooker, Markham and Wickham had organized the deed, but, as any criminal will tell you, the problem of realizing financial gain from a burglary can be no less troublesome than the theft itself. Taking rubber seeds was one thing. Making money from them was quite another, needing a person like Henry N. Ridley to lend his talents to the cause.

Manaus did not care when news came up-river that a large *Hevea* consignment had left Pará and arrived safely in London. Its Chamber of Commerce scoffed at the possibility of its lucrative monopoly being withdrawn (though eight years later it did impose a tax of £60 per kilo upon exported rubber seeds). Great Britain seemed equally casual in realizing its brand-new form of asset (acquired at a total cost of some £1,500). Wickham, who did know a thing or two about the subject, did not travel to Ceylon with the precious plants. Instead, and without explanation save restlessness, he moved to northern Queensland and tried his hand at tobacco and coffee, about which he knew no more than about the Australian land in which he failed to grow them. This project was to lose him everything he had earned in the rubber snatch, his share of those £1,500.

The rubber plants left England on 12 August 1876 in the company of William Chapman, a Kew gardener. The *Duke of Devonshire* was bound for Colombo and its rubber for the Peradeniya Botanical Gardens. So far, in a sense, so good, with little time wasted and a goodly number of the seedlings still in vigorous growth. Before he left for Australia Wickham had written a report in which he passed on all his available *Hevea* knowledge. He even suggested, most prophetically, that Malaya might be the most suitable location for rubber plantations. This report must have been either disregarded or lost, because its many recommendations were not initially applied. Instead the belief grew that *Hevea* would grow most satisfactorily in swamps. This notion arose from a mistaken idea of the Amazon in general and the fact that much latex was gathered within easy reach of rivers. A major plantation experiment was not started until 1888, and this was located in a frequently flooded, high-rainfall area near Ceylon's Kalu Ganga river. Not one of the many thousands of young trees survived. The local planters, well-established in tea, did not rush to grow the new crop when confronted by such governmental failure. And the rubber-men, half a world away in the forests around the Amazon, continued to thrive on their monopoly. So what if some *inglés* had stolen seeds a dozen years beforehand?

While those in Ceylon were watching saturated *Hevea* drown, there was a young man in Singapore, later to be known as 'Rubber' Ridley, who was determined to make this difficult New World tree succeed. Trained at Kew, he directed the botanical gardens at Singapore, almost on the Amazon's latitude. There were three principal problems to overcome. First, to make the trees grow. Second, to extract their latex profitably. And third, to persuade planters to think of rubber as a future source of revenue. He knew the last difficulty would be overcome the moment he had conquered the initial two, and the second was a greater problem than the first. An existing belief, perhaps even nurtured by Wickham (who had travelled to Ceylon after failing in Australia), was that rubber could only be tapped infrequently. This was, after all, the procedure in South America, where the men searched out the trees, slashed them for their latex, and returned months or even years later to slash them yet again. It was also believed that only large trees yielded rubber, because the tappers around the Amazon sought out the bigger specimens. Ridley succeeded in destroying both fables. He showed that even four-year-olds could be milked *every single day*.

Ridley's principal discovery was the herring-bone method of tapping

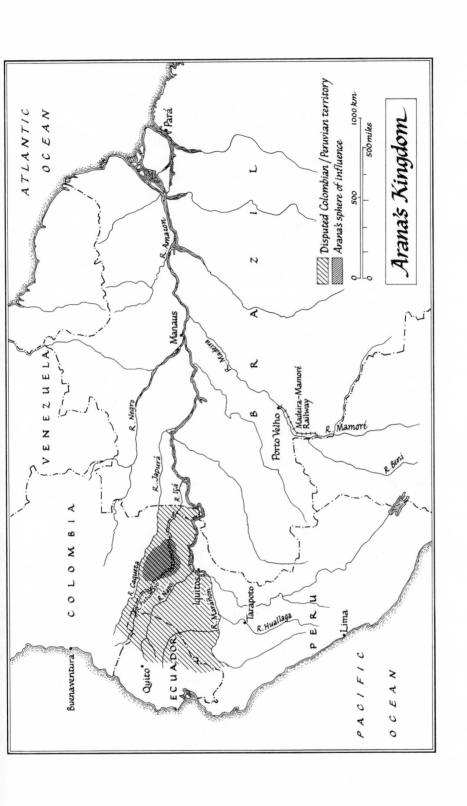

Arana's Kingdom

Disputed Colombian / Peruvian territory

Arana's sphere of influence

0   500   1000 km
0   500 miles

trees. (This is such a feature of rubber acquisition, conspicuous in every photograph on the subject, that one can forget it had to be discovered.) If latex could be acquired daily from young trees, the economics of tapping looked vastly different – many hundreds of times more appealing than waiting perhaps for a quarter of a century before extracting rubber once every other year or so. In 1895 Ridley persuaded a couple of Malaya's coffee planters to risk putting two of their acres into rubber. When these trees were tapped twenty years had passed since the *Amazonas* had sailed from Pará, but the Amazonian monopoly was at last being cracked, if only modestly. This early Malayan rubber sold in London for 2s. 8d. a pound. The quantity involved was small but the price was critical. The Pará rubber of Malaya cost less than that coming from Pará. (A peak price of 12s. 9d. per pound was to be paid to Manaus in 1910.)

It is not recorded whether Douglas and Ronald Kindersley made much money from their two-acre investment, or whether they were quickest off the mark in planting further trees, but Ridley did not stop with them. Before a dozen more years had passed some ten million trees had been planted in 500 square miles of Malayan soil. Many thousands of immigrants from other parts of Asia were imported to help with the tapping of this extra revenue. Rubber had become Malaya's primary crop, and was to stay that way.

Ridley had been born in the year that Richard Spruce had returned to Manaus, there to discover that rubber had boomed. He was five years old when Markham and Spruce were abducting cinchona from Peru, and was achieving his majority when Wickham pulled off the same *coup* with the yet more lucrative species from Brazil. Ridley was eventually to see planters falling over each other in their twentieth-century haste to switch from coffee to rubber. He watched the new plantations come to fruition when the automobile industry was proving avaricious for more and more of this bouncing latex, so tailor-made for inner and outer tubes. Ridley was also there when the First World War boosted demand, and he knew only too well of the catastrophe as the Japanese swarmed south through *Hevea* plantations one war later. Synthetic rubber helped to plug the gap, but after the Second World War demand for the natural product permitted Malaya to become, once again, principal supplier of this commodity. Finally, having spanned and made a piece of history, Ridley died. He missed by one year Malaysia's independence, but he had done more than any other individual to establish the country's primary crop and a major source of its wealth.

So when did the tide turn in the Amazon? When did everyone realize, along the Manaus waterfront, at Pará, at Santarém, or within the *Hevea* forests far from any town, that something had happened to the rubber boom? To a degree it was understood even before the event. There was always a kind of madness in Manaus, a lack of comprehension concerning the explosive demand for rubber and an accompanying assumption that such beneficence could not last. The citizens of Manaus did not behave as rich men. Instead they were sweepstake winners, astounded at the bounty to come their way, and, foolishly, carelessly, they did their very best to vanish the affluence. They did not invest; they spent. They did not care for the future; the present was sufficient. Rubber was a boom that could only disappear, either slowly or as fast as it had come.

In the end the boom's dying was as none had foreseen. For a few years the signs of impending death had been fairly plain, but along came a *coup de grâce* no one could have visualized. It was not directly connected with the burgeoning plantations in the East, but straightforwardly linked with a youthful American, a proud Peruvian, and an Irish homosexual. Rubber had always been an odd commodity. The eclipse of its Amazonian empire was in total keeping with that strangeness.

During the latter half of the first decade of the twentieth century these three men could not have been placed more differently. Nor were their aspirations similar. Not one was Brazilian, but it was within Brazil that their various actions had greatest effect. To some extent they were all broken by the interchange. One was knighted, and therefore brought to a prominence that assisted in his downfall. One suffered from loss of earnings, and of time, as he pursued justice with no ulterior intent. And the third never seemed to understand why the first two had hounded him into relative poverty and definite obscurity.

Walter Ernest Hardenburg was, without doubt, the most straightforward of the three. He was also the youngest and most likeable. When he enters the story, late in 1907, he is twenty-one. It had been his childhood ambition, first in Illinois and then in Youngsville, New York, to see the greatest river in the world. As soon as opportunity permitted, he and a friend left the United States, worked their passage through Central and South America, and then heard that engineers were wanted on the Madeira–Mamoré railway. Hundreds of men had died in two earlier attempts to link Bolivia with a navigable portion of the Amazon system, and a third effort to complete the connection was then in progress. It needed men, preferably with engineering experience, and W.E. Hardenburg and W.B. Perkins were on their way. While journeying south they encountered the river Putumayo.

Julio César Arana, the Peruvian, had been born in 1864 (and was therefore forty-four when Hardenburg and Perkins met that river). Initially he worked in the hat business, as did his father. He travelled widely, notably down the Amazon. It must have been difficult peddling hats when everyone else seemed to be in rubber, tapping it, curing it, and selling it at great price. Arana could not resist the new challenge and set up a small trading post at Tarapoto on the Huallaga (where Spruce had worked so happily before being commissioned to collect cinchona). By 1890, loathing the forest and resenting the lowly life enforced upon himself, his educated wife and their brand-new daughter, Arana was growing more ambitious by the hour. He steeped himself in the rubber business, borrowing money, causing more and more tappers to be in servitude to him, and gradually becoming powerful. Most of the leading rubber men held sway over great tracts of land, and woe betide anyone who trespassed on to them, let alone tapped a single tree. By the middle of the first decade of the twentieth century Arana's principal domain was a piece of land claimed by both Colombia and Peru. A particular river was said by some to be the frontier. That river was the Putumayo.

Roger David Casement had been born in the same year as Arana, but near Dublin rather than in Peru. His parents died when he was a child and he moved north to Ulster, living with a guardian there. Employment with the Elder Dempster Line introduced him to western Africa and then to the Congo. There he worked with the explorer Stanley, and achieved a name and work with the British government. Official Foreign Office postings then took him to the Niger Coast Protectorate, Uganda, Lourenço Marques, the Upper Congo, South

Africa, and the Congo once again. During this final visit he reported upon the hideous maltreatment of the Congo Free State's native population. Punishment by death of workers who had failed to bring in some necessary quota was frequent. So too was mutilation, the chopping off of hands and feet. This Free State, he wrote, 'was no more than a gigantic and ruthless enterprise'. That was in 1904. He was then posted to Lisbon, to Santos and Pará (both in Brazil), and, as consul-general, to Rio. While holding that post he received orders to accompany a Commission of Inquiry that would investigate alleged atrocities in the rubber industry. It had been reported that Indian workers were being maltreated, with torture and killing a frequent occurrence. This was the Congo all over again, and he should proceed to the source of all the allegations. This region was on either bank of the Rio Putumayo.

The intertwined story of these three men has to begin in Manaus, the boom town lying some 450 miles downstream of the point at which the Putumayo flows into the Amazon. For centuries this settlement, founded as a fort by the Portuguese, was most tranquil, as the black waters of the Negro flowed past to meet the brown Amazon a few miles to the east. When it became the entrepôt of the rubber industry, flaunting excessive wealth, it also became the centre for every extravagant tale. Myth and legend are difficult to disentangle, but this jungle city, not even then connected by road to anywhere else, did thrive in a most astonishing fashion.

The hard facts certainly make many of the tales believable. Rubber had been only a few pence a pound, and only a few tons of it had been exported, during the first decades of the nineteenth century. Following the efforts of Macintosh, Goodyear and industrialists of distant lands, not only did the price rise but demand escalated. The trade was already booming when Spruce re-encountered Manaus in the 1850s, and it continued to reverberate. In each ten-year period between 1880 and 1910 the quantity shipped down-river increased by 10,000 tons. Far from satisfying demand this merely whetted it, and straightforward arithmetic can explain the dizzy rise of this extraordinary city. A production of 10,000 tons at 2s. a pound meant an income of £2,240,000. A production of 44,296 tons (the peak figure) at 12s. 9d. a

The boom town of Manaus at the turn of the twentieth century, with steamships collecting its vital commodity, and the dome of the opera house showing how some of its money had been spent.

pound (the peak price) meant £63 million. The twenty-eight-fold rise in income between 1880 and 1910 from this one source led to considerable prosperity, whether lavished wisely or indulgently.

Manaus chose indulgence. A flock of ladies descended from Europe (always said to be courtesans rather than some lesser name). One police report alleged that two of every three houses were brothels. Cobblestones were imported at great price to improve the streets. Slabs of marble also arrived, partly to be walked upon and partly to adorn the houses. An entire tramway system came as well, the first to be constructed anywhere in South America. The first telephone service along the Amazon was installed. As Manaus had nothing, save for the Amazon and its all-encircling trees, virtually everything had to be imported – chandeliers, street lights, pianos, clothing, food (other than the most basic produce), drink (other than the local kinds), jewellery, yachts. If something had to come from such a distance it might as well be good, or so seemed to run the argument. Therefore it became the very best, the most flamboyant, the ultimate extravagance. (Even in his hat-trade days Arana had realized a prodigal streak in the local character. After failing to sell some costly items he abruptly raised their price five times. At once he made a sale to a formerly reluctant purchaser who did not wish it to be known he thought the price excessive. For the same reason a drinking partner bought a similarly expensive hat for himself.)

The famous opera house was entirely in keeping with the Manaus love of ungrudging ostentation. It had started as a modest project, £3,600 being allocated as suitable expenditure. Then, not only was funding for the city increased through a twenty-per-cent tax on all exported rubber, but there arrived a new governor for the state. Eduardo Gonçalves Ribeiro was young, power-hungry and happy to spend the Manaus wealth in an appropriate manner. He saw to it that the city changed from a frontier assemblage of shacks to a well-planned, right-angular collection of *boulevards* and streets. He planted trees as befitted a capital. He imported the electric lights and sixteen miles of tramway. He organized good drinking water, fine governmental buildings, a formidable Palace of Justice, lakes, bandstands, parks, gardens and a race-course, all for the 'village', as he called it, that he had found. To crown everything he raised the status of the planned opera house from little more than a modest hall to a prestige symbol that would surely attract the greatest and the best.

It should not be forgotten that, for all its wealth and fame, Manaus was still in the middle of the forest, still unconnected by road to anywhere, and still possessing no more than 30,000 inhabitants. Ribeiro ordered the opera house's ironwork from Glasgow, its external tiles from Alsace-Lorraine, its chandeliers from Italy, its marble pillars from Carrara, and did not baulk at costly porcelain, curtaining, seating and art-work. He raised the original paltry budget again and again until it approached £500,000. The resulting building could accommodate an audience of 1,600, which meant that one in eighteen of the Manaus population would be needed to fill it on any evening. There was also the problem of filling the stage, or finding suitable performers for such a resplendent setting. (The Manaus population today is nearing a million, and the opera house is less startling in its brash effrontery, but it is still an oddity, being used for performances for less than four weeks in each year.)

Certainly Ribeiro's starched front, possibly starched in Portugal

The opera house's opening performance was in 1897. It had seating capacity for 1,600 in a town of 30,000 ebullient citizens.

where many sent their linen, must have protruded proudly on opening night, and so must 1,600 others. The date was 6 January 1897, and the Grand Italian Opera Company was there to perform Ponchielli's *Gioconda*. Fortunately this cast departed from Manaus without sickness invading its ranks, but other groups were not so lucky when yellow fever took its toll. Extra enticements were therefore necessary: jewellery for the prima donnas and encrusted batons for the maestros. The Austrian consul (who had started as a clerk in Stuttgart) determined that the world's most famous tenor should grace the Manaus Opera House. Either Enrico Caruso did not answer the many beseeching cables or he did so with refusals. Herr Scholz had therefore to content himself with munificent parties, in which girls bathed in champagne while guests lapped at the doubly precious liquid. (Many notables, such as Anna Pavlova and Sarah Bernhardt, are also alleged to have performed at Manaus, but, alas, these two did not visit the place any more than did Caruso.)

Manaus life-styles were not in keeping with those of other frontier towns up and down the two Americas. Waldemar Scholz did not stop at effervescing ladies. He had a lion, a yacht, a motorboat. His servants were in livery. If one man burned money to light a cigar, others had to do so. If some girl became fashionable, or extremely costly, she grew instantly desirable. As Victor von Hagen phrased it,

[Manaus] had actually become El Dorado. Gold flowed like water through its streets. The whole city throbbed to the recrudescence of the dream of wealth. Indians who once became fearfully besotted on sense-racking rum now drowned their *Weltschmerz* in champagne. One had *pâté de foie gras*, Crosse and Blackwell's jams, Huntley and Palmer's biscuits, imported wines. One could sit down to a dinner at which the butter came from Cork, the biscuits from Boston, the ham from Oporto, and the potatoes from Liverpool.

The fact that food arrived from such distances may seem one more excess, but the steamships collecting rubber from Manaus' £1,000,000 floating dock (the river rises fifty feet during each year's flood) had come from Europe or North America. Whether laden with cobblestones, women or wine, they had to bring something. Trade between Manaus and the rest of Brazil, which also lay at a considerable distance, was extremely modest and far less exciting. Who wanted whatever Rio could provide when stuffs from Paris were available, cars from North America, pearls from the Orient? Besides Manaus had high hopes, and the firm intent, of becoming Brazil's next capital. It should therefore be supreme in every way.

Julio Arana, the Peruvian, moved his headquarters to Manaus in 1904. To be elsewhere was to be second best. By then his principal rubber-tapping domain was along the River Putumayo. This was an excellent site, rich in trees and also free from prying eyes. The border dispute, and occasional sabre-rattling from both Peruvians and Colombians, discouraged casual interference. Arana did not employ ordinary rubber-tapping *seringueiros*, recruited from the casual workforce to be discovered up and down Amazonia, but used Indians, mainly from the Huitoto tribe. And instead of using local men to act as overseers he imported 200 West Indians from Barbados. He knew they would be both ruthless and entirely under his command. Besides, they were British subjects and he had recently transformed his business into a British concern, the Peruvian Amazon Rubber Company (later renamed the Peruvian Amazon Company to make it less specific). To have foreign capital supporting his enterprise was valuable and highly prestigious. The company had British directors as well as British employees from the West Indies.

On reaching Manaus and hearing a thing or two about the employment for which they had signed, some of the Barbadians jumped ship.
The British vice-consul affirmed they had no right to do so, their
contracts being binding. Together with the local police he ushered
them back on board. At about this time, bored and irritated by the
Putumayo dispute, Peru and Colombia agreed to remove all military
presence from the area, with neither side claiming it for the time being.
The region would be left to itself, and therefore to Arana. He quickly
saw to it that no one entered *his* river, save his employees or those with
the authority of one of his agents. A couple of hundred thousand
square miles were now under his control, a piece of land four times the
size of England. He was therefore poised to become the greatest
rubber baron of them all.

Only in this ambition was he like his rivals, like A.G. Araújo who
controlled most of the Rio Negro, like Colonel Nicolás Suárez with
25,000 square miles by the Beni river, like Scholz with his stranglehold
on the import business. By contrast Arana was a man of culture, or
wished to be. He revered his wife and family. He longed for Paris
rather than the jungle and whatever raucous entertainment Manaus
had to offer. His life-style was puritanical. Notwithstanding the heat he
dressed impeccably, donning starched collars and dark suits. His beard
and moustache resembled those of British or Tsarist royalty rather
than the well-waxed extravagances of his Latin contemporaries. Only
his relatives were appointed to key positions in the Arana empire,
although he loathed their wayward antics. Hard work and a beloved
family were, for him, all that mattered. He might have been thought a
model, upright and highly principled citizen, save for the Putumayo.
The deeds along that river were about as foul as any in mankind's long
history of abusing other human beings.

Walter Hardenburg and his friend Perkins had been advised not to
go down the Putumayo on their way into Brazil. The Colombians said it
was a difficult region where they were likely to find themselves in
trouble. Far better, they added, to take the Rio Napo, a parallel and less
troublesome route. No doubt some of the warnings attracted the
youngsters, hazard exerting its own appeal for the adventurous, and
they determined upon the Putumayo. The date was 1 October 1907
when they left Buenaventura, on Colombia's Pacific coast, and headed

for the Andean passes that would take them to the allegedly difficult river.

Hardenburg was to publish a book about his adventures five years later. Called *The Devil's Paradise*, it starts off in a most insouciant manner, as a relaxed travelogue, and no hint of anything devilish enters the first 100 pages. He and Perkins take note of the passing scene, drink a lot, shoot animals (in the spirit of the age), and steadily progress downstream with their eyes wide open: 'The dress of the Incas is very picturesque . . . The food of these aborigines consists chiefly of maize, collards, and game.' Their drink 'has a sour, bitter taste, very palatable to the Indian, but disgusting to most white men'. Hardenburg is impressed with the local *bodoquedas*, blow-guns accurate 'up to about thirty metres' and having 'a great advantage of noiselessness'. On meeting the headwaters of the famous Putumayo the two travellers encountered a torrent, some six feet wide, which they crossed on the first day 'no less than thirty-four times'. When the Andes were finally behind them they 'invested in a couple of bottles of wine and, retiring to our hut . . . duly congratulated one another on the successful termination of the first stage of our journey'. Young men all over the world have behaved likewise; such travel can be great fun.

So far as rubber is concerned, and how a paradise became the devil's domain, Hardenburg enters the subject precisely as he witnessed it. Shock does not surface all at once, the story being unfolded as it unfolded itself to him: 'A small traffic with the rubber-collectors of the Upper Putumayo and the neighbouring Indians is, however, still carried on' (p. 68). 'There are two distinct kinds of rubber – that produced by a tree that must be cut down to extract the milk, which is called *caucho negro*, or black rubber . . . and that which is the product of a tree that can be tapped indefinitely, which is known as *jebe* or *siringa*, and is collected from the Hevea brasiliensis' (p. 94). The third mention of rubber is equally non-committal, with no presage of future involvement: 'In addition to his regular employees he had several Indians also at work collecting for him, whom he paid in merchandise' (p. 110). Even by page 133 there is still no hint of things to come: 'I learned that all the rubber produced in this section of the Putumayo is an inferior kind of *jebe* or *siringa*, known technically as *jebe débil* or weak-fine rubber.'

In between these references, and most tantalizingly, he continues with his traveller's tales:

The ugly and unusual custom of pulling out the eyebrows, eye-lashes, &c., and cutting the hair short is observed by both sexes. The women are, if possible, uglier than the men, which is saying a good deal . . . Gonzales, after a glance at the wound, informed me that it was the work of a vampire bat . . . What a pleasant sensation it was to sit calmly in the canoe, while the swift current bore us steadily onwards . . . I took deliberate aim with the shot-gun, and at a distance of some ten metres let fly at him. The hideous monster jumped up and, after lashing his tail wildly about two or three times, plunged with a splash into the water but a few metres from our canoe . . .

Hardenburg judged this boa constrictor to have been 20–25 feet long (he was reliably inconsistent with units of measurement) and more exciting to shoot than mere tapirs, lizards, toucans, capybaras, pec-caries, doves, parrots, caymans. (At one point in this text the 'Editor' butts in with an unnecessary aside: 'The travellers seem to have encountered a numerous *fauna*.') Everything visible and likely to be edible was worth a firing, although the possible edibility was not crucial.

Their greatest adventure in the travelogue came when marooned on a sandbank. Jaguars, vampires and piranhas may seem more dangerous, but inability to move in an area where fellow-voyagers are in short supply can be more frightening. One morning they awoke to find 150 'metres' of sand between their boat and the water, the river having dropped two 'feet' during the night. No amount of pulling narrowed the gap. Hastily improvised rollers sank in the sand. A complete trackway of wood also proved inadequate. There was nothing to be done on this Friday 13 December 1907 save wait for the river to rise. If that did not occur before the next Andean rainy season they might not live to see the day. In the meantime they explored their sandbank, discovering it to be three kilometres in length and sur-rounded by 'enormous alligators'. Shooting other game was no longer possible, and chess became a substitute: 'Whether my mind was distracted by our shipwreck, or whether Perkins had done some studying up, I cannot say; the fact remains that during all the time we were shipwrecked I only won a single game, and we must have played over fifty.'

Julio Arana

Play was interrupted in a two-fold manner. A small boatload of police arrived, all happy to lend a hand 'after dinner'. No sooner was the marooned boat emptied of its contents and transported to the water than the river rose, aided by a sudden storm. The 'sickening task' of heaving all their goods could have been avoided had the travellers waited (and had they fully appreciated how much they had accumulated). By now the book is steeped in that mannerism so beloved by many a traveller of using lovely foreign words where English words would do: 'We had had originally seven *bultos*, weighing about four *arrobas* each; now in addition to this we had a barrel of *aguardiente*, our Indian souvenirs, Perkins's mineralogical specimens, our *danta*, &c.' (The four words mean, respectively: packages, about twenty-five pounds, local rum, and tapir.) One begins to suspect that English may be totally discarded after a few more months of travel, what with *corregidors* already being entertained on the *playa* underneath their *pamacari* with eggs of the *charapilla* and *piuri* found in a *quebrada* at the end of the *trocha*. It is possible, at times, to lose the thread.

The devil then comes into his paradise. The book's tone changes as its facts grow less agreeable. A Huitoto Indian informs Hardenburg 'that the Peruvians treated his countrymen "very badly", and . . . he gave me to understand that in case the Indians did not bring in a sufficient amount of rubber to satisfy the Peruvians they were flogged, shot, or mutilated at the will of the man in charge'. The American took this information 'with a grain of salt', but there was soon confirmation. A Colombian settler, David Serrano, told how he owed some money to the Peruvian Amazon Company. A 'commission' then arrived, chained Serrano to a tree, dragged his wife on to the porch, 'outraged' her before his eyes, and vanished, taking his entire stock, the 'unfortunate woman' and their small son. Allegedly she became concubine to the company's local manager while the 'tender son acted as servant to the same repugnant monster'. Hardenburg was no longer taking salt, and had changed from the docile, casual traveller he had been hitherto. It becomes clearer by the page that he and the boss of the Peruvian Amazon Company will surely meet one day. The Americans had stumbled into Arana's kingdom by the back door, as it were. Their thoughts of working on the Madeira–Mamoré railway were diminishing with every mile (and kilometre) they travelled, with everything they saw.

In the rubber-tapping business it was generally the custom to keep all tappers in debt. Of course such men had no money when signing their indentures, and were grateful to be capitalized with a protective gun, ammunition and food, the wherewithal for collecting rubber. The snag, as these men realized soon enough, was their inability to tap and cure sufficient rubber to repay the original loan. A further loan therefore had to be agreed, and then another. This was bondage of a most displeasing kind. Working conditions were also unfavourable. The forest's rubber trees did not grow in clumps but individually, at a distance from each other. That tropical forest species should grow in this fashion must have seemed most disagreeable, necessitating as it did a constant back and forth and side to side for the tapper, much as dogs consider proper for a walk. The environment itself is none too pleasant. It is dank and dark. The vegetation can be most spiteful. There are diseases – malaria, yellow fever, leishmaniasis, Chagas. There are venomous snakes, such as bothrops and the corals. The land is not necessarily flat and the trees can induce claustrophobia. There is no sky save where a giant has toppled recently, permitting an instant entanglement of weed-like growth. There are insects that suck, bite, invade or merely irritate, lapping up sweat, walking into ears, finding eyeballs irresistible. And of course there are the bigger animals, like cougar and jaguar, that can unnerve even if they pose a lesser threat.

To walk and stumble through such a place is not everyone's ideal. To do so knowing that the wretched latex is not being accumulated sufficiently rapidly to repay debt must have been loathsome. No wonder the *seringueiros* sometimes turned and fled. The peril of being caught, flogged and returned to the forest was always a possibility, but so was freedom. No wonder that rubber managers found labour difficult to recruit. And no wonder they turned instead to Indians, to docile tribes already in shock from disruption to their world. These people could be subjugated far more easily. They did not know that justice might be available many days' journey downstream. They were pulverized into submission, and nowhere more so than around the Putumayo.

About 40,000 Huitoto Indians lived by that river. They were tractable, and less inclined to either laziness or belligerence than other local tribes. At first Hardenburg did not find words in favour of them,

Collecting rubber was never an easy business, neither the tapping nor the curing, when the raw material was dripped on to a pole that slowly rotated in smoke from smouldering palm nuts.

but he then alters that tune:

The Huitotos are a well-formed race, and although small are stout and strong, with a broad chest and a prominent bust, but their limbs, especially the lower, are but little developed. Their hair, long and abundant, is black and coarse, and is worn long by both sexes ... That repugnant sight, a protruding abdomen, so common among the 'whites' and half-breeds on the Amazon, is very rare among these aborigines. Among the women the habit of carrying their young on their backs makes them adopt an inclined position, which they conserve all their life. Their feet are turned inwards, and when they walk their thighs generally strike against each other as though they were afraid. Notwithstanding these defects, it is not rare to find among these women many really beautiful, so magnificent are their figures and so free and graceful their movements.

Hardenburg was increasingly seeing things from the Indians' viewpoint, and a new experience only reinforced that attitude. When canoeing downstream, together with an amiable bunch of Huitotos, he and Perkins were suddenly surprised by two launches. The Indians jumped overboard before vanishing in the forest. Orders were shouted to 'sink' the canoe. Bullets, quick to accompany these instructions, whizzed through the air. 'We heard a voice ordering us, in the most vile and obscene words, to approach the launch,' wrote Hardenburg after being on the receiving end of gunfire for the first time. 'We were jerked on board, kicked, beaten, insulted and abused in a most cowardly manner by Captain Arce Benavides . . . and a gang of coffee-coloured soldiers, sailors and employees of the "civilizing company", without being given a chance to speak a word.' Having been told earlier that the Peruvian Amazon was a 'civilizing company', he never fails henceforth to refer to it in this fashion. The maltreatment of Indians was one injustice. To be abused oneself made the insult personal.

Both Americans were then imprisoned, and while captive they witnessed an assault upon a pregnant woman caught on the same punitive up-river expedition. The man in charge (whose name the editor decided to delete) was a 'human monster, intent only on slaking his animal thirst of lasciviousness . . . and, in spite of the cries of agony of the unfortunate creature, violated her without compunction'. The farmer's boy from New York state was learning about life from the wrong end. He and Perkins were 'plunged in the most gloomy reflections and expecting to be shot or stabbed at any moment, for our captors were drunk and in a most bloodthirsty mood'. They watched Indians at work, staggering under loads, and all 'branded with the infamous *marca de Arana*', the flogging scars upon their backs. Later on Hardenburg listed his observations:

1. The Indians received no pay other than food.
2. They were kept naked.
3. They were robbed of their women and children.
4. They could be sold in Iquitos for £20–£40.
5. Floggings often laid their bones bare.
6. They received no medical treatment, and many died.
7. Their ears, fingers, arms, legs and testicles were sometimes cut off as punishment.
8. They were tortured and crucified head downwards.
9. Occasionally their children would have their heads smashed against trees.
10. The old ones were killed when they could no longer work.
11. Some were shot 'to provide amusement or to celebrate the *sábado de gloria*' (the day following Good Friday).

Julio Arana

Huitoto Indians and their employers in Arana's kingdom at the time of the rubber boom.

A few weeks earlier the same reporter had been patronizing about the local Indians, sneering at their drink and disdainful of their ugliness. He was now a vigilante on their behalf. The possibility of working on the Madeira railway had been totally forgotten.

The Americans then had to part company. Hardenburg was forcibly transported to the town of Iquitos on the Peruvian Amazon, while Perkins stayed behind hoping to locate their stolen baggage. He was also ill. For a time Hardenburg was kept prisoner at Iquitos, but he talked his way to freedom by posing as the chief executive of a major company. Once released, his first call was on the dentist, Guy T. King, acting American consul. Such representatives could be more loyal to their localities than to their distant governments. Hardenburg was incensed, and said so in his book: 'This gentlemen, considering solely and exclusively his own interests and forgetting the duties that his position as Consul incurred upon him, contented himself with congratulating me upon my narrow escape from death at the hands of the assassins of Arana and informing me that, owing to various circumstances, he could do absolutely nothing for us.'

The tone of *The Devil's Paradise* now becomes increasingly shrill. He calls the area a living hell. He talks of blood and crime and bleached skeletons, and wonders if the vegetation is so luxuriant for having been deluged with this blood. He realizes that there is an 'unparalleled system of wholesale bribery', with every complaint neglected, passed over and finally pigeon-holed by the judicial authorities. Even the book's editor, who had commented previously on such items as the quantity of fauna observed by the travellers, now feels obliged to delete certain passages, notably when the author is rising in crescendo: 'Think of nine-year-old girls torn from their homes, ravished, and afterwards tortured or flogged to death; of sucking infants snatched from their mothers' arms and their heads smashed against a tree; of a wife having her legs cut off merely for refusing to become one of the concubines of these bandits; of men flogged until . . .' – and here the editor intervened with the blunt statement: 'This account cannot be printed.' One wonders, of course, about the omission, but the message is already clear. Arana's managers were exercising a ruthlessness in their inter-territorial no man's land that shamed even the Congo. They enforced the playing of a kind of football, shooting all those in the opposing team who looked too dangerous. The children were tied to trees while gunmen dislodged their various appendages until, as the sickened author phrases it, 'an unlucky bullet strikes a vital part and puts an end to their sport'.

Hardenburg's book was written long after his days in Iquitos, although he never makes this point. He perhaps made notes at the time, but much happened before he contemplated publication. In the first place, having given up prospects of railway employment, he had to acquire some funds. He cabled home for $300, started teaching English at a secondary college, and received rather more money for helping to design a new hospital on the Amazon. His purpose now was to carry on a personal crusade. He had seen the infamies of the river Putumayo and could not forget what he had seen. Perkins's arrival at Iquitos after he too had gained his freedom, though having lost all sight of their possessions, not only emphasized the difference between the two men but made Hardenburg more adamant. How dare they treat Perkins like that! (Every man imprisoned with him had been executed.) How dare they steal precious equipment, and clothes, and valued tourist trophies! In Perkins's head there was only one thought: to leave the Amazon for ever. He was still ill, he was disenchanted, and he had no wish to enter into lengthy negotiations that might or might not extract reparation from the Peruvian government for lost goods and injured pride. From his $300 Hardenburg proffered the necessary sum for one steamer ticket back home and bade his friend farewell. 'I admire your spirit,' Perkins said, 'but I don't think you will succeed.'

Walter Hardenburg had no idea in that month of May 1908 whether he could bring any justice to the Putumayo. He was, after all, a single individual. He had sufficient income to keep himself in food and lodging, but hardly campaign funds. His education had advanced abundantly since he had set forth from Youngsville, but he was still a youngster, rich in both the courage of the young and their inexperience. Ingrained idealism told him that Julio Arana could not possibly know what was being done in his name. Clearly the man should be informed. Then suddenly the news was current that Arana was in town. Hardenburg was half the other man's age and possessed a minute fraction of his Amazon experience, but he decided instantly to ask about the Putumayo in general and its Indians in particular. He therefore knocked upon Arana's door.

The young idealist stood before the Peruvian rubber-man, two alien species with little in common save their presence in that room. Arana insisted on speaking in Spanish, although well-versed in English. In an urbane manner which also helped to confuse the young American, Arana promised to enquire about the missing baggage, although he rarely visited the area in which it had been lost. He then asked Hardenburg what he thought of the situation upon the river, and the younger man knew this was one more game of chess. Therefore he did not blurt out all manner of accusations. He did not even tell of his own rough handling. Instead, now treading carefully, he suggested that Arana should look into the facts himself on his next visit to the region. The interview then ended coldly and dispassionately, with nothing showing on either face.

Hardenburg achieved his twenty-second birthday shortly afterwards. He was learning every day about the task he had set himself – the degree of corruption and fear, the crooked practice from top to toe. He knew that only his American passport stopped him from becoming one more body in the river. What he did not know was how to proceed. What can a mouse do against a cat?

A youth named Miguel Galvez, allegedly the son of Benjamin Rocca, then came to see him. Hardenburg knew about Rocca, having watched his small printing works being destroyed one night. The man had published statements from individuals with a grudge against Arana's company, and Arana had taken the obvious step. With Miguel claiming to be Rocca's son, Hardenburg suspected a trap. The young man explained that there were further testimonies as yet unpublished. Did Hardenburg want them? Of course he did, and there seemed no way of acquiring them other than trusting this seventeen-year-old. They met again most secretly. The papers were handed over, and Hardenburg at last had some solid evidence, all duly signed: 'The heads of the Indians were wrapped in banana leaves.' 'A girl of 15 was shot to celebrate Easter.' 'Honest men! Avoid the Putumayo!' Hardenburg chose not to tell the consular dentist of this good fortune.

Only a few of the documents had been signed in the presence of a lawyer. Nevertheless they were better than nothing, and the American decided to have them photographed. The photographer, having taken one look, decided otherwise. They were plainly evidence against Arana, and he asked the American to leave his studio at once. Hardenburg was coming to realize the extent of Arana's grip, as when he questioned a particularly obliging pupil among his fourteen students of English. The man proved to be none other than Arana's personal lawyer. Iquitos was a difficult place in which to do anything that did not have Arana's blessing. The American knew he was spied upon at every turn and thought of trying his luck in Manaus, a thousand miles downstream. As further inducement to move, the young Miguel suggested a promising approach. He knew his father had attempted an interview with a carpenter named Aurelio Blanco. The man apparently had tales to tell but had left for Manaus before Rocca could reach him. Hardenburg, no doubt wanting a change of scene, caught the paddle-boat heading east from Iquitos. He was thus moving from Peru into Brazil, as determined as ever upon his personal crusade.

No one had heard of carpenter Blanco. For days Hardenburg asked bar-tenders, fellow-drinkers, hoteliers. He grew dispirited and watched solemnly, but then excitedly, as a hearse rattled by in the street. Of course, coffins are made by carpenters – and not long afterwards the American was speaking with a man three times his age. Yes, he was Aurelio Blanco, carpenter. Yes, he had worked for the Peruvian Amazon Company and had been told to round up Indians. He had been shot at for his refusal, had seen Indians dying from their sentences of 600 lashes, had managed to escape down some rapids, and had eventually attempted to bludgeon the cost of his lost carpentry box from none other than Arana; but he could see no point in Hardenburg's current endeavours. He would not swear anything in front of a lawyer. Such men, he knew, were in Arana's pay, and he would end up inside one of his own coffins. He did offer to write a letter to Hardenburg – sometime, when the time was right.

In weariness Hardenburg returned to Iquitos, where further evidence against Arana was more likely to be found than in down-river Manaus, even if he now doubted his ability to collect it. Blanco had been no timid employee, having even demanded recompense from Arana, but he had shied away from incriminating himself in an official document. Nevertheless Hardenburg continued to build up an impressive factual dossier. He learned that Arana's managers received no wages save in commissions – hence their enthusiasm for extracting work from the Indian employees. He was told how very young Indians were taught to use rifles against their elders. And he heard of the Putumayo motto: 'Kill the fathers first, enjoy the virgins afterwards.' His accumulated evidence eventually included several depositions, and he naively asked the American consul to forward them to the United States representative in Lima. The dentist's inevitable refusal helped Hardenburg to make up his mind. Iquitos was full of enemies and unhelpful fellow-countrymen. The Peruvian Amazon Company was British, with British directors and British influence. Surely London would be more supportive? Justice must be more possible to obtain there, however far away it might be, and would be worth the £40 a ticket would cost. So he left Iquitos, and on 17 June 1909 watched the fetid glamour of Manaus recede into the trees. It was the last Walter Hardenburg would ever see of the rubber capital. It was not, however, the last it would hear of him.

On arriving in London he took lodgings in Sandwich Street on the opposite side of Euston Road from St Pancras station. Each day he told

Walter Hardenburg, who stumbled so accidentally upon 'The Devil's Paradise'.

anyone who would listen, even for a moment, of atrocities over 6,000 miles away. In particular he approached the editors of Fleet Street and publishers everywhere. He told of the borderland between Peru and Colombia, of the Huitoto Indians, of vile practices in the rubber trade, and of a Peruvian named Julio Arana living mainly in Brazil. From the viewpoint of the various editors, here was a very young American talking of crimes in a different part of the world that was not even in the Empire. Where were Peru and Colombia anyway? Weren't they always having revolutions, and weren't lots of people killed when those happened? Besides, what about the law of libel? It was quite possible, extremely possible, for a rich Peruvian to resent being named disparagingly in a London publication. Wily lawyers were always picking on defamatory articles, discovering the one who had been defamed, and acquainting him not only with the facts but with the rewards that might accrue. Please – in effect – show Mr Hardenburg the door.

After a month the young crusader began to suspect that London was no better than either Iquitos or Manaus. He realized that exciting things were happening to occupy each editor's attention. Flying machines were all over the place. Suffragettes were forever doing something. The military rumblings from Germany were growing louder all the while. And Edward VII was still on the throne, always good for a story. If good causes were required there were plenty within Britain, in the factories, in the slums, down the pits. In short, Hardenburg failed with the British press. He therefore tried the Anti-Slavery and Aborigines' Protection Society, and the tide began to turn. John Harris, aged thirty-five, was the official who welcomed and listened to the American. It seemed, immediately, as if this was the terrible Congo all over again. In the early years of the new century Harris and Roger Casement, British consul in King Leopold's African domain, had reported on awful crimes committed there, of – in some areas – half the local population being destroyed. The official of the Anti-Slavery Society sat bemused as Hardenburg told the same old stories of outrageous behaviour, but from South America instead of Africa.

Having listened, John Harris then acted. He introduced the American to everyone who might be interested. In particular he introduced him to Robert Bennett, editor of *Truth*. Henry Labouchere had done more than anyone to make this the most vigilant and feared weekly magazine, and on taking over the editorship Bennett was intent on keeping up that prickly reputation. *Truth*'s offices, in Carteret Street, were placed strategically, midway between Buckingham Palace and the Houses of Parliament. It acted as gadfly to both, and to any other organization requiring some investigative and courageous journalism. Bennett and Sydney Paternoster, his deputy, were eager to publish Hardenburg's story, but they first made enquiries of their own. They discovered that the Colombian representative in London possessed supporting evidence from distinguished Colombians who had worked in Arana's territory. The British consul at Iquitos, home on leave (and plainly a different person from the vice-consul in Manaus who had ordered the West Indians to obey their contracts), was able to offer similar confirmation from the viewpoint of those British citizens, the Barbadian overseers. Another form of proof came from the Peruvian government when it awarded Hardenburg and Perkins a total of £500 as compensation for the problems they had encountered when in that country. *Truth* had learned a thing or two about libel in its turbulent history. It knew it had to check and check again its facts. It also knew that writs quickly arrived after any sloppiness in procedure. Consequently, only after taking all suitable precautions did it go into print with 'The Devil's Paradise: A British-Owned Congo'. Edwardian Britain then had another scandal on its hands.

Truth did not publish one article: it published the story for week after week, keeping it on the boil. In revenge the Peruvian Amazon Company opted for blackening Hardenburg's character. Cleverly distorting what had happened, rather than fabricating tales from scratch, it referred to certain events in Iquitos and Manaus. In one the American had supposedly demanded money to defame Arana, and in the other he had allegedly forged a banker's draft. This was Arana's way. Both incidents had been set up long beforehand, in case they were needed. He believed everyone was a potential enemy, particularly those asking awkward questions. Therefore agents had been set upon Hardenburg to follow him, to ask for loans, to suggest he signed some papers, to gather material that might incriminate the man. When *Truth* published its allegations the time had come, or so Arana believed, to turn the tables on Hardenburg. These counter-allegations were interesting to competing publications, notably the *Morning Leader*. After being given some of this rival material a reporter wrote the story and his paper printed it. The same reporter repeatedly visited the offices of the Peruvian Amazon Company in the City of London, suspecting there was more to come. Eventually he was ushered into an inner room. A company official expressed gratitude to him and his newspaper, said no more such information was available and proffered an envelope. One astonished glance by the young man revealed that it contained money. Instantly the envelope plus contents were handed back as if smeared in cyanide. The company official was nonplussed. So too, in a different fashion, was the reporter, but the *Morning Leader* knew exactly what to do. 'Our Congo,' it headlined; 'Strange Story of a Banknote; Peruvian Amazon Company and the *Morning Leader*'.

Thus it happened that the British directors of Arana's company learned of a reporter actually visiting their offices. They were as aghast as anyone that a bribe had been attempted. Some of them knew South America, and all knew business, but none knew anything about the Putumayo. Of course the American was lying, but why, with this envelope of money, had the company brought suspicion upon itself? They immediately hit back at *Truth*, saying they did not believe the alleged atrocities had ever taken place. For good measure the British directors added that they were not even in office at the time of Hardenburg's passage down the river. Defend the company, but do not forget to defend yourself, might have been their motto. The point about not being in office was true, even if irrelevant should litigation ensue. In any event no director visited *Truth*'s offices to examine the evidence it had on file. Instead the men listened to a junior clerk, recently returned from the Putumayo after improving the company's up-river book-keeping system. He was shown the *Truth* articles and repudiated them utterly. The relieved directors promptly raised the man's official status. Henceforth he would be 'secretary and manager' instead of accounts clerk. His income would rise in commensurate fashion from £150 per annum to £1,000, which gave immediate delight to the twenty-eight-year-old.

Walter Hardenburg's finances were doing less well. *Truth* had explained, and he had accepted, that it did not pay for crusading material. The compensation money from Peru, which so assured *Truth* that the allegations were correct, had not yet arrived. The American asked his father for repayment of £78 sent home much earlier on his travels. The magazine loaned £20 to Hardenburg, but stressed eventual repayment. One blessing, in the face of this penury, was Mary Feeney. She was a young friend of the couple who ran his boardinghouse, and Walter saw more and more of her. Early in 1910 the two were married. Despairing of London, and feeling that others could pick up his crusading baton, Hardenburg abruptly decided to emigrate to Canada. He and his bride arrived there in March of that year. It must have seemed to both of them that the struggle had been lost.

However, others did pick up his baton, or rather it had acquired a momentum of its own. The Foreign Office in London was believed to be considering some form of investigation. Arana had amassed a dossier against his 'blackmailers', but his British directors did not like it when they saw it. They dissociated themselves from events on the Putumayo, saying that only Arana knew about them. (It was nice collecting director's fees of £200 per year, plus half-yearly dividends, but no one wished to be involved in anything distasteful.)

Arana also wanted to disconnect himself from such events, but for different reasons. He knew the rubber industry in South America was reaching a crisis. World demand for the product had become insatiable. Manaus was greedily, desperately, insanely pricing itself out of the business. Worse was to come. The motor car was about to leave the garages of the wealthy. Henry Ford's Model T, the people's car, had been created in 1908. Thousands had already been sold and millions would be. Everybody also wanted galoshes. Each ship-load of rubber from the Amazon gained in value between departure and arrival. Simultaneously there was a rush to invest in the new plantations of the east. Shares had reached ludicrous values. Suitable land in Malaya was changing hands at many times its original value. In Manaus more and more hungry men were still arriving, part of the 'black gold rush' wishing for a piece of the fortune before it vanished. The Chamber of Commerce attempted to restrict export, hoping to drive the rubber price even higher. To Arana it was all madness. He wished only to ensure that his family continued to enjoy the prosperity it had merited. Not one of them should suffer, and he installed his wife, his five children, their governesses and their servants most comfortably in a house to the north of Kensington Gardens. Within this household (and most incongruously) was also a Huitoto boy brought from the Putumayo. Arana wanted the lad to become a doctor, the first Indian to be so qualified.

Three months after the Hardenburgs had sailed for Canada the

Julio Arana

British Foreign Office set up a commission of enquiry 'into the Putumayo allegations'. The river had become the most famous, after the Amazon, in all of South America. It began to appear on maps. The clamour that something should be done had proved irresistible. Sir Edward Grey, Foreign Secretary and a man more aware than most that lights would soon be going out in Europe, had yielded to pressure. It was a lesser problem by the standards of the approaching First World War, but it would not go away.

As for Arana, he wished to be rid of his Putumayo interests, but he would not suffer injury to his pride. If there was to be a commission of enquiry he would fight it. If people were to insult him, or threaten to bring disrespect upon his family, he would be fiercely unforgiving. His first task, as he saw it, was to object to each proposed member of the commission. He did so, but eventually could object no longer, the final list being arguably worthy from everyone's point of view. In charge was a mining engineer, a friend of one of the directors. Under him would be an agriculturalist who already knew Brazil, a businessman, a botanist who knew about rubber, and the company's secretary and manager. This last member, so recently promoted from £150 to £1,000 per annum, now had his wage increased to £2,500. There was still money in rubber, he must have concluded, even while assisting on a commission that might halt the flow, once and for all.

Arana could relax with this assortment of individuals, but then Sir Edward Grey wrote one more name on the list. Britain's consul-general in Rio would, he believed, be most suitable. The man knew Brazil, and also knew from his Congo investigation what mankind could do to its fellow human beings, particularly if the victims were no more than simple natives. A telegram was despatched to Roger Casement, and Arana realized this governmental enquiry would now be no casual scrutiny. The two men had met when both were sailing to Pará in an earlier year. Each therefore knew a thing or two about the other, and Arana certainly knew he was up against an inflexible opponent.

Without doubt Roger Casement, now forty-five, was in quite a different category from, for example, the young clerk so grateful (and so perfidious) for a sixteen-fold rise in salary. Casement's report on the Congo had impressed everybody. His intellect was considerable; so too the range of his knowledge. Agriculturalists, botanists and business-men, however worthy, did not carry the prestige of this ambitious Foreign Office employee, a most respected servant of the largest empire the world had ever known. Walter Hardenburg's labours were at last earning their reward. He was now in Toronto, trying to acquire sufficient funds to head west, while the British consul-general to Brazil's capital was reading through his hard-won testimonies. It may seem curious that a British commission of enquiry was about to investigate alleged malpractice in Peru, but no one thought so at the time. Casement certainly had no qualms on this matter as he sailed from Britain, where he had been on leave. Instead his thoughts were frequently in quite another quarter.

'July 12. Hotel. Splendid testiminhos. Soft as silk and big and full. No bush to speak of. Good wine needs no bush.' His ship had docked at Madeira, *en route* to the Amazon, and Casement's journal reflected all his interests. The so-called black diaries, to be used at his subsequent trial, to be considered by some as forgeries (to this day) and released for public view in 1959, were a pot-pourri of personal material, some of it about his homosexual encounters. Casement already knew Pará, first port on the Amazon, having been its British consul, and he did not waste the ship's first evening there: '. . . after dinner to Vero Peso, two types, also to gardens . . . then Senate Square and Caboclo (boy 16–17) seized hard. Young, stiff, thin. Others offered later.' Later in the four-day stop-over he meets with a friend from earlier days. 'Shall I see João, dear old soul! I'll get up early . . . To cemetery, and lo! João coming along – blushed to roots of hair with joy.' If Arana had wished to blacken Casement's name within a society that had imprisoned Oscar Wilde for being similarly honest only fifteen years earlier, his spies could have had a field-day. Case-ment must have been aware of the risk, but disregarded it. He never had been, or would be, short of courage. (Or of carelessness, for his wayward actions were jeopardizing the committee's purpose and intent.)

At Manaus the story was similar, save that the visit lasted one day: 'One lovely schoolboy, back and forward several times . . .' Then it was Iquitos, where the proper work could, and did, begin. Casement enquired particularly after the Barbadians, the British subjects, and

Roger Casement, in consular uniform, shortly before his visit to the infamous Putumayo.

made extensive notes. The stories he collected were of the calibre and unpleasantness given to Hardenburg two years earlier. The commission departed for the Putumayo on 14 September 1910, reaching the company's first outpost six days later. The diary then changes its theme, noting that the Indians who carried the baggage had scars on their buttocks, 'weals for life . . . this is their welfare, their daily welfare. All slaves.' From the Barbadians who would talk, and from the evidence it saw, the Casement commission steadily learned the truth. Scars, floggings, wooden stocks, beatings between the legs, blisters from punishment by fire, murders – there were sufficient facts soon enough, but Casement had been criticized for lack of perseverance in the Congo. The commission had therefore to continue, visiting more and more of Arana's up-river settlements, hearing and seeing more at every turn.

Westerman Leavine, a Barbadian eager to talk, told of Armando Normand's crimes. This station manager had allegedly killed hundreds of Indians 'by many kinds of torture; cutting off their heads and limbs, and burying them alive. [Leavine] more than once saw Normand have Indians' hands and legs tied together, and the men or women thus bound thrown alive on the fire. . . ' Casement was hating everything, and having to suffer the hospitality of those he wished to accuse. He loathed the food, the insects, the climate, but above all the interminable interviews. Most of the Barbadians wished to leave, and by 28 October it was time for the commission to depart, having completed its job. Ahead lay the faster journey downstream, and then Pará again, and João with 'big bunch of flowers, very nice indeed'. Soon Casement disembarked at Cherbourg, reaching Paris in time for New Year's Eve: 'Later, in Champs-Elysées, soldier, and then in B. des Capucines, green hat and small, last two no copper but Denis 10s. Mild evening, great crowds . . .' And so began 1911.

One week into the new year Casement presented a preliminary report to his Foreign Secretary. It fully vindicated Hardenburg, *Truth* and Sir Edward Grey's wish to send out a commission of enquiry. That immediate statement was amplified during the next four months until it reached 135 pages. A copy of this document reached the Peruvian Amazon Company's directors on 13 May. In it Casement did not do precisely what he had been instructed to do, namely report only on

Many Barbadians were imported to oversee the Indian labour force, who provided the raw material from which fortunes were being made.

sufferings to British citizens. However, the company was a British concern and the maltreatment of its workers could not be ignored. Casement estimated that the Indian population had been reduced 'by possibly four fifths of its former total' within five years. He concluded that the Peruvian Amazon Company was to blame.

Whatever the other directors may have thought on reading this crushing indictment of their company, Arana was still busy plotting, scheming, conspiring. He demanded an astonishing £898,000 from the Colombian government for 'disturbances' in the area. He arranged that the 'Putumayo estates' should be mortgaged for his wife. The British directors, reeling from every revelation, now learned that much of the company belonged to her. There were many to whom money was owed, and the company did not have assets worthy of the name. Four months after receiving the 'Casement report', the Peruvian Amazon

Company decided to wind itself out of business, but appointed as liquidator none other than Julio César Arana.

Meanwhile the British government was acting at a different level. It urged the authorities in Peru to investigate the situation, and Lima responded by sending its own commission to the Putumayo. This moved slowly, or perhaps realistically. So many warrants were issued that the Iquitos gaol could not have coped with the influx, and most of the miscreants were given ample time to reach the security of Manaus and Brazil. Only nine of the 237 warrants for arrest were actually served. The British government was incensed that criminals were not being brought to book: 'Of all the things I have ever read that have occurred in modern times . . . the accounts of the brutalities in Putumayo are the most horrible,' expostulated Sir Edward Grey. Another Liberal politician stressed that it was still a British problem, whatever Peru might or might not do, as British subjects, recruited through a British government agent, and serving a British company, had committed many of the deeds when involved in collecting a product for Britain that was transported by British ships to British industry for sale in Britain. As a final source of rage, no one could understand how the company's managing director, presumed guilty to a greater or lesser degree, had become its liquidator.

The United States government was not faring much better. Peru was not its territory, and Arana's company not its affair, but, as Grey wrote in a private letter to the *Manchester Guardian*'s editor, 'It is American public opinion that must be the most potent factor in either American continent.' The new American consul in Iquitos (who had replaced the dentist) went on a tour of the Putumayo, but it was a pointless exercise. In theory he should have travelled in a Peruvian government launch. In practice, when this failed to materialize he accepted the hospitality of one of Arana's vessels. He therefore saw nothing except happy Indian dances, and heard everyone referring to 'Papa Arana'. Casement had scoffed at this visit before it happened. He scoffed even louder on learning of its progress up the Putumayo. As he had been knighted for his work upon the Amazon, and as his report had received far more respect than anything the Peruvians or Americans had to offer, everything he had to say on the matter received considerable attention.

Julio Arana

Public clamour in Britain would not drop the Putumayo issue. A canon of Westminster Abbey named and denounced the Peruvian Amazon Company's directors from the pulpit. The matter was vigorously debated in the House of Commons. It was almost as if the revelations were recent, yet Walter Hardenburg had arrived in England with his evidence over three years before, and *Truth* had started its campaign not long afterwards. It was twenty-two months since Casement had travelled on the river and well over a year since his report had become generally available. Nevertheless the fury mounted. What was the government going to do? Something more was necessary; something should be done.

The new prime minister, Herbert Henry Asquith, saw the Putumayo report among the items at the top of his in-tray. To reduce the heat, and possibly discover some solution, he resorted to a well-tried parliamentary procedure. On 6 August 1912 he announced that a Select Committee of the House of Commons would be established to decide what could be done. Were changes in the law, for instance, demanded by the Putumayo findings? Were foreign employees of British companies established by foreign nationals outside British jurisdiction, and if so, should they be? The Committee's chairman, Liberal Member of Parliament Charles Roberts, immediately wrote to Casement saying that his knowledge and experience would be of crucial assistance. The Committee could not imagine working without his aid.

Over in Canada the continuing Putumayo scandal was of little consequence save, of course, for Walter Hardenburg. After a year in Toronto he had moved with his wife and baby son to Red Deer, midway between Calgary and Edmonton. His portion of the Peruvian government's compensation had arrived and he could have let the matter drop, but this became out of the question when he began to hear of blackmail charges against him. Hardenburg caught the train back to Toronto and there corresponded with relevant acquaintances in London and South America. He learned of the Select Committee, but realized it would do nothing until Parliament reassembled after the summer recess. He angrily returned to Red Deer, but a piece of him, if not the whole, longed to be in London. It was five years since he and Perkins had opted for travelling down the Putumayo, and he was

distantly aware that justice was at last being done, albeit at the pace of a
Select Committee.

Its members formed an imposing list. There was Raymond Asquith,
son of the prime minister, a member of the *Titanic* court of enquiry,
already marked for high office (and terribly mourned when killed in the
First World War). John Astbury, KC, would plainly become a judge
before too long. Douglas Hogg would become Lord Hailsham and
Lord Chancellor. William Joynson-Hicks would be Lord Brentford
and Home Secretary. Also on the Committee were Lord Alexander
Thynne, son of the Marquis of Bath; William Young, born to a farmer
but now a merchant banker; Willoughby Dickinson, another lord-to-
be; and Swift MacNeill, another KC and MP for South Donegal. He,
so it was said, would be the best fighter of them all. Eight other MPs
completed the array, and this Committee began its formal work on 6
November 1912.

Sir Roger Casement presented his case all over again, assisted by
some frightening photographs. With his prompting, the right questions
were asked of other witnesses. The accounts clerk, so swiftly promoted
to company secretary when he had kept quiet about the Putumayo,
received particularly rough handling. Did he not think it odd that a
rubber company should spend £7,000 on rifles? Was he not 'a little
financial babe in the wood'? As for the scars on Indians, he answered
that they were on a part of the body at which one does not normally
look. The committee learned that only two of the company's directors
had ever visited the Amazon, namely Arana and his brother-in-law
Alarco. It discovered that the London directors had no notion whether
Indians were ever paid, nor any means of finding out. There were
disconcerting payments for the hunting of fugitive Indians. Was it not
against British law to hunt down employees, even if this was permitted
in Peru? As for Hardenburg, and the allegations against him, was it not
likely that such assertions would be made by those who understood
what the American had brought to London?

Gradually, as that winter of 1912 became the spring of 1913, the
case was built up that everything had been left to Arana. He knew what
conditions were like. He could explain the accounts. He could always
satisfy his gullible directors. The news then surfaced that Julio Arana
would be coming to testify, amazing both the Committee and the

newspapermen covering the proceedings. Their activities had been too much for the Peruvian, who had been in Manaus during that northern winter. He had read the London papers, had realized how his name was being besmirched, and saw how the tables were being turned against him. He had never yet lost a battle and had no intention of losing this one. They were treating him as if he were some miscreant, a nobody, a man without substance. He would show that he was metal of quite a different kind. Nothing could be done, he realized, save travel to London and there present his case and himself to the Select Committee. He caught a Booth liner and arrived at Fishguard on 4 March 1913.

It so happened that over in Canada another man now reached more or less the same conclusion. Events too momentous to be disregarded were taking place in Britain. The distance from Alberta to London was about as far as from London to Manaus, but Walter Hardenburg had also had enough of sitting on the sidelines. The Anti-Slavery Society thought in similar fashion. Its valiant crusader, who had visited their

It has been Hardenburg's intention to work on the Madeira–Mamoré railway, a line finally opened with an inaugural train in 1912.

offices seeking help, was not even party to the enquiry which he, more than any other individual, had instigated. The Reverend John Harris wrote to Hardenburg offering to pay for a third-class return ticket and some expenses, should he decide to travel from Canada. The American delayed no longer. He bade his family farewell – there were now two sons – caught the train heading east and soon embarked for Liverpool.

The Peruvian arrived in London before his implacable opponent, and learned that a bankruptcy court had decided he was the last man to whom the task of liquidation should have been entrusted. If he did not know of the atrocious practices 'he ought to have known', and he could not possibly be the liquidator. Then word came that Eleonora, his wife, was extremely ill at their home in Switzerland. Arana hurried over and discovered there was nothing seriously wrong, save for terrible anxiety. She too was on the sidelines, but knew too much about the London proceedings, what they were already doing to her husband and would continue to do until (and after) they were completed. Arana returned to England where, although his bearing had earlier been commended, the facts were ridiculing him. He too was made to suffer over the matter of the rifles. He was forced to withdraw allegations that Hardenburg had been a forger. If Casement had encountered brutalities within a few weeks, why had Arana not discovered them over several years? He was also questioned over Hardenburg's visit to him in Iquitos, and what each man had said. At this point the MP for South Donegal, Swift MacNeill, was only too happy to play an ace. Would Arana please look round to see a newcomer in the audience. There, plain for him and everyone else to see, was Walter Ernest Hardenburg.

The American made an excellent impression when the time came for him to present his evidence. Arana, on the other hand, possibly unhinged by Hardenburg's presence, became increasingly confused. He contradicted himself, saying he had evidence among some papers, saying he would bring it on the next day. Eventually he refused to reply to questions, not even with a yes or no. The Committee continued with its work, enquiring, questioning and learning from others, until it suddenly realized the Peruvian was no longer in his usual seat. The man had gone.

When the parliamentary body delivered its findings, almost a year after it had been established, they were quite clear. The British directors were guiltless of the atrocities, in that no direct charge could be brought against them, but their negligent ignorance of the company's affairs deserved severe censure. Company directors 'who merely attend board meetings and sign cheques . . . cannot escape their share of the collective moral responsibility when gross abuses under their company are revealed'. They should have appreciated this obligation and 'not lightly have exposed to risk the good name of England'. As for Julio Arana, he 'had knowledge of and was responsible for the atrocities perpetrated by his agents and employees in the Putumayo'.

These deliberations did not receive the publicity they should have earned, considering the long-running interest in the Putumayo scandal. On the previous day a young woman, Emily Davidson, had thrown herself under the King's horse as it rounded Tattenham Corner in the Derby. She then died from this most violent action ever undertaken by any suffragette.

Within a few years a British consul visiting Manaus reported that it was like a ghost town. Momentum had continued to bring rubber through its warehouses for a time, but the old days had expired at about the time of Casement's visit. In 1911 and 1912 the price of black gold leaving its floating dock remained stationary, a sure sign of things to come. Every liner leaving the city during those years was full to capacity, with people leaving as hurriedly as they had arrived. Bankruptcies were frequent. Tickets were paid for in jewellery. The former clerk who had bathed ladies in champagne went up-river and killed himself. Another 'baron', the owner of a most magnificent yacht, died from beriberi. Yet another, once owner of fourteen rubber-laden ships, stayed on to sell lottery tickets in the street. Manaus crumbled, and rubber from Malaya was being produced at ninepence a pound.

As for the three principals of this story, Sir Roger Casement was the first to die. During the First World War he went to Germany. There he tried, unsuccessfully, to persuade Irish prisoners of war to fight against Britain. He then travelled in a German submarine to Ireland, where he hoped to continue the struggle on behalf of Irish nationalism. He was speedily caught, tried in London for high treason, and hanged in 1916.

Although the rubber boom had ended, the jungle city of Manaus still smacked of grandeur when this aerial photograph was taken in 1921.

Walter Hardenburg returned to Canada when the Select Committee had done its work, and died there in 1942, aged fifty-six. Julio Arana, the survivor, lasted longest, dying peacefully in Lima in 1952 at the grand old age of eighty-eight. As for the River Putumayo, its disputed territory was ceded by Peru to Colombia in 1922. Most of it looks much the same today as it did when Arana learned of it and thought it had excellent possibilities, likely to be much more profitable than hawking hats. A curious memorial to its history lies in the fact that in many atlases published at about that time only three rivers in the northern half of South America are given names. These are the Amazon, the Orinoco, and the Putumayo.

Postscript

The events described in this book span over four centuries, and yet all the individuals concerned would be able to recognize portions of the Amazon even today. It would not be like asking Peter Stuyvesant, governor of New Amsterdam, to feel at home around New York City. Nor asking Captain John Smith to recognize the Virginia landscape he came to know so well. Instead the huge river, explored since 1540, can still be explored. It is still possible to be lost along its tributaries, to feel at one with the early investigators, to encounter hazard, and to die. There was no real map of the Amazon basin until aircraft completed the task in the second half of this current century. Each year, following the seasonal flood, the landscape is altered, with tremendous lakes and backwaters where such things had not been before. There is steady change, with ox-bows forming and then drying, and all the Amazon rivers altering course when they alone think fit.

The basin is still frontier territory. Even on the great river itself the major conurbations of Belém, Santarém and Manaus, although well established, do not seem settled in their ways. Perhaps their long-standing lack of connecting roads to other portions of Brazil has imbued them with this sense of isolation. They have always been outposts of a kind. Rio de Janeiro, São Paulo and Santos can all believe they are the centre of the universe, and their inhabitants care little for the basin of the Amazon, most of them never having seen a single part of it. The creation of Brasilia was a major leap towards the interior, but the pull from Rio and the coast was sufficiently strong to prevent even this giant step reaching the drainage area of the world's greatest river system. The Amazon collects its water from a piece of land the size of the United States but manages curiously to conceal this great domain. The number of people living near its banks, near all its banks combined, is minute compared with the tens of millions who cluster by the world's other major rivers. Think of the Nile, the Ganges, the Yangtze Kiang, the Mississippi. I myself travelled last year down a thousand miles of one colossal Amazonian tributary, the Araguaia, and was astonished by the lack of people. There were small towns, but great stretches were without a sign that human beings exist upon the planet, let alone in multitudes.

Long after Francisco de Orellana considered he had put Amazonia on the map, and even within the current twentieth century, there have been voyages of discovery around the Amazon. They merit no lesser name, being expeditions involving risk as well as ignorance of the route they would pursue. Percy Harrison Fawcett vanished with two younger companions near the headwaters of the Xingu in 1925, causing other explorers to search for their remains. (The Fawcett 'mystery' is mainly mysterious for the amazement that it caused. There is still no problem about vanishing by those headwaters, with or without the assistance of other human beings.) Theodore Roosevelt was undoubtedly of the opinion that his journey down a Brazilian river in 1913 formed a major exploration. Admittedly, in the subsequent book he was not averse to stressing perils, with piranhas, snakes, cougars and disease all receiving considerable treatment, but two men did die on his journey, one from drowning and the other by murder, when expedition bickering reached breaking point. The river on which he and his party travelled, the Rio do Dúvida (or river of doubt), flowed into the Madeira, but no one knew where. When that doubt had been removed this waterway became the Rio Roosevelt, and its eponymous hero expressed astonishment that something 'the size of the Upper Rhine or Elbe' should have had an unknown course 420 years after the New World's discovery.

Perhaps North Americans, so adept at quelling their own landscape, find the Amazonian scene particularly difficult to contemplate and assess. Henry Ford, confident in his ability to solve virtually any problem (and making over a million cars a year by 1925), saw an obvious solution to the Asian monopoly in rubber: he would plant his own trees and evade a cartel imposing its prices upon his business. His

Postscript

The former president of the United States, with companions and the day's bag, when on the River of Doubt, now the Rio Roosevelt.

agents chose a piece of land by the Rio Tapajós, near where Wickham had collected seedlings and where he too had believed a plantation system might flourish. Not for the first (or last) time an enormous stretch of forest was devastated, as always the easiest part of the task. The locally recruited workers proved troublesome and dismissals were frequent. Consumption of alcohol became a particular problem, but a minor one compared with leaf blight. The rubber trees did not do well in the very region where Pará rubber had originated and, like many an individualist, did not appreciate being organized in rows.

A second site was chosen, nearer to Santarém and the mouth of the Tapajós. There was now a kind of desperation that the plan should succeed. (Had Ford ever failed?) Different varieties were tried. So too grafting, and pesticides, and everything the 1930s could provide. Another war loomed, demand grew, and so at last did Henry Ford's trees, three and a half million by the early 1940s. Unfortunately the actual production of rubber was still at a modest level, a mere 750 tons during America's first year in the war. One small shipload was pathetic compared with the requirements of an economy abruptly transformed from depression into desperate urgency. The men on the spot argued that the British had taken far longer, almost forty years, before their trees had begun to yield interesting dividends, but patience was not Ford's longest suit. After eighteen years he had had enough of his South American venture, and a rising xenophobia in Brazil was keen that he should go. The huge properties of Fordlândia and Belterra were sold back to the Brazilian government in 1945.

Another American to make another attempt was Daniel K. Ludwig. He had earned a fortune in the shipping business, and hoped to make another in wood-pulp. Fordlândia had been two million acres, but in 1967 Ludwig acquired almost twice as much land by the Jari river, which flows into the Amazon from the north. He intended also to grow rice and mine kaolin, but his main interest was in wood, as he believed a severe shortage of wood-pulp was imminent. Ludwig was an autocrat and a resenter of outside influence, virtually closing Jari's doors to the inquisitive, such as journalists. Henry Ford's experience must have loomed large in his thoughts, partly as warning but also as challenge to do better. Agro-forestry had advanced by the 1970s and more was known about every aspect of the subject, but many of Ford's problems began to arise at Jari. Plantations of a fast-growing Indian tree, Gmelina, were disappointing. The species did not like the soil and was attacked by insects. The extremely toxic Caribbean pine, believed to be immune, proved to be susceptible to leaf-cutting ants. The value of pulp rose dramatically in the mid-1970s, giving Ludwig confidence to order a $270 million mill from Japan. This vast machine was towed across the Pacific to Jari, and was soon consuming ten acres of trees a day. These came almost entirely from the native forest because the plantations could not yet cope with such an appetite, albeit a fraction of the mill's capacity. Ludwig, like Ford before him, eventually decided to cut his losses. Another Brazilian enterprise could be left henceforth to the Brazilians.

They too were not immune to misjudgement. In the 1960s, when the first highways were being constructed across this undeveloped third portion of the country, the possibility of access became suddenly exciting. For years people had been buying and selling bits of hinterland as if they were plots upon the moon. The prices had always been minute for the basic reason that nothing could be done with such distant, inaccessible territory. When roads arrived the value of nearby land leapt tenfold, a hundredfold, and those whose land was now

Postscript

approachable were quick to avail themselves of a further kind of exploitation. In North America the key word had always been development, the taming of the wilderness. Around the Amazon, and in much of South America, the spirit of the *conquistadores* still seemed to reign: take what could be taken and then move on again. This certainly applied to the new ranch-owners, the *fazendeiros* with perhaps a million acres suddenly at their disposal.

The system they applied was simple. First make a track between the new road and the available land. Then send men with axes (and not much else) along the track with instructions to clear the forest at its end. Cutting down a sizeable portion of a tropical forest is not excessively difficult, some of the trees being balsa-soft and others not much harder. This work continues from April to August, throughout the dry season around the great river, and the axes leave behind them a destruction that men on a battlefield would recognize. The hard trees, such as the iron-woods, are left standing, but everything else creates a spilled match-box of fallen timber. This dries quickly in the heat, becoming tinder almost instantly. The axe-men never jettison lighted matches or smouldering cigarettes; everything is stubbed into extinction. Any carelessness could cause a conflagration that would have these sweating, poorly paid *caboclos*, the peasants of Brazil, speedily incinerated.

Matches are struck, most purposefully, in mid-August. By then the powder-keg is more than ready. Everyone in the vicinity has been warned that several hundred acres, or even several thousand, are to be ignited. There is no difficulty in starting the fire, no cosseting of a precious flame as with bonfires in damper areas. The fire catches hold with frightening speed; the analogy with gunpowder is not inexact. Very soon, within minutes rather than hours, the entire region that has been felled, whether hundreds or thousands of acres, is alight. Within one hour, at most, the work of destruction has been accomplished. An observer can then walk within the forest ruins, kick at smouldering stumps, see termite mounds glowing in the heat, and weep at such a quantity of loss; but, from a *fazendeiro*'s point of view, the first stage has been satisfactorily accomplished.

Stage two is a second rendering of that first event, but without the need for axes. A tremendous growth springs up the moment some water falls upon the terrible acres of ash. These remains are rich in nourishment, the forest having husbanded minerals over the centuries, and the secondary growth speedily takes advantage, with weed-trees like Cecropia achieving fifteen feet a year. When the next dry season begins, some eight months after the burning, the halt in rainfall is generally devastating. Most of the vegetation dies to recreate the tinder of one year earlier. Once again a match is struck in August and a further fire rages over the ground, diminishing the surviving trunks and killing the forest yet again as if it had not already died. A third year of such treatment is probably sufficient for the place to be called *campo* rather than *mata*, field and not forest any more.

The area is then sown with grass. When that has grown – to some six feet – cattle are introduced, the hardy Zebu cattle that flourish under most tropical conditions. The *fazendeiros* of huge ranches think in terms of tens of thousands of cattle, or even – when sufficient felling has been achieved – hundreds of thousands. This is undoubtedly big business, but it is exploitation rather than development. Just as the secondary growth flourished on the accumulated mineral wealth that had been the forest's lifelong possession, so does the grass grow on all that precious capital. And, just as the grass grows well, so do the cattle; but only for a time. When they are exported, on the hoof or as carcasses, they take much of that capital with them. Nothing is put back, and there are no plans to use fertilizers. (Such a scheme would be impractical, physically and financially.) The soil is not rich on its own account, however abundant the original forest, and the cattle schemes begin to fail as the land becomes increasingly impoverished. Everyone now realizes (as a few had been proclaiming all along) that such ranching was not a good idea. It was another form of failure to conquer Amazonia, or one more form of exploration proving that this, the largest tropical forest of them all, will not yield easily.

A current plan for profiting from the Amazon basin is to tap its hydroelectric potential and then acquire its minerals. There are said to be over 100,000 megawatts of power waiting to be used within the tributaries alone. (No one has yet suggested damming the river itself.) This quantity of electricity, greater than the needs of many an industrialized society, would be vital for extracting minerals from power-hungry ores such as bauxite. Lock-gates within the dams, plus the inevitable reservoirs upstream, would make it possible for big ships to approach each mineral site and take away the ore. Many a major tributary, however wide and impressive, is now un-navigable for much, or most, of each year, save for vessels of extremely modest draught. The dams would therefore provide the power *and* the means for a further round of exploitation. Many observers believe that these major schemes are designed by and for the mega-rich with the aim of making them mega-mega-rich.

The largest dam so far built within the Amazonian basin, and the fourth most powerful in the world, exists at Tucuruí on the Tocantins river. Its reservoir has flooded the land up to Marabá, 125 miles distant. The next colossal project of this kind will be at Altamira on the Xingu, where 13,500 megawatts are to be created. Once again an enormous tract of forest will disappear, but everyone seems to have a reason for cutting down the trees. The big ranchers remove great swathes, and so do the squatters, who work on a smaller scale but are more numerous. Every aspect of invasion, whether military or civil, unplanned villages or well-planned towns, is partnered by tremendous felling as if trees are anathema. Perhaps they are. Perhaps, however much lip-service is paid towards forest conservation, people in general dislike great tracts of trees, their darkness, their damp, their obscuring of clear blue sky. The Indians made the place their home; for them there was no other way. Modern Amazonians favour a different form of life, and the forest is no part of it. The official government figure states that $2\frac{1}{2}$ per cent of the surviving *mata* is going every year; the true quantity is probably greater. There are schemes for preservation, with no land-owner supposedly cutting more than half the trees upon his land, but it is not easy to have much faith in such proposals. The world at large has not exercised restraint, and there is little prospect of Amazonians behaving differently.

The United States only woke up to the wilderness concept when 98 per cent of its land had been transformed. Optimistic scientists around the Amazon expect no more than 10 per cent of the trees to be left standing, but think 5 per cent much more probable. When that situation has been reached, in two or three decades from now, the Amazon will have been altered beyond recognition. All those whose exploits form the substance of this book would no longer be able to see the place as they saw it in their day. Instead, like Peter Stuyvesant gazing upon Manhattan now, or John Smith in modern Virginia, they would be at a loss. There will still be the water (although lack of trees will lead to lower levels), and it will still be the greatest river in the world – in size, in flow, in the area it drains – but it will no longer be a place for exploration, not even in its smallest tributaries. The age of its discovery, which lasted for centuries, will finally have drawn to a close.

Illustration Acknowledgements

MAPS DRAWN BY REGINALD PIGGOTT

BLACK AND WHITE ILLUSTRATIONS: p. 20 Archivo General de Indias, Seville; *photo*: Mas. pp. 28, 31, 42 Fotomas Index. p. 53 Illustration from George Millar, *Orellana*, Heinemann, 1955. pp. 67, 75 Fotomas Index. p. 83 Biblioteca Nacional, Madrid; *photo*: Mas. p. 127 Prado, Madrid; *photo*: Mas. p. 143 Fotomas Index. p. 166 Roger-Viollet. p. 170 Mas. p. 172 Hulton Picture Company. p. 209 A. and J.-C. Lemonnier. pp. 223, 248 Hulton Picture Company. pp. 257, 263 Royal Geographical Society. p. 282 Kimball Morrison Archive, South American Pictures. p. 284 Hulton-Deutsch Collection. p. 292 Kimball Morrison Archive, South American Pictures. p. 294 J. Allan Cash Ltd. pp. 301, 303 Kimball Morrison Archive, South American Pictures. p. 308 By courtesy of Richard Collier. p. 315 Mansell Collection. pp. 317, 321 Kimball Morrison Archive, South American Pictures. p. 324 Royal Geographical Society. p. 327 Theodore Roosevelt Collection, Harvard College Library.

Index

Figures in *italics* refer to captions

Index

Index

337

Index

Index

Index

340

Index

341

Index

Index

Index